The economics of quality, grades and brands

Virtually every decision to produce, buy or sell is influenced by the quality of a product, so the importance of quality in economics and marketing cannot be overemphasized. The firms and countries that have done best in the past twenty years have been those with a quality-based competitive strategy. When quality plays so critical a role, it is surprising that there has been little attempt until now to produce a methodology which can be adapted to the needs of people working in the real world.

The Economics of Quality, Grades and Brands aims to correct this. Peter Bowbrick shows that as quality is critical in competition, it is too important to leave to guesswork. A rigorous, practical theory is needed. This book brings together different traditions of quality analysis from economics, marketing economics and marketing itself into a coherent whole. An important aspect is identifying the weaknesses and limitations of the different traditions of quality economics and the different approaches to analysis. The book progresses logically, defining the subject and clarifying the underlying concepts before going on to more complex issues and a rigorous analysis of the subject. Brands and grades are an integral part of quality and are integrated into the analysis at all stages. As quality does not exist in isolation – what to buy and what to sell are strongly influenced by the market – quality, grades and brands are placed firmly within the market context. The book is written in a clear and straightforward style, and the author has kept the presentation simple in order to avoid confusing an already complex subject.

Peter Bowbrick is a marketing consultant specializing in food and agricultural marketing and price policy. He has both practical and research experience as a marketing economist, and has published extensively in this area.

The economics of quality, grades and brands

Peter Bowbrick

London and New York

658.562
B784e

First published 1992
by Routledge
11 New Fetter Lane, London EC4P 4EE

Simultaneously published in the USA and Canada
by Routledge
a division of Routledge, Chapman and Hall, Inc.
29 West 35th Street, New York, NY 10001

Typeset in Baskerville by LaserScript Limited, Mitcham, Surrey
Printed and bound in Great Britain by
Biddles Ltd, Guildford and King's Lynn

British Library Cataloguing in Publication Data

A catalogue record for this book is available from the British Library

ISBN 0–415–07848–2
     0–415–07847–4 (pbk)

Library of Congress Cataloging in Publication Data

Bowbrick, Peter
   The Economics of Quality, Grades, and Brands/Peter Bowbrick
   Includes bibliographical references and index
   1. Quality of products   2. Commercial products – Standards
   3. Brand choice   4. Consumers' preferences   I. Title
   HF5415.157.B69   1992
   658.5′62–dc20

ISBN 0–415–07848–2
     0–415–07847–4

Contents

List of figures

List of tables

Introduction

WHAT THIS BOOK AIMS TO DO

This book provides the basic economic theory and concepts necessary to analyse quality, grades and brands in the real world, and to develop their use as tactical and strategic weapons in production and marketing. It provides a broad general framework into which product-specific and firm-specific analysis can be fitted.

It aims to provide working economists in business, marketing and government with the basic theory and concepts needed to analyse the specific products and markets they deal with and the theory on which market research techniques must be built. Academic economists will find it useful as an exposition of the concepts and theory which underlie the economics of quality and as an opportunity to discard some of the dead wood in the subject.

WHY QUALITY IS IMPORTANT

Quality is important. Virtually every decision to produce, buy or sell is influenced by the quality of the product. In real life we almost never face the choice between two competing goods which is the basis of classical economics: instead, each product is divided into many competing product lines of different quality. A modern supermarket contains very few 'goods' like meat, yoghurt or wine, but thousands upon thousands of competing product lines, each providing its different quality. This means that an economics that does not take quality into account assumes away factors of key importance in most economic decisions.

Modern marketing and technology make these quality differences ever more important. Where Henry Ford could say of the

Model T, 'You can have any colour you like as long as it's black', today's Fords have so many variants, so many optional extras like cassette players and air-conditioning, that there are millions of possible combinations. Where the corner grocer used to weigh out biscuits and sell them in a paper bag, the modern supermarket sells hundreds of competing lines and dozens of brands of packaged biscuits. Today, any economic analysis that talks of 'cars' or 'biscuits' as though they were homogeneous products, misses the point.

Quality is a critical element in competition. The cut-throat competition between supermarket chains over the past thirty years has been largely a fight to provide the best quality, and only those who managed it survived. Tesco, for example, grew up in the 1950s and 1960s by a policy of 'Pile it high and sell it cheap', but realized that it had to switch to a policy of excellent quality to survive into the 1980s and 1990s. When the Argyll Group of supermarkets bought the relatively small Safeways group at the end of the 1980s, it switched its existing shops to the Safeways name, to cash in on its excellent reputation for quality.

The effect of quality on competitive performance is shown by several studies. For instance, a comparison of the marketing strategies of British, US and Japanese firms operating in the UK, by Wong, Saunders and Doyle (1988), has shown significant weaknesses in the marketing effort of the British. The Japanese were succeeding because they were

> marketing oriented not in terms of spending more on marketing activities or deploying more aggressive pricing and marketing tactics, but rather by way of offering good quality products, specifically targeted at well defined segments in the market, backed by strong customer sales and service support.

That is to say, they produced similar products to higher quality standards, they introduced new qualities, and they produced a quality appropriate to the market segment. Jacobson and Aaker (1987) showed the strategic role of product quality in competition in the USA. Garvin (1988) and Ouchi (1981) re-emphasize the critical importance of quality as a determinant of Japan's success in the US market.

Japan's rise to economic power was paralleled by her increasing commitment to quality. Before the war and in the early post-war years, Japan had great difficulty in exporting what were generally believed to be shoddy, badly-made products. There were even rumours that a town in Japan had been renamed 'Britain', so that goods made there could get the coveted label 'Made in Britain'.

Today, of course, Japanese products are renowned for their quality and Japanese manufacturers do not advertise the fact that some Toyota cars or Sony televisions are made in Britain or the USA.[1] Their constant improvement in quality standards and their innovation in quality has meant that other countries which concentrated on cost-cutting or improving conformance to obsolete quality standards have been unable to compete.

WHAT THIS BOOK COVERS

This book is concerned with quality, grades and brands in the real world. In this context, rigour of analysis means not just that the conclusions follow logically from the assumptions, but, far more important, that the assumptions are a close approximation to the real world. Rigour implies an open-minded approach, listening to economics, marketing and business practitioners and to researchers in other traditions and trying to incorporate their experience into the theory, rather than just assuming it away. Rigour also implies an attempt to treat all phenomena in a single theory, rather than have special theories for inconvenient exceptions. In this book, for instance, brands are not treated as a separate subject for separate theory, as though one could produce products without brand labels and leave the market unchanged: instead they are treated as just one aspect of quality, and are integrated into the analysis at all stages.

The first step in the analysis is to clarify the underlying concepts, because if these are understood, many of the problems that arise are easily managed, and some can be resolved without too much economic analysis. Confusion over these concepts causes conflict and misunderstandings within a firm, when the marketing department is striving after one concept of quality while the production department is searching for another. Confusion over concepts also invalidates much of the theory in the literature: where theory is based on inappropriate concepts, on false or contradictory assumptions, that theory is necessarily wrong, and examples will be given of commonly-used theoretical models which are flatly wrong. The Japanese quality controllers have a quality control concept of 'Poka Yoke': when they are building

Toyota cars, they stop the production line immediately they identify any defects and go back to where the defects occur to rectify the process.[2] They do not carry on building defective cars and repairing them at the end of the process. In the same way, this book concentrates on seeing that the basic concepts and assumptions are right, rather than building a large theoretical edifice on assumptions and concepts that are clearly wrong or unrealistic. There is always the danger that once one has built a large theoretical model, one has invested so much in it that one continues to use it even where its assumptions do not apply or even when it has been proved wrong.

One approach would be to start with an examination of the concepts and assumptions in minute detail for five chapters and only then start the analysis, but this would be unreadable and would cause confusion. Instead I have started with some basic concepts and have worked from there, using a more detailed analysis only for the chapters that require them. For example, it has been possible to use a very simple concept of product for nearly all the book without losing much in generality. Had I discussed each of the alternative and more realistic concepts of Chapter 14 in relation to each aspect of quality, the book would have been many times longer.

The book presents the disassembled components that can be used to assemble a product-specific, market-specific, model. It presents the basic concepts and shows how they fit together. It is, of course, impossible in any economics, and particularly in the economics of quality, to take an off-the-shelf model and to expect it to apply to your product in your market even as a rough guide. When a firm can lose millions by the wrong product launch, the wrong product positioning, or the wrong quality strategy, no economist will want to make decisions on rough guides. Accurate models require realistic assumptions and appropriate concepts.

Quality does not exist in isolation, so it is not acceptable to have a theory which confines itself to consumer preference at the time of purchase. The decisions on what to produce, what to buy and what to sell are all strongly influenced by the market. Grades and brands are marketing tools, and they exist only because there is a market. They affect the structure and operation of markets, at the same time as the structure of the markets affects the possible grading and branding systems. Accordingly, this book sets quality, grades and brands firmly in the context of the market.

An important objective of this book is to identify some of the approaches to quality which are inappropriate or flatly wrong. Chapter 9 draws attention to some of the weaknesses of public policy on consumer protection. Chapter 10 shows the weaknesses of the research programme on price as an indicator of quality and Chapter 12 shows inadequacies in the existing theory on quality in production. However, the most important targets are the closely related 'characteristics approach' and 'hedonic approach' to quality. These are important because they are the dominant theories in economics, and their influence has spread to marketing economics and marketing. The limitations of these approaches become increasingly apparent through the book. Chapters 15 and 16 concentrate on the fundamental problems of these approaches, and these criticisms are supported indirectly by earlier chapters on the basic concepts, such as Chapters 1, 2, 3, 4, 13 and 14.

Why is it so important to get the theory and the concepts right? It is sometimes argued, against this, that a very simple model based on regularities in buying behaviour, and with no economic content, can give more accurate results than economic models and that economic models are, therefore, a waste of time. It is even argued that 'Fred in Marketing has a flair for these things and usually gets it right, so we do not need any fancy models'.

It is true of course that bad economic models can be expected to produce worse results than flair and experience, but on the other hand good models should produce better results. Similarly, models based on unrealistic assumptions can be expected to produce unrealistic conclusions. Obviously a good rule of thumb is better than a bad or unrealistic model. However, a good, realistic, model is better than a simple, illogical, model or Fred's flair *even when it is a less accurate predictor*. With hindsight we may see that Fred was right, but we have no reason to rely on his predictions. Perhaps he has been right on the last four or five occasions, but there is little reason to believe that he will be right the next time, when conditions may have changed, and there is a good possibility that his flair will be hopelessly wrong. A solid model, soundly based on reality, will at least give some confidence that the prediction is in the right direction and of the right order of magnitude, so there is less risk. Equally important, when things do go wrong, we can work out why, rather than just watching Fred scratch his head. In most economic prediction, the most *accurate* forecast is that things will be exactly the same next year as this year, but the costs if this forecast is wrong are so high that we prefer the (possibly) lower accuracy and higher reliability of an economic analysis.

WHAT THIS BOOK DOES NOT COVER

This book cannot cover all aspects of quality, grades and brands, because they are an element in all production, buying and selling decisions. To cover them all would mean covering all microeconomic theory and then adding the multidimensional problems of quality to each bit of this theory. Accordingly, it leaves out some subjects that appear in the literature but are unlikely to interest the average economist, like quality in index numbers and government control of the quality supplied by regulated monopolies, and it does not attempt to provide a list of reasons why quality or grading is a 'Good Thing'. The quality aspect of production economics is given only a short chapter because there is almost no work on it in the literature. Statistical quality control, quality assurance and quality management are, at present, a totally different subject, with no links to the economics of quality. The market research techniques for quality are a subject for another book: in this book the aim has been to identify what should be measured and what is measured under some circumstances and to provide a conceptual base. Even on those aspects that have been covered, there is a lot more that could be said. From time to time, notably in Chapters 15 and 16, the possibility of a very interesting theoretical analysis arose, but I had to say that the analysis could have no practical implication, and I stopped short.

PRESENTATION

This book is written as clearly and simply as I know how: far too many writers on the subject have tried to achieve academic respectability by writing obscurely, and have confused themselves and their readers. The subject is complicated enough without trying to make it difficult: it starts at the frontiers of microeconomic theory and then adds dimension after dimension, as different quality characteristics are taken into account, and as different brands are brought into the analysis.

I have stuck to the economists' convention that the only references cited are ones which I believe would help someone wanting to study the point in more depth. It is not helpful to the reader to cite all I have read, useful or not. As the book is theoretical and conceptual, I have not given references in support of my empirical statements. These would in any case be of little value as evidence: I could give 130 references in support of my statement 'Some people sometimes appear to judge quality by price' but these are of no help at all to the readers who have to carry out their own research to find out if the statement refers to their own product in their own market (see Chapter 10).

In order to facilitate the use of the book as a textbook, it has been written so that, as far as possible, each chapter is self-contained or is closely linked to one or two other chapters, and this has meant that a certain amount of duplication is necessary so that readers are not constantly flipping back and forth. While it is certainly possible to read Chapter 15 as a separate entity, it does draw on theory developed throughout the book.

THANKS

I must thank David Price for his helpful criticism and advice, Dan Twohig, with whom I have discussed many of these problems over the years, and with whom I did a lot of empirical work on quality, and Sam Feeney with whom I did the work for one chapter.

Chapter 1

What is quality?

DEFINING QUALITY

Everybody believes that 'Quality is a Good Thing', but nobody is terribly clear what they mean by quality. We all use the word in very different senses from time to time, and it is only too easy to switch from one meaning to another and then back again in a single sentence without noticing it. This causes confusion. It also causes serious misunderstandings and conflicts when groups of people are using the word in different senses, when the marketing division is pressing for one kind of quality, while the production division is striving to produce another, or when customers want one kind of quality and the firm is trying to provide another. When both sides of an argument are striving for quality, but do not realize they are talking about something different, they suspect each other of bad faith, and this can seriously damage the efficiency of a firm.

Many people get a large part of their job satisfaction from the knowledge that they are producing excellent products. There can be a strong, and understandable, emotional reaction if they are asked to produce a product that is third rate in their terms. This can cause serious conflicts, many of which can be avoided by using a more specific definition of excellence. For example, if the plant breeder can be brought to think that an excellent strawberry is one that the consumer wants to buy, rather than one that is disease resistant, resistant to bruising, storable, and with a long shelf life, he can change his objectives to include flavour and aroma. All too often scientists think there is something vaguely discreditable ('rather like advertising or selling double glazing door to door') in producing what consumers want rather than 'what they ought to want'. Even if they cannot be brought to believe that the marketing department is right, they can be brought to understand the marketing department's point of view.

In this chapter some of the concepts of quality will be examined, and their differences brought out. I have selected eight concepts, based mainly on who is using the concept – self-evident, inspector-based, user-based, buyer-based, distributor-based, producer-based, input-based and product-based.[1] The distinctions have an arbitrary element and do overlap to some extent, so other classifications are possible. It is important to note, though, that I am not pushing any one approach as the right one, and still less am I going to attempt to define quality in a way that makes it easy to model mathematically. The fact that a concept is hard to model does not mean that it can be ignored.

Quality is self-evident

'It is self-evident what quality is. You cannot define it, but you know it when you see it.' When this statement is made, it may just mean that the speaker has not given any thought to what he means by quality. He may, however, mean exactly what he says in this context. I can recognize a Rubens as having an innate excellence, and I will let my taxes be used to ensure that it stays in a British Museum, but I will never visit that museum, and I would not have a Rubens on the wall of my house. I can recognize that Jane Austen is excellent, and demand that other people's children should be forced to read *Persuasion*, even though I read thrillers myself. I can recognize that a Rolls Royce is far superior to the latest Metro, while accepting that it would be commercial suicide to produce the Metro to Rolls Royce standards. I can recognize that, in some sense, round, brightly coloured, unblemished tomatoes are excellent, in spite of their thin coating of insecticide, and lack of flavour.

Inspector-based

Government inspectors, EEC bodies, consumer organizations and, not least, the quality control departments of factories, have an idea of quality which is seldom the same as anyone else's. This may be partly because they have not thought through the question of what quality they want to inspect for and why. It may be because they fail to realize that there is a relationship between quality and price, or that people do not always buy the quality they say they prefer. It may be because they are trying to provide people with what is good for them. Often it is because they are trying to take into account the quality objectives of a wide range of interested parties, the factory managers, the marketing departments, the retailers and the consumers. Inevitably, any attempt to take everybody's ideas into account produces a hybrid 'inspectors' quality' which is nobody else's.

Inspectors are also faced with the problem that they have to define quality in terms of measurable, objective characteristics that can be used in statistical quality control. Taste, beauty and feel cannot be measured directly, so quality must be redefined in terms of other characteristics. (Would the Venus de Milo have passed quality control?) The results are usually a definition of quality that is odd, but workable in their terms. The danger is that, as has happened often in the past, this odd definition has come to be accepted as the quality we should be aiming for.

It is easy to laugh at some of the excesses of inspector-based quality, but some economists are guilty of exactly the same error. It will be shown in later chapters that one or two of the concepts of quality used by economists have been chosen and elaborated with the single objective of being easy to manipulate in a mathematical model. They are even more restrictive than the inspectors' quality. The danger here is that economists trained in this tradition will accept a concept of quality that bears no relation to the concepts used by anyone else, and which is totally unrealistic.

User-based

User-based concepts of quality are based on products meeting a need. Someone who is hungry can meet that need in many ways, using different products, even when that hunger has crystallized into such a precise form as 'I want to eat a bar of chocolate'. Here a great many product lines can meet a need, and ranking them in order of quality is at the fancy of the individual.

At the same time, a single product line can meet different satisfactions. A Mars Bar may satisfy hunger, it may give oral satisfaction, it may substitute for love and affection, it may be a reward to a child for keeping quiet while her father is talking, it may be part of the experience of going to the circus, or it may be one child's superiority over his friend, who only has chewing gum.

Here one product line can be many different 'goods' each with different substitutes. The quality of the Mars Bar compared with other products depends on which satisfaction is the goal. Even so, the product may be providing several satisfactions at once, so a product that is moderate in several respects may be preferred to one that is excellent in only one. Similarly, two products may be consumed jointly, either as substitutes or as complements, to produce a single satisfaction.

As users vary in their preferences and financial situation, they can be expected to have different optimum choices, even for simple goods (the theoretical single-characteristic product with a single use, for instance), and these preferences can be expected to vary over time. In fact, there is no reason to believe that any two people have the same preferences for goods, and if by chance they should have, their financial position is sure to be different. This means that it is seldom possible to say unequivocally that one product is better for *all* consumers, and even less often possible to say that it would be the best buy at that price. Marketing recognizes the importance of this diversity, and a main thrust of consumer research is to find identifiable groups of customers (segments) whose tastes differ from those of the majority.

User-based concepts of quality, unlike inspector-based concepts, recognize that consumers may not get their satisfactions from the objectively measurable characteristics of a product, and they may not base their purchases on them. This is partly because consumers generally cannot identify or measure characteristics at the time of purchase, and often cannot identify or measure them at the time of consumption (when consuming vitamin pills for instance). It recognizes that some goods are bought on entirely imaginary attributes like 'luck' or 'miracle ingredients'. Others are bought for 'beauty', 'style', 'flavour' or 'social acceptability' – and I do not suggest that these are not real or important just because they are not objectively measurable. They are part of user quality.

These concepts are basic to advertising, and are a recognized part of market research, where a product is tailored to meeting consumer tastes. They appear intermittently in marketing economics, and are generally ignored in economics derived from utility theory.

Buyer-based

The buyer-based concepts of quality recognize that the person who buys the product may not be the person who uses it, as a home-maker buys the food for all members of the family, including himself, as governments buy public goods, and as procurement departments buy for firms. Most goods are bought for someone else, or, at least, by a home-maker buying for the family at the same time as he buys for others.

The home-maker who is trying to produce a meal satisfactory to all members of the family, or who is trying to buy consumer durables to meet the demands of all members of the family will not act as though the demand function was a simple addition of the demands of the users. The outcome may be a bland solution that pleases no one, but annoys no one.[2] Alternatively, preferences may be weighted by some criterion such as which child screams loudest. Some home-makers buy the products they like themselves; others, self-sacrificingly, buy only what other people like. The solution is not likely to be a mathematical function of the demands of the users.

The users, the children, may not feel that they face any of the financial or logistical constraints that the buyer does, and so they may ignore price and value for money when pressing the buyer to buy one quality rather than another. A similar problem arises with public goods, where the general public has a concept of quality which may be very different from that of the public official who procures the goods.

The home-maker also gets important satisfactions out of the buying process, the satisfaction of making a 'good buy', of reaching a satisfactory resolution of a difficult management and logistic problem, of being essential to the family's well-being, of his contribution being recognized. The purchase of special foods, wholefoods for instance, and the preparation of special dishes may be satisfying these needs and may in fact be contrary to the wishes of his family who want junk food. Marketing and advertising practitioners work on this with advertisements showing that a caring home-maker protects the family with margarine made of polyunsaturated fats, rather than trying to persuade the eventual consumers that they like it.

Purchases are determined partly by *direct* satisfactions arising from the buying activity, and partly from *indirect* satisfactions of the user (including the home-maker as well). Depending on the product and the market, the indirect satisfactions may be of very little importance indeed, or they may be the main determinant of the purchase.

Most marketing statistics cover what buyers actually purchase, not what the eventual users would like them to buy, so economists tend to work at this level for market analysis, calculation of elasticities, and so on. Formally, analyses using utility theory are concerned with what the buyer purchases, but it is almost universally assumed that the buyer is the user. This is a serious cause of confusion in utility-based quality theory, as will be shown in later chapters. Marketing and advertising often recognize the importance of the distinction, though not as often as one might expect.

Distributor's quality

To the wholesaler and retailer, quality may have a whole new set of connotations.

A quality good is one which increases the store's prestige, even if they do not sell much of it. Safeway, for instance, sells a few bottles of wine at £67 a bottle to improve the reputation of their wine department, their store and, less directly, to boost their share price.

A quality good gives no trouble. It comes when ordered, and it can be ordered at short notice. It need not be checked on delivery, there is no shrinkage, and it can take rough handling. There are no dissatisfied customers. A quality good is cheap to handle. It has a long shelf life and no waste. It takes up very little shelf space or aisle space.

A quality good gives high turnover at a good margin. This is partly determined by the buyer's perception of the quality of that good, but also by the whole policy of the shop – ambience, pricing policy, reputation, location and so on, rather than by the quality of that product alone.

Much of the value of a product can arise from its ability to meet these requirements of the distributor. It can be argued that a large part of the pay-off from grading schemes and minimum quality standards arises in this way. If the standards were designed with distributor quality in mind, rather than with a hotchpotch of user quality, inspector quality and self-evident quality, as is often the case, they would be a great deal more effective than they are now.[3]

The relative importance of the *direct* aspects of quality, such as the handling costs, and the *indirect* effects arising out of buyers' and users' satisfactions will vary according to the product and the market. For example, one fruiterer with a shop outside a hospital sells mainly to buyers who give presents to users, the patients. He expects very little repeat custom, as there is a constant turn round of patients. The patients certainly will not complain about the poor quality of the gifts. He defines quality as something that looks wonderful, that meets specification on entering the shop, and that has no waste in the shop. He was delighted by the Italian Jonathan apples he was selling one February: 'They taste like cardboard, but they look beautiful – red, shiny, and perfectly shaped'.

Production-based

In the manufacturing context quality means that the product conforms to specifications, even if the specifications are meaningless to the buyer and user. A product that is designed to be cheap and nasty is only unacceptable if it is *not* cheap and nasty (If the end product is a mix of good and bad, the buyer in the shop will scrabble through the display looking for what is good. This causes congestion in the shop, disorganizes the display and damages the product. To the distributor the product may be of worse quality than one that is uniformly cheap and nasty.)

It is common for the production specifications to be aimed at criteria of no interest to anyone but the producer: easy assembly, low rework costs, minimum sorting, low cost, and so on. All these lead to lower production cost but they do not help the consumer or distributor. Conflicts often arise between the production departments who are meeting their specifications superbly, and the marketing department which cannot sell the product.

Economists often use a purely production-based definition for their own output. A publishable paper is one which meets its production specifications by being perfectly consistent logically from its arbitrary assumptions to its conclusions, by using the house style for references, and by being within the journal's word limit. User-based concepts may be ignored: does anyone want to read it? Will anyone be able to read it? Can it be applied to the real world?

The production-based concept, where quality is conformance to specifications, is essentially the one used in quality assurance, total quality management, statistical quality control and the costs of quality and it is the one used in the British Standards.[4] Its advantage is that of inspector-based quality – that it is based on easily measurable objective characteristics. The concept is almost never used outside this, and it hardly appears in the economics literature. Its disadvantage is that it completely ignores user-based, buyer-based and distributor-based concepts of quality. It encourages producers to concentrate on producing efficiently rather than trying to produce the right product for the market. This is a fertile source of conflict.

The approach is not wrong, any more than any one of the others is wrong, and as long as it is recognized that it is only one way of looking at the problem, it can be helpful. Here again, we have the *direct* quality arising from cheap and efficient meeting of specifications and the *indirect*, arising from distributors' willingness to purchase the product and the even less direct influence of buyers and users.

Input-based

If the product is taken to be an input for a production process, its value is derived entirely from its use in that process. Because of this, and because the technical and chemical input/output relationships are more or less known, this type of quality is amenable to formal analysis. Farm management economists have developed it to a considerable degree. Margarine manufacturers, again, use mathematical programming to determine which particular mix of oils and fats will produce the right end product at the lowest price each day.

Product-based

Precisely because it is possible to achieve so much with input-based analysis, there is a temptation to apply similar measures to areas where its application is not so obvious, applying linear programming to buyer behaviour, for instance.

Characteristics-based

An approach that arises directly out of the inputs models is the characteristics approach, where the product itself does not produce any satisfactions, but its objectively measurable and rankable characteristics do. In effect, the product is taken as a raw material and is processed by the user, by cooking for instance, before consumption. This approach is amenable to mathematical analysis if enough simplifying assumptions are made, and the bulk of the more mathematical economics is in this tradition. Its strengths and weaknesses will be discussed in later chapters. It is, perhaps, questionable whether this is a concept of quality rather than a set of simplifying assumptions for dealing with product-based quality.

Joint consumption and several ingredients[5]

Many products are jointly consumed, as when a film is seen by the whole audience at once, and a meal is eaten by the whole family. At the same time there may be several characteristics that combine to make one end product. Either of these situations can result in strong pressure to make the final product or its ingredients bland and insipid.

This can be seen from David Ogilvy's work with Gallup in the 1930s:

> I discovered that some stars had a *negative* effect at the box office; their names on the marquee repelled more ticket buyers than they attracted. The list, which I called Box Office Poison and classified TOP SECRET, included some of the most famous names in show business, and ruined their careers[6]

This is not just a matter of one film star leaving some of the audience cold, and nor is it just a matter of one star having a negative valuation which may be offset by another having a positive valuation. If a film has two stars, and each is strongly disliked by half the population, then the chances of the film being successful is small. If each of the *Seven Samurai* were avoided by a seventh of the population, each by a different seventh, then nobody at all would have seen the film. This means that no film can afford to have starlets or supporting actors who are hated: they must be bland. It is quite a big risk even to have two stars who are powerful enough to repel large numbers of the population. There are a small number of stars who are not bland, but who nevertheless do not repel many potential viewers. They are immensely valuable, and they are the superstars.

This effect is multiplied by the fact that people often go to films in couples or family groups. If one single person in the group hates one single star, then everybody in the group avoids the film.

When portable radios replaced families sitting round the wireless set, there was a big change in the market for music. It was no longer necessary to have the broad appeal and the lack of irritating factors which made Bing Crosby a superstar. A new generation of musical stars came into prominence, people whose music was definitely unacceptable to the family group as a whole, but who survived because the teenagers could now listen separately.

This phenomenon is equally important in food marketing. Restaurants have to provide meals with every course acceptable to every customer: if one customer hates it, he will avoid the restaurant and take his group with him. Similarly, food manufacturers can get away with a product that is bland, but they cannot get away with a product that most people think is excellent, but a few people hate. Again, a single hater can change the consumption patterns of the whole family.

This model works particularly strongly if a consumer evaluates the product on its worst attribute and will reject a stew with any garlic, say. It is less important where there is additive evaluation, and the film-maker can compensate for a repulsive star by putting in three starlets who are liked. This explanation for blandness works instead of, or in conjunction with, Hotelling's classic model.

The effect of joint consumption and several ingredients in determining perceptions of quality, and in determining sales, will be shown to be of critical importance to some quality models in later chapters.

HOW THE APPROACHES FIT TOGETHER

In Table 1.1 the relationship between the different concepts of quality is shown. It is particularly important to note the direct and indirect effects, with manufacturers getting direct benefits as well as benefits arising from the fact that the distributors and consumers get benefits from the product.

Table 1.1 Concepts of quality, and their direct and indirect components

Concept	Direct	Indirect
Self-evident	Some which does not appear to get in anywhere else	Quality which other people's children would benefit from. May overlap with others
Inspector's quality	Amalgam of other people's quality. Self-evident.	Quality of pressure groups taken into account.
User-based	Product lines producing satisfactions. Different products meeting the same satisfactions. One product line meeting different satisfactions.	Ecological factors benefit others.
Buyer-based	Buyer buys for several users. Buyer gets satisfaction from good buy, being seen to be good home-maker, keeping family happy, and so on.	Buyer combines wants of users, some of whom have no financial constraints.
Distributor quality	Prestige goods. No shrinkage, no waste, good shelf life. Low handling cost, low floor, shelf space requirement. Takes rough handling. High margin.	Fast turnover/high margin, both deriving from buyer's quality and, less directly, users'.
Production-based	Meets specifications. Low product cost, high yields, few outgrades, low pest and disease incidence, not dangerous or unpleasant.	Sells easily at a good price, deriving from distributors' quality, and from buyers' and users'.
Input-based	None	Quality and value determined by its use to producers.
Product-based	?	?

WHAT THIS CHAPTER HAS SHOWN

This chapter has shown that there are many concepts of quality, and eight of them have been explained. None of these are right or wrong: they are different ways of looking at a complex and amorphous concept. Typically, producers, consumers, buyers, engineers and marketing people have different concepts of quality – taking a view strongly influenced by their personal interests.

This means that there is an enormous scope for confusion when two people discuss quality. Often someone writing on quality will switch from one concept to another and back again within the course of a page – and I am sure I do so from time to time: it is virtually impossible to discuss quality in the real world without such switches.

Because people believe passionately in the need for quality and because there are so many concepts of quality which are not wrong, there is scope for major conflicts. These are damaging when the production and marketing departments engage in open warfare about what is or is not good quality or when regulatory bodies have a concept of quality that is not the distributors' or the users'.

This chapter provides the basic framework for removing the confusion and for resolving the conflicts by showing that people are arguing at cross purposes. Any economics of quality that says that there is just one concept of quality is wrong.

Chapter 2

The product as a variable

In elementary microeconomics it is convenient to assume that a product is a product, that wheat is wheat and there are no variations in quality and no close substitutes. Textbook models are constructed where the only alternatives are wheat and steel. At a slightly more advanced level product differentiation is introduced 'in which the products of different sellers, though different, are all *given* so the only variables studied are price and quantity'.[1] In this book the much more realistic tradition of product variation (as opposed to product differentiation) introduced by Chamberlin in the 1940s and 1950s is used. In this

> 'Product' is used in the broad sense to include all aspects of the good or service exchanged, whether arising from the materials or ingredients, mechanical construction, design, durability, taste, peculiarities of package or container, service location or seller, or any other factor having significance to the buyer.[2]

> Products are not in fact 'given'; they are continuously changed – improved, deteriorated, or just made different – as an essential part of the market process.[3]

The distinction between product variation and simple product differentiation is of key importance in the economics of quality.

The product as a variable is a realistic approach, incorporating many of the approaches used in practical and theoretical marketing. Of course, it is valid for a model of a specific market for a specific purpose to make simplifying assumptions and to concentrate on only a few aspects of the Chamberlin approach. What is not acceptable is to build up a large body of pure theory, stated to have general applicability, which starts off by assuming away nine-tenths of these sources of variation.

In this chapter Chamberlin's original concept is taken and enlarged upon considerably, with sections on attributes and characteristics, risk, external quality, substitutes, purchasing costs, selling costs, and so on. It will be shown that the product is infinitely variable, that even a product as uniform in its physical characteristics as tins of baked beans can vary enormously in aspects like consumer purchase and consumer satisfaction as a result of variations in the marketing mix. It will be shown that even where there is no evidence of price competition, and where the physical characteristics of the goods sold by rival companies are the same, there can be cut-throat competition using product variation. This chapter is introductory, and the concepts introduced here will be expanded on in later chapters.

Since the most obvious sort of product variation is a variation in physical characteristics, with one computer having more memory than another, for instance, it is easy to jump to the conclusion that they are the most important product variations, or even the only variations, and build up an economic theory of quality based on them alone. To avoid this error, this chapter will emphasize other forms of product variation, ways in which products which are identical in their objective measurable characteristics can have quite different values.

Of course, the physical characteristics of products supplied by competing firms are often very different, with an enormous range of quality even within one good, for example, motor cars. Even that one good is not a fixed concept: if it is thought of not as 'a motor car', but as 'transport', then bicycles, taxis, trains, ox-carts and trucks become part of the same good. If it is thought of as status, then gold watches, jewellery, houses and holidays are part of the same good.

ATTRIBUTES

The consumer's satisfaction with a product is in his* own mind, and no outside observer can measure this satisfaction directly or,

---

* I am advised that the often-used convention of calling the consumer 'she' is sexist, branding womankind as housewives. The old usage, recently revived, of using 'their' instead of 'his' or 'her' is confusing when, as in this book, the difference between the individual and the crowd is of critical importance. Accordingly, I stick, with apologies, to the conventional 'he' and 'him'.

as will be shown below, indirectly. We cannot, therefore, talk about average levels or market levels of satisfaction.

An individual's purchasing behaviour is not determined by the objective measurable characteristics of the product. It is determined first by what the buyer believes his own wants to be (and in the last chapter several different perceptions were discussed). These perceptions may be inaccurate: I may think I want a fast car when I really want status. The perceptions at the time of purchase may not be the same as the perceptions at the time of consumption.

Second, the buyers have a subjective impression of what product elements will satisfy these wants. They may believe that ginseng, make-up or love stories will satisfy their need for romance. Again, the perception may or may not be an accurate perception of the satisfaction that will be achieved. A complicating factor is the placebo effect: if I believe a pill contains a pain-killer, it may kill pain.

Third are the consumer's perceptions of the degree to which products on the market can provide these elements. Again, the perception may be quite wrong.

Fourth is the perception of the price of the characteristic – a perception which is inevitably flawed because of imperfect perception of the price of the product (It is well recognized in marketing that people perceive 97p as being a higher price than 99p and both as being much lower than £1.00) as well as imperfect perception of the characteristics of the product and their level.

How does this affect our tin of baked beans? Some people perceive themselves as wanting flavour, some as wanting nutrition and, to complicate the analysis, most people see themselves as wanting both. Some people perceive beans as a fattening food, with high carbohydrate and high starch, and some as a slimming food with high fibre and moderate calories.

The upshot is that even when consumers have identical tastes and incomes and face an identical set of choices in terms of objectively measurable characteristics and prices, they will end up with different purchases. A very large marketing effort is aimed at consumer perceptions, because they can be changed. They can be changed by persuasive advertising, or by putting informative labels on the can for instance, as well as by experience.

External quality

In this section, external quality is discussed, those elements of quality that are important but do not directly relate to the objective characteristics of the item bought.

The shop

The shop in which a product is bought has an impact on its perceived quality. While it may not be true that a can of Heinz baked beans bought in Fortnum and Masons will be perceived to be better than the same can bought in the supermarket down the road, it seems likely that a pound of Stilton bought there will be.

The ambience

The ambience of a shop affects the perception of quality, a fact particularly noticeable in restaurants.

Service

The service when the product is sold, and after it has been sold, changes the value of the product, both by changing perceptions of the product and in ways like helping the customer get the right product for the purpose, teaching him how to use it, and reducing risk if it breaks down.

The brand

The brand is a quality element in its own right. Levi jeans are valued differently to identical jeans with a different label, and a pair of trousers bought in Saville Row may be perceived differently to an identical pair bought in the local shopping centre.

However, even apart from this, the brand has quality attributes which are not the same as those of the specific item bought by the individual. For example, there is a perception of the distribution of quality within a single product line of that brand. This perception may make it seem less risky to buy one brand than another, and it may affect a consumer's satisfaction with his purchase. Somehow, a product of a given quality from a brand with a reputation for erratic quality does not give the same satisfaction as an identical product from a brand with a reputation for consistent quality.

Similarly, a new product from Sony will have a quality image which is not the same as that of an identical new product with an unknown brand.

Trader quality

As was shown in the last chapter, traders value a product for elements quite different to those a consumer values. Traders generally think not in terms of a given item, the one item an individual buys, but in terms of the characteristics of a product line. They are concerned with the wastage rate in store, with shelf life, with the storage life after the customer buys the product, with the level of complaints after purchase and so on.

Time-dependent quality

There are several ways in which quality varies with time. Many products, durables in particular, are consumed over time. There have been many economic models of the quality of consumer durables, mostly using life expectancy as the only measure of the amount of its objective quality characteristics – a vacuum cleaner that lasts six years gives twice the utility as one that lasts three years. While this is an interesting stratagem to avoid the problems of measuring characteristics like vacuuming ability, and to avoid looking at product variation, it is not clear what applicability it has. Chamberlin comments:

> It may be remarked in passing that a product, say an auto-mobile, by reason of its many aspects, may, at any one time (unlike a price) be a *composite* of decisions with reference to different time periods.
>
> (Chamberlin 1953: 12)

The substitutes for durables are not just other durables with the same life expectancy. Instead of buying a radio with a twenty-year life expectancy, one may choose to buy one with a five-year life expectancy. This implies some belief about improvements in the performance of radios over the period, and about the continuing fall in prices, as well as some belief in the quality of programmes in ten years' time.

Prompt delivery is an important time-dependent quality element, accounting for the rise of the fast-food business, and explaining why some manufacturers survive and others fail. 'Just In Time' strategies of input delivery have proved important for Japanese manufacturers in particular, enabling them to operate a factory with only a few hours' supply of raw materials, and virtually no storage or interest charges.

Some products like strawberries have a value that is time-dependent. The very first home-produced strawberries have a special value and prices remain high for the first few weeks, and then tail off over the season, even when supplies start to dry up. There is a pleasure in the first of the new crop, which might be novelty, or the first sign of the advent of summer, or boredom with the fruit available in winter. A similar price structure occurs for the first apples of late summer and the first Brussels sprouts of winter. The laboured arguments about whether consumer surplus would be maximized if supplies were steady throughout the year fall away once this is recognized.

Availability is also important: the tin of baked beans bought in a neighbourhood store at 10 p.m. on a Sunday does not have the same value as the tin of beans not available from a supermarket until Monday morning.

There is also a very human desire for variety. This has several elements in it which will be discussed in later chapters, particularly Chapter 13, such as a constant desire for variety, a fall in desire because of boredom, a fall in desire because of satiation, and a constant desire for novelty.

Consumer satisfaction from an item also varies over time. The satisfaction is different in anticipation, in actual consumption and in recollection.

Substitutes

The perceived value of an item or a product line is affected by the availability of substitutes. This may be a function of rarity, like penny blacks or Dior models. Inevitably, too, the existence of close substitutes changes the elasticity of demand for a product.

Use

The value of a product depends on what it is used for. A product which has many uses can give an enormous range of satisfactions.

The range of satisfactions which can be produced by food is shown in the following list derived from market research[4]

1 Satisfy hunger and nourish the body
2 Initiate and maintain personal and business relationships
3 Demonstrate the nature and extent of relationships
4 Provide a focus for communal activities
5 Express love and caring
6 Express individuality
7 Proclaim the separation of a group
8 Demonstrate belonging to a group
9 Cope with psychological or emotional stress
10 Reward or punish
11 Signify social status
12 Bolster esteem and gain recognition
13 Wield political and economic power
14 Prevent, diagnose and treat physical illness
15 Prevent, diagnose and treat psychological illness
16 Symbolize emotional experiences
17 Display piety
18 Represent security
19 Express moral sentiments
20 Signify wealth

Other people might choose a less abstract set of examples. One extreme is Fort Tuli on the border of what are now Botswana and Zimbabwe, whose walls were built from 1890 to 1896 out of tins of bully beef: two regiments stopped there one week; the supply orders were not cancelled, and the half dozen people left there could not think of anything else to do with the rations.[5] Another is the old Spanish practice of slapping a hunk of smelly cheese on the wall to keep the flies from pestering the customers eating at a restaurant. A household example is using flour and water paste to stick wallpaper.

A single item may be used for many of these uses. This means that it is infinitely variable. Marketing, of course, emphasises this variety of uses, packaging, advertising and marketing a product in several different ways to encourage its use for different purposes. Advertising can be used to alert customers to new uses, or to emphasise one use.

Purchasing cost

At a basic level of economics, and for many practical applications, it is convenient to assume that the cost to the consumer is identical to the price. This is never entirely correct, and for many marketing applications it is grossly misleading.

Location

Location is the most obvious example. A can of beans at a neighbourhood shop is not the same as a physically identical can of beans at a supermarket on the other side of town. A can of beans on a shelf at eye level is not the same as a can of beans on the bottom shelf: sales will be far higher at eye level. There is a very large literature on location economics, regional, within cities, within shopping areas and within shops.

Search

A similar cost is the search cost: the time and trouble it takes a customer to find out the quality and price of competing product lines and choose between them. There is a thriving body of theory on this, and it will be discussed in later chapters, particularly Chapters 4, 5, 8 and 9.

These purchasing costs are specific to the individual. That is to say, if a new superstore is opened down the road from me it will have a big effect on my locational costs, but other shoppers may not be affected at all. Similarly, a reduction in search is not equivalent to an across the board reduction in price. Some people like search, some people have a low opportunity cost for time, some people find search difficult. The cost of an item to an individual (price plus travel plus search) is a variable. Reducing search or reducing travel costs is not equivalent to the same cut in prices to all buyers. It cannot be looked upon as being a simple shift in the supply curve.

Risk

Risk can be important in many buying situations. In practice, products vary and the buyer can never be perfectly informed. If the risk is too great, which may be at as low a level as one egg in 10,000 having dangerously high levels of salmonella, consumers may avoid the product, causing a serious fall in sales – as happened in Britain in 1989. Risk has two elements which are important in quality, the probability of the product deviating from expected specifications, and its value to the buyer at each level of deviation (with the diseased egg having a strong negative value).

The simple approach to risk is to construct models where the buyer knows the statistical variation of characteristics. A few possible approaches are:

1 Variation of quality from one product line to another on the assumption that each product line has a single homogeneous quality (that is, that there is product differentiation rather than product variation) and that information is such that differences in quality cannot be perceived until the product is consumed.

2 Variation of the characteristics of a product, when it is known what the manufacturing specifications are and what the statistical deviations from specifications are. The assumption might be that the buyer gets a random item from the production line. Simple models are based on objective characteristics rather than subjective perceptions, and do not allow for differences in the characteristics valued, or used, by consumers, buyers and manufacturers.

3 Variation of the characteristics of a grade, which may be specified by, say, the upper and lower limits of its characteristics. This type of problem implies a variation within the sample purchased, a variation between samples and a variation over time. Each item purchased may be within the grade specification, but there may still be a significant variation from item to item.

4 The value of an item at different levels of characteristic might be plotted. At some levels this might be negative, if the baked beans contain arsenic for instance. If one then assumes that the buyer gets a random item and one assumes a statistical probability of getting that item, one can calculate the probable value of that choice.

However, most of these statistical risk models deal with an ideal situation where statistical probabilities of deviation, statistical probabilities of purchase, and consumer's valuation of different qualities are known. In the real world we must assume that the consumer's (or buyer's) perception of both probabilities are not the same as the objective statistical probabilities – many people work on Murphy's Law, while millions of others will bet on horses when the odds are strongly against them. We must also accept that some people do not mind a bit of risk in their lives, while others are strongly risk averse.

The manufacturer and distributor between them may be able to calculate the probability of deviation from an ideal specification, and even the probability of a given buyer getting a given quality, but they certainly cannot tell how a given consumer will evaluate each quality, or how risk averse he is.

The perceptions of risk can be changed in several ways. First, of course, the actual probability can change, with perhaps higher specifications, or closer conformance to the same specifications. People can be given information (correct or not) which will change their beliefs about the probabilities. They can be given information which will change their perception of the cost of a deviation from specification. Marketing strategies to reduce risk or to transfer risk (such as manufacturers' guarantees) can be adopted. All these are major changes in the product, and most of them arise even when there is no objective change in the physical quality characteristics of the product.

Selling costs

Just as basic theory ignores purchasing costs, it ignores selling costs, assuming that the price is the same as the seller's revenue. This assumption is often a reasonable simplification for practical economic analysis, but it is never strictly correct, and it is wildly misleading for many marketing applications.

Competition between sellers is often not a matter of cutting the price, or of changing the physical characteristics of the product, but rather of changing the selling costs. The most obvious example is advertising, but there are others like providing service and the right ambience. Distribution to locations convenient to the consumer increases distributors' cost at the same time as it reduces consumers' cost. Risk reduction, by providing guarantees and warranties, is another way in which the costs to the seller rise as benefits to the consumer rise.

These differences in the cost of selling mean that items with the same physical characteristics vary in the value to the consumer and in the net revenue to the seller. The value is specific to individual purchasers, and the supply cost can vary from item to item. This means that changes in selling costs cannot just be treated as changes in the price of the product: the effect is different, both in who buys and in its effect on total and net revenue.

Price

Simple price competition is a matter of charging a lower price, or of supplying more for the same price. Price is more than just the cost of purchase – indeed, it has been argued above that it is only part of the cost.

Price has other effects though. It affects peoples' perceptions of the quality and quantity on offer. Customers often believe that a more expensive packet contains more, so the unit price is the same, or that a bigger packet has a lower price per unit. They may also believe that a more expensive product is of a better quality – 'if it wasn't, the seller wouldn't be able to charge a high price would he?' (this is examined in Chapters 4, 5, 8, 9 and 10). It is quite common, in the fashion world for instance, for firms to compete in this way, charging more to indicate the quality of their product.

It also affects the satisfaction people get from the product. If it was expensive and it is good, consumers may persuade themselves that it was superb and the money was well spent. If it was expensive and not very good, customers may be furious at the waste of money. Some of the satisfaction may come from a deep-seated belief that you can only get top quality by paying for it. Some may come from the knowledge that all your friends can see what you paid for it.

This means that price is both one of the costs of buying a product, and part of quality in its own right.

CHARACTERISTICS

In this section I look at some of the physical characteristics of a product. Again, I am emphasizing the concept of the product as a variable, and I want to avoid the straight product differentiation model where a product can be defined by its physical characteristics alone.

Single item

Let us look at a single item of a product line. It is often convenient to define, or describe, it in terms of its physical characteristics. We will be looking in some detail at characteristic models in Chapters 14, 15 and 16.

Ingredients

The most obvious way of using objective physical characteristics is to list the product's ingredients, using a recipe or a formula for instance. With some products this gives a perfectly accurate and useful description, H_2SO_4 for instance. Generally, however, an accurate description of the physical content of a product or of the way in which it was produced is not easily related to the satisfaction the product gives. There are some products where one can use ingredient characteristics as an indication of quality. When mixing pig food, for instance, one tries to achieve a certain balance of protein and carbohydrate plus calories. The value of each product going into the pig food is determined by the level of the ingredient characteristics going into the mix. One may say that to some limited extent the octane level of petrol indicates the satisfaction it gives.

Manufacturing specification

However, it is patently foolish to describe a motor car in terms of its ingredients: 84 per cent steel, 5 per cent rubber, 2 per cent leather, 6 per cent glass and so on. It is far more useful to know how it was constructed than what its ingredients are. Some aspects of a manufacturing specification are often very important in influencing consumer choice (organic, hand painted and so on), and of course, at some stage in a product's life a manufacturing specification is needed.

What it does

A product may also be described in terms of another set of characteristics, what the product does. A motor car, for example, does 0-60 mph in eight seconds; it does 35 miles per gallon; it provides seats for four people, and so on. Defining a product in this way has advantages over ingredients or manufacturing specifications. For example, it means that traditional corkscrews, CO_2 openers and wine waiter cork removers are seen as different product lines of the same product, even though they have quite different ingredients, work on quite different principles and vary in their effectiveness when used with old or broken corks. Similarly, a whole range of computer spreadsheets do much the same job with similar commands, though they work with very different programs.

What needs it satisfies

Another possibility is to define a product in terms of what needs it satisfies. Again, it permits all cork removers, all mousetraps or all spreadsheets to be thought of as a single product group. On the other hand, while all personal computers do much the same thing, they can satisfy many needs, being used as typewriters, accounting systems, games, control systems for industrial robots and so on. Defining computers in terms of what they can do, rather than the multitude of satisfactions they can produce, seems reasonable. Some of the many satisfactions that food can produce have been listed above, but it is hardly helpful to try and define a product line in terms of its seduction potential, its oral satisfaction, its social status, its 'in group' message and so on. These can certainly be used as a basis for an advertising campaign, but not as a basis for a characteristics model of quality.

Taste, beauty, feel, smell and harmony are important elements of products, and of the satisfactions that the products give, but they do not fit easily into the approach of defining a product according to its ingredient characteristics, its performance characteristics or its use characteristics. Indeed, the most commonly cited economic models based on objective characteristics specifically assume them away.[6] Again, they are critical elements of competition which cannot be handled by simplistic models. They are in the eye of the beholder, and so are infinitely variable.

It has been pointed out above that consumers draw inferences about the quality of a product from the fact that it has been branded or graded or has a price label. The brand or grade label influences purchases and the satisfaction obtained. It is an objectively determinable fact that the label is or is not there. In one sense, therefore, there is an objective characteristic which is related to the individual's satisfaction – though the label itself may give no satisfaction, and may be a proxy for other attributes or characteristics which do.

RATIONAL OR IRRATIONAL CHOICE

Traditionally economists work on the assumption that man is totally rational and that all decisions are made as a result of full and careful calculation. We know that this is not true, but we continue to do analyses based on the assumption for one good reason. People are seldom totally irrational, and if our model shows up irrational behaviour, it is a sign that very careful reworking and reappraisal of the model is needed before the conclusion is accepted. Most backward-sloping supply curves, for example, show rational behaviour if properly analysed. On the other hand, even if people do act irrationally, they are generally fairly consistent in their behaviour, so market research approaches which analyse regularities in buying behaviour can act as useful predictors of behaviour. If these predictions clash with the predictions of economic analysis, or if observation shows a sudden marked switch in buying behaviour, a very careful reworking of the analysis, and a close examination of the market research techniques are in order.

CONCLUSION

This chapter showed that product differentiation is only a part of product variation and is not a necessary part at that. Cut-throat quality competition can exist even when there is little or no physical product differentiation. The importance of buying costs and selling costs has been emphasized. So has the distinction between the objective physical characteristics and the subjective attributes. A major implication is that product variation, including variation by reducing buying costs, or increasing selling costs, is not the same as an across-the-board reduction in price – each individual consumer is affected differently.

The variations discussed here are not remote possibilities of theoretical interest only: they are part of the day-to-day business of marketing, and there are few firms which do not make use of them in some way.

The implication is that an economics of quality that is based on physical product differentiation alone, with each producer producing a physically different product, is inadequate. A large and rich economics of quality can be created without assuming this differentiation. This means, of course, that the models of quality based on physical characteristics alone cover only a small part of the economics of quality. They have their part to play, of course, but they are not the whole of the subject, nor even a key part of it.

Chapter 3

What are brands and grades?

This chapter presents working definitions for a discussion of brands and grades and a few of the other concepts that will be used in the rest of the book. These definitions are adequate to follow the flow of the argument, though some of the definitions will be examined critically and in detail in later chapters.

The chapter will distinguish between different types of brands and grades and show how they differ and how they overlap. This is important because of violent arguments that arise in practice when people are talking at cross purposes. It is common, for example, for one person to think of grading as sorting, another of grading as labelling and another of grading as minimum standards. If the combatants can be persuaded that they are talking of quite different things, they may be able to come to an agreed solution. Similarly, if an economist is aware of the distinctions, he can build a model which is consistent in its use of terms – and a lot of the papers in the literature are inconsistent. Most readers will find it easier to follow the rest of the book if they take one product, their firm's main product perhaps, and categorize it according to the definitions here.

One major conclusion of the chapter is that while grades may exist without brands, brands usually exist in conjunction with grades, and some grading process, even one invisible to the consumer, is implied by the fact that a manufacturer has branded his product.

It will also be suggested that it is rather pointless to spend any time on analysing 'pure quality', where there are neither grades nor brands, because these situations are rare in practice. The message of the last chapter, that the product is a variable even when there is no physical product differentiation, will be reinforced.

In the next few chapters these concepts will be used to look at questions like

How do brands and grades help consumers choose? How do they help reduce buying cost?

How do they reduce risk? How do they give consumers added reassurances of quality and reliability?

How can the brand itself, or the grade itself, become something the consumer is willing to pay for?

What kinds of increases in selling costs (advertising, labelling, distribution, and so on) are likely to help the seller and the buyer?

How can sorting, for example, change the quality of the product?

WHAT ARE BRANDS?

It is easy to give examples of brands which everyone will agree are brands, like Heinz, Peugeot and Nestlé, but there may be more disagreement about 405, General Motors, Marks and Spencer or Thompson's Tomatoes. For the purpose of this analysis a brand is a label which indicates that all products carrying a label have a common manufacturer, distributor, retailer or country of origin. It does not necessarily give any information about who that manufacturer, distributor or retailer is, nor about the quality characteristics of the product. A brand is often intended to convey information on, or persuade the consumer about the quality, reliability, social status, value for money or safety of a purchase. It would be pointless to split hairs about this definition, in the light of the distinctions and overlaps that arise later in this chapter.

Main types of brand

The main types of brand that will be looked at here are as follows:

Umbrella brands, like Lever Brothers, General Motors and so on

These brands may indicate the holding company, but not give much indication about the product or the manufacturer. Often the names are not known to the final consumer at all.

Generic brands

Generic brands, like Danish bacon, or Outspan oranges, with generic advertising like 'Drinka Pinta milka day', are used for marketing a generic product, produced by many manufacturers. Hoover is an example of a proprietary brand which has been absorbed into the language to become a generic description of vacuum cleaners. Generic drugs are perhaps just within this category: they have no manufacturer's brand, just the generic description 'aspirin', 'penicillin' and so on, and so are somewhere between a brand, a grade and a product description.

Manufacturers' brands, like Nestlé and Cadbury

These unambiguously identify the manufacturer.

Retailers' own brands, like St Michael or Sainsbury

These do not identify the manufacturer, but give the buyer some indication that the product has met the standards imposed by that retailer.

Retailer's names

The fact that a product is bought in a certain shop gives some indication of quality, reliability, social acceptability and so on. One can draw a lot of conclusions (right or wrong) by noting whether a product is sold in Woolworth's, British Home Stores, Harrods, or all three.

Other cues

Other cues, like 'bought in Saville Row', 'Harley Street doctor' are, again, generic rather than specific to one manufacturer, and are barely brands at all.

Many of these brands fall in several of these categories at the same time. 'Boots', for instance, is an umbrella brand for a wide range of pharmaceuticals and related products; it is the manufacturer's brand for those products manufactured by the company; it is the retailer's own brand for products manufactured by others and marketed under the brand 'Boots'; it is the name of the retailer – and the fact that another brand is sold by Boots gives customers a certain confidence: hence the advertisements for cosmetics and so on which end 'Stocked by leading department stores and Boots the Chemists'.

Levels of brands

Another way to look at brands is to consider how they work at different levels.

Umbrella brands, like Unilever, General Motors or Mitsubishi

These may or may not be visible to the ultimate buyer, but they certainly will influence the purchasing decision of wholesalers and retailers. They at least can see the brand on the outer wrapper or on the invoice, and form judgements on quality as a result.

Main brands, like Ford or Brooke Bond

These may be recognized and used by the final buyer, and the decision to purchase may be made on these main brands alone, or on these plus sub-brands produced by the same manufacturer like Sierra and PG Tips.

Sub-brands

Ford has sub-brands like Grenada, Sierra, Escort, Fiesta, and so on. Coca Cola has Classic Coke, Diet Coke and Cherry Coke. These sub-brands are often more powerful selling tools than the main brand. The sub-brands are likely to refer to one product, or even one product line, while main brands often cover a range of products.

Product line

Product line is used here as one line within a product group produced by one manufacturer, one variant of a Ford Escort, for instance. In practical marketing this can get very specific indeed: the Gillette Contour five-pack, but not the ten-blade pack, nor the special offer, and certainly not the Wilkinson equivalent.

Cues

Cues are subjective indicators of quality. Cues such as the quality of the packaging, the location of the shop selling the product, the colour of the egg, the ambience of the shop, and so on, all affect consumers' perceptions of quality. They overlap with the main subjective indicator of quality, the brand, when, for instance, it is assumed that any product sold in a certain shop must have excellent quality. While it may be perfectly rational to believe that a certain shop would not dare sell shoddy goods, it may be completely irrational to predict the taste of an egg from the colour of its shell.

Again there are overlaps. Nestlé is a manufacturer's brand for instant coffee, but an umbrella brand for a range of foods. A manufacturer may use different brands for different product lines: the major soap manufacturers, for instance, have dozens of lines, but advertise them as competitors, rather than as having a single common origin. Elsewhere, the same brand may be used for products as different as pianos and motorcycles.

Brand recognition

At first sight it may seem that just putting your name on a box of cabbages is not branding it: a brand is not really a brand unless there is brand recognition. However, a rigorous application of the definition used demands that this should be called a brand. In practice, too, Campbell's Cabbage is likely to have some small value at least, being recognized (or avoided) by a small group of customers buying from Mr Campbell's market salesman, even when only a tiny proportion of the retailers using Covent Garden have ever heard of him. In later chapters examples will be given of situations where sales can be increased just by the fact that a product is branded, even if there is no brand recognition.

At the other extreme, my aunt, being a Dubliner, cannot fail to recognize the brand Guinness, and she is firmly convinced that 'Guinness is good for you'. However, she is, like many Irish, a lifelong teetotaller, so she has never touched a drop.

Labelling with a brand

At first sight it seems that the product should be labelled with the brand if it is to be a brand at all – allowing for a few apparent exceptions like the Adidas stripes and Dunhill's white dot. However, the examples given above show that this is not so – General Motors, Van den Berg and Jurgens, 'Bought in Bond Street', 'Made in France', and so on. Sometimes it is enough that the user knows that the product is of top quality, even if he cannot prove it by looking at the label, or showing it to other people.

WHAT IS GRADING?

The word 'grading' is relatively new: Marshall always put it in quotation marks. Because of its newness, perhaps, its meaning has not really settled down, and it is not used in any consistent sense in the literature, or even in single publications, and this causes a great deal of confusion in the analysis. In this book grading is taken to mean:

Classification, or
Sorting, or
Grade labelling, or
Price labelling, or
some combination of these.

Sides of beef at an abattoir, for example, may be classified, but not priced or sorted. Pictures may be classified (Genuine Picasso, Rose Period), but not grade labelled or sorted. Tobacco bales at auction are classified and labelled, but not sorted or priced. Apples may be sorted, classified, given a grade label and given a price label.

The word 'grade' appears to have been used consistently in the sense of 'a class of things having the same quality or value'[1] since the 1880s at least, and does not have the same variation of meaning as 'grading' so it can be safely used here.

All products have grades

It is important to remember that all products have grades. No process produces totally homogeneous output, so some sorting always takes place. In agriculture, the output is typically heterogeneous, and it is sorted to produce several more uniform products, often sold to different markets. The raw materials for industry are often sorted from a heterogeneous product in the same way, but the manufacturing process is intended to make a uniform end product. While economists often choose to assume that the end product is homogeneous, the quality control manager and the after sales service staff are only too well aware that it is not. There is a range in qualities produced, some items being produced to specification, most deviating from specification but being within acceptable tolerance levels, some being outside tolerance levels and some being frankly defective. A product with 5 per cent of its units defective is not 'to all intents and purposes homogeneous' and in an industry like microchips, the acceptable error is in parts per million: a single defective chip can mean that a computer malfunctions at great expense.

Quality control

Quality control in a manufacturing process is formally a sorting process which is part of grading. At its simplest it is sorting the product into two grades 'accept' and 'reject'. The sorting may be integrated into the manufacturing process, with quality checks at all levels from acceptance of raw materials to final delivery: this makes it difficult to identify the sorting process, but it is there nevertheless, and it has its effect on the final product shipped out of the factory.

Classification

Classification means measuring the *characteristics* of a good and determining what grade, class or category it falls into, according to the *grade specification*. The grade specification is based on the level of some characteristic or characteristics of the product. Classification sometimes has the implication of testing the product as a whole rather than its characteristics: 'Does it work?', 'Is it drinkable?'.

If a product is classified by just one single characteristic, and that characteristic varies continuously, then the grade may be specified by the upper and lower level of the characteristic, or by the lower limit alone, or by the mean and some level of dispersion, usually the range or tolerance. Nearly all the theoretical analysis in the literature has taken the simplifying assumptions of a single characteristic, constantly varying and with the grade defined by a top and a bottom limit (this and alternative methods are examined in Chapters 6 and 7).

Generally, of course, products are classified according to several characteristics at one time, some continuous, some discrete, some defined by limits, some by means, some by tolerances.

Another complicating factor is that many products are not single items, but a collection of items in a package. Here the grade specification may require that each item in the package must meet grade specifications, or alternatively it may require that the mean of items in a package must meet the specifications. The two approaches result in very different distributions of quality. In many ways this is like random selection of samples from a parent population with the packages forming a sample.

Characteristics and attributes

In the last chapter a distinction was drawn between the objectively measurable characteristics of a product and the subjective attributes, which are in the eye of the beholder. The importance of this distinction will become increasingly obvious as the book progresses.

A producer will normally be in a position to classify a product by some of its objective characteristics – size, shape, sweetness, and so on. Characteristics are normally assumed in the literature to vary continuously from low to high, with high levels being more highly valued. In fact, many characteristics do not vary continuously but discretely, like variety of apple, country of origin, leaded or unleaded petrol and so on. In fact, too, consumers often think that too much of a characteristic like sweetness or acidity in wine is as bad as too little.

A consumer's perception of a product may be closely linked to the characteristics a producer used for classification, but may be quite different, either because the consumer's satisfaction is based on a different set of characteristics, or because the consumer's perception of the product is not closely related to the objective characteristics.

Sometimes characteristics are divided into vertical and horizontal, on the assumption that everyone agrees that more of a vertical characteristic is a 'Good Thing', but there is no agreement on a horizontal characteristic like the colour of apples. This distinction causes more confusion than it removes. A product can have a horizontal quality even when its component characteristics are vertical. With fertilizer, for example, the main nutrients N, P and K are vertical over a big range, in that more is better, but the proportion in which they occur is critical: the mix suitable for a lawn is quite wrong for rose trees. This means that there is a horizontal quality difference between different fertilizer mixes. What is more, too much of the right fertilizer can also be harmful, so again quality is not vertical. Very few characteristics are vertical at all possible levels. There is nearly always some level at which any increase reduces the value of the product. In effect, vertical and horizontal are subjective perceptions of the individual, and great care should be using in applying the concepts to objective characteristics.

It does no harm to start an analysis with the presumption that the quality of the product (not the characteristic) is horizontal, and that any change in formulation will make the product more acceptable to some people and less acceptable to others. While it may not be strictly true always, it is psychologically easier to move from this perception to a realistic appraisal than it is to switch from the assumption that more is always better.

Sorting

Sorting may be a purely mechanical process, with different sizes going into different grades according to objective characteristics, but it may require some judgement and appraisal, or some arithmetical combination of measurements of characteristics. Sometimes the sorting may be based, not on an objective characteristic, but on the sorter's subjective perception of quality – which may not be at all like the buyer's!

At first sight it appears that sorting implies classification; that a product is necessarily classified before it is put into a grade. In practice, though, it is more common for a product to undergo a series of separate evaluations on different characteristics, sorting for size, then for colour, then for defects perhaps. The product may never be classified as a complete product: instead the end product is a series of items meeting grade specifications.

In the short run, suppliers have the options of doing full sorting, of leaving part of the bulk product unsorted or of doing partial sorting (when, for instance, it pays to sort a mixed product to Class 2, but high wastage would make it too expensive to sort it to Class I). They may also sort to closer tolerances than the grades require.[2] In the long run, when a given, mixed, product is being sorted, it is impossible to change sorting specifications to increase the supply of one grade without altering the supply of adjacent grades. Even in the long run, when production methods can be changed, it is probable that changing the supply of one grade will change the supply of adjacent grades.

Grade labelling

The quantity of information that is given on a product varies enormously:

1 The product may not be labelled at all.
2 The product may not be labelled, but it may be obvious to the shopper that it has been sorted or classified according to some unstated specifications.
3 The grade may indicate no more than that the product has been sorted or classified to say, 'Choice' or 'Export Grade', where the buyer does not know the specifications.
4 The grading system may be one that the consumer does not know about, but could, in principle, find out about if he put enough effort into it, writing to the EEC in Brussels for instance.
5 The grade may indicate the ranking of the grades, with Class 3 being, in some unspecified way, inferior to Class 1.
6 Exact specifications in some or all relevant characteristics may be marked.
7 The seller may label his better grades, but leave the cheaper grades unlabelled.
8 Any of the above may be combined with a brand label.

Combinations of the above exist: The label 'English apples, Cox's Orange Pippins, EEC Class 1, 60-65mm, Organic' gives precise information on size, variety and country of origin, less precise information on the use of insecticides, and very vague information about the characteristics covered by the EEC standards.

Price labels

Price labels can give the buyer a great deal of information about the quality, even if there are no grade labels to support them. For example, the product may be labelled with:

- The price per kilogram, a price related to a single characteristic.

- The price per unit. If all items on display have the same price, there is an implication that they are all of the same quality and quantity.
- A different price for each item on display. This suggests that in some way their different characteristics have been measured and the price has been adjusted accordingly, so they are the same value for money.

A high price gives the consumer several contradictory messages. First, it is undesirable, with a high price meaning that he has less money to spend on other products. Second, it is desirable, with consumers getting some satisfaction from the fact that they have paid a high price, and they can afford it. Third, it is undesirable, with consumers upset that they have paid too much for a product. Fourth, it is desirable, with consumers attributing quality, desirability, social acceptability, and so on, to a high-priced good.

Single firm grades and market grades

Some grading systems apply throughout a market, with all firms using the same system. Others are used by one firm alone, usually in combination with a brand. Sometimes, products will have combinations of the two.

Single manufacturer

A single manufacturer may have his own grading system within a single product line, independently of what other manufacturers do. For example, he may have a jumble display of frozen chickens, differentiated by price and weight label.[3] A car manufacturer may sell cars identical except for the grade: 1000cc, 1300cc, 1600cc and so on. A hair shampoo may be 'For Dry Hair', 'For Greasy Hair' or 'For Normal Hair'. A computer may have 20Mb, 40Mb or 60Mb disk storage.

The grades may be so different that they become separate product lines: large, unblemished oranges may be sold loose in one shop, small, unblemished oranges may be sold six to a net in the same shop, while medium-sized, blemished, oranges may be sold in a different type of shop entirely. One grade of car (left-hand drive) may be sold in Europe, while another, (right-hand drive) is sold in Britain. The different grades may even go to different end uses and so be, in effect, completely different products. Petrol and kerosene, for instance, are different grades sorted out of crude oil.

On the other hand, a manufacturer may use one grade description over a range of quite different products: 'low calorie' or 'ozone friendly' for example.

Market level grades

Market level grades may exist when there are no brands, when some firms brand or when all firms brand. The grade may not be labelled, or it may be used as well as the brand – where all petrol companies use the same octane ratings for instance.

There are many possible forms of these grades. They may apply only within one product line for instance. The same basic grading system may be applied to a range of product lines within a product. The same system may cover entirely different products, apples and bananas for instance. The possible combinations are endless: a firm can have a main brand, differentiating its products and product lines by market grade, or it can have each line separately graded.

A combination of grades

In most markets there is not just the choice of either everybody using the same grading system or of each manufacturer using his own grade. Instead, there are parallel grading systems, with Classes I, II, and III, as well as Grades A, B, and C and Categories Fair Average Quality (FAQ), Choice and Select. Individual producers or groups of producers may use their own grades instead of, or in addition to, the market standard. It is very seldom indeed that a product is described by a single grade label 'Grade A' and nothing else. Even when there is a single grading scheme in operation with government forbidding any alternative scheme (as is often the case in France), there are usually parallel grades and other sources of information. When there is a Flavour grade, there is still likely to be an EEC grade, information on the variety, size, origin and so on, and a brand, all of which add to the information available.

Market transparency and levels of the marketing chain

Grades are often used at some levels of the marketing chain, but not at others. Sometimes grades with completely different specifications are used at different levels. One sometimes sees violent criticism of this on the grounds that it does not give 'market transparency'. It is argued that an efficient system uses the same grades and specifications from producer to consumer so that consumers' preferences are communicated direct to producer. This argument has a certain appeal if one does not look at it too closely, and it is one of those value-loaded concepts that arouse strong emotions. In fact, if one looks at the concept closely, it is clear that the reason that different grades are used is because this is more efficient: market transparency is a side issue. It has been pointed out above that wholesalers, retailers, buyers and consumers have very different requirements; factors like low waste in store, uniformity within deliveries and fast turnover, which are of key importance to retailers, are of no direct importance to consumers. A grading system which reflects consumers' preferences does not reflect wholesalers' preferences. Similarly, when a product has different end uses it may be appropriate to use different grading systems for each. One of the main aims of grading and sorting systems is to produce qualities that will appeal to different market segments, so a single grading system reflecting the demands of one segment would be a disaster. The marketing system and the sorting system are so complex that consumer preferences would not be fed back accurately to consumers. This is perhaps seen more clearly with manufactured goods. It is of no interest to the consumer to know what grade of wheat was used to make his bread, or what grade of steel was used to make his desk lamp. Even if consumers had very strong preferences for one grade of steel for desk lamps, it could hardly have any effect on market prices or communicate consumer preferences to producers.

CONCLUSION

This chapter has shown that for most products grades and brands are inextricably linked. It has also shown that there are many possible structures for branding systems, and many more for grading systems. There are tens of thousands of combinations of the two. It is not possible therefore for any economist to come up with any broad generalizations and conclusions which will apply to all products. What has been done here is to present a framework for identifying the characteristics of a specific market and a specific product. This is a necessary precondition for any analysis designed to guide action in the real world.

The outline provided here will be used in later chapters. Some of the concepts will be expanded and analysed in more detail there but it would be boring to expand the concepts in any detail before it becomes clear why they are important, and before the market has been discussed in a way to make it clear why the refinements are relevant.

Chapter 4

What is search?[1]

INTRODUCTION

In previous chapters it has been shown that a product does not have one single, unambiguous, quality. Manufacturers, distributors, buyers and consumers all have different concepts of quality (Chapter 1). Moreover, consumers have different perceptions of the quality of a good, different tastes and different incomes, so they will not all agree on the ranking of grades of any one product (Chapter 3). In Chapter 2, on 'The product as a variable', it was shown that a product that is totally homogeneous in objective characteristics, with no product differentiation, can still vary enormously: its value can vary with location, with the shop's reputation, with the time of day it is available and so on. Apart from variation in physical characteristics, search is probably the most important of the factors causing product variation. It applies to products that are homogeneous, and to those that are differentiated, so there are few products for which it is not important.

Much of economic theory is based on the premise that consumers buy the goods that give them the greatest satisfaction for the least cost. The reality is different: it takes time and sometimes money to identify the prices and the quality of the product lines on offer, and it may be impossible to acquire the necessary knowledge to maximize satisfaction. As a result, people are willing to make suboptimal purchases if this reduces search cost. The search cost can be high enough to make a market cease to function, when, for example, some of the food on offer is known to be dangerous, and the consumer cannot identify which is dangerous and which is safe. It is a lot more time consuming to find out what qualities of rice there are in an African market, and their prices, than in a supermarket, so people with a high opportunity cost for time are happy to pay a higher price for the same product in the super-market. If search cost can be reduced, the cost of buying falls and sales increase: individual consumers may perceive it as being analogous to a fall in prices (though the effect at market level is very different from a fall in price). Sellers recognize this, and have a host of strategies to reduce search cost, such as minimum safety standards, grades, brands, quality control, guarantees, and public relations for their stores. The amount spent on these strategies and their ubiquity confirms their central role in modern marketing. No useful economics of quality can be constructed which does not take search into account at all stages.

One of the most important arguments in favour of brands and grading systems is that they reduce search. They can make search easier by reducing the variance in the quality of the goods in the market, variance over time as well as variance within and between product lines, by reducing the variance in the quality of a product line between shops and by facilitating price/quality comparisons. They can, in fact, increase the pleasure of search, reduce the pain,

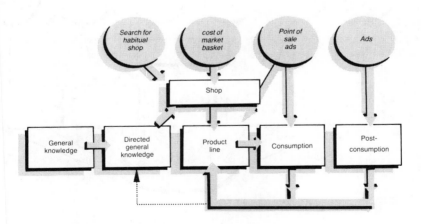

Figure 4.1 One possible search for cornflakes

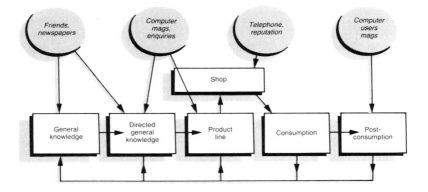

Figure 4.2 One possible search for a computer

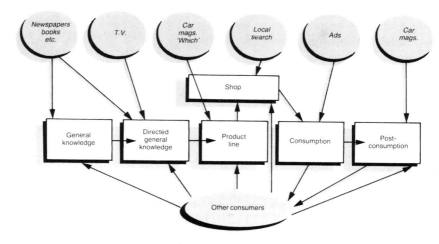

Figure 4.3 One possible search for a one-off purchase of a car

and reduce the expected pay-off from further search. Some of these effects will be discussed in this chapter, some in later chapters.

A body of theory has developed on the economics of search, based on the premise that rational buyers will search until they believe that the probable increase in utility from the better product that may be found by continuing the search will just equal the probable decrease in utility from carrying out that search. This equi-marginal position will be influenced by their beliefs about the probability of getting a better buy, allowing for variations in price and quality, and their beliefs about the amount of search needed to find that better buy. Costs of search include time taken, travelling, information collecting and information processing. Interesting and illuminating models have been constructed to elucidate particular points. However, to make modelling easier, they have been based on a very narrow range of assumptions, with the result that (a) each model is highly specific, (b) very few models share the same assumptions, (c) all models implicitly ignore factors of some importance in real world situations, (d) the models are not generalizable and (e) some of the models apply to situations which could not exist in the real world.

Some of the models are neither interesting nor illuminating: they are quite unrealistic in assuming that people can do linear programming in their heads and do this routinely in the daily shopping, that they know the distribution functions of price and quality, that they know probable search costs, that everything is linear, that sellers' quality is exogenously determined, that consumers know the distribution frequency of all price/quality pairs in equilibrium and so on. Much of the search theory in the literature is of the order of:

a consumer wishing to buy a unit of a certain good at a minimum expected total cost should shop around until he finds a price $p = R$ such that

$$c = \int_{o}^{R} F(p)\, dp$$

where c is the cost of search and $F()$ the distribution function, assumed known.[2]

This type of approach does not seem to have any practical application, or to be a useful model for consumer search in the real world.

The purpose of this chapter is to lay out one possible framework of search which will link the useful approaches, and set out which searches must be covered in a complete model. Most of the specific models in the literature remain as special cases, though it becomes clear what parts of a complete model they do or do not cover. The totally unrealistic models will be shown to be unnecessary. A more complex, and more realistic, sequence of searches will be substituted for the one-off search of most models, and a perfectly normal process of evaluation substituted for the computer analysis of perfect information that is sometimes assumed. The emphasis will be on deconstructing the search and decisions, because it is not possible to construct a useful model of a real market without an appreciation of the constituent elements. It will be shown that the process is more complex and more interesting than the specific models allow, and that the implications for marketing are more far reaching. The problems of quality identification and evaluation, in-store choice, consumption technology, information processing, advertising, grades and brands will be left to later chapters.

In this chapter, advertising is treated as a form of information only, a simplifying assumption. The fact that some brands, for designer jeans, for example, have a value independent of the characteristics of the product is a complication that must be dealt with later. The chapter also concentrates on the economist's rational buyer, as search theory was built around this. Search patterns are presented as hypotheses which may or may not apply to any particular market, so it is considered inappropriate to refer to papers in the marketing literature which show that similar searches have been found in one or two specific instances. Indeed, the searches are so widely recognized that there are few issues of marketing journals that do not have at least one paper elaborating on one aspect of one kind of search. This chapter is concerned with the economic implications of the search pattern, and is not concerned with questions of the underlying consumer behaviour, with methods used by consumers for processing information, with regularities in search or purchasing behaviour or with marketing's behavioural models.[3]

SEQUENCE OF SEARCHES

In this chapter search is not treated as a one-off activity leading to a single purchase. Instead, it is recognized that in the real world there are many phases of knowledge acquisition – general knowledge, directed general knowledge, pre-purchase search, search for a shop, search between shops, consumption and post-purchase search. Out of pure curiosity, most people gather information about a range of goods which they may never want to purchase. If, however, they are vaguely thinking of buying a car, they may start to direct this search towards a general interest in cars, which later becomes a specific search as the need and opportunity arise. It is only at a late stage in the search that they go around car dealers trying to identify the best buy in the way modelled in the literature. They savour the car as they use it, they seek more information to reassure themselves that they did not make a mistake, then they advise their friends on what to buy. This is shown in outline in Table 4.3.

This model gives rise to many feedback loops, from consumption to general knowledge and from post-purchase evaluation to choice of shop or choice of product, for example, so search may be considered as an iterative dynamic process. Not all decisions involve all types of search: buyers may go straight from general knowledge to purchase if there is no time for other searches or if the probable pay-off seems small in relation to the cost. There is also an overlap, with a shopper in a supermarket gaining general knowledge about one product while searching for the cheapest line in another product and, indeed, doing several stages of search for one product at the same time.

This approach to search is very different to the one in most of the literature.[4] In the rest of this chapter the search procedure will be elaborated on and the economic and marketing implications noted.

GENERAL KNOWLEDGE

Consumers do not start their search in total ignorance: they have an enormous fund of general knowledge about products, prices and places to shop at. This covers products they will never buy, including sports cars and old masters. The accumulation of general knowledge may be thought of as being an unconscious

Table 4.1 The different stages of search

Stage of search	Information acquired
General knowledge	How good is a Rolls Royce? Are there any new products in the shops? Which are the best neighbourhoods to live in? Which is better, a CD or tape?
Directed general knowledge	What types of car are on the market? Which brands have a reputation for reliability? Which cars have my friends had trouble with? What extras would I like on my present car?
Which retailer?	Which garages have a reputation for cheap cars, and for being willing to negotiate? Which offer me the best trade-in? Which have a good reputation for after-sales service?
Which product?	What are the different qualities offered in this model? cc, extras, size, luxury? How do they compare in value for money?
Final purchase	Which car offered by which retailer offers best value for money?
Consumption	How is it now I have bought it and driven it for a few months?
Post-purchase search	Perhaps I should have bought a Jaguar after all?
Feedback	Should I buy the same car as last time?

strategy of storing up information which may possibly be of future use, a strategy that is so basic to human life that it may be considered a survival trait. People store information about the desirability of different residential districts, note their friends' complaints about their cars, and note that someone was pleased with a certain plumber. Negative information is as interesting as positive. As they walk around a supermarket buying the items on a shopping list, they note what other lines are stocked, and note the existence of new products.

While it is normal for economists to model search as a costly activity, search can be a pleasure, knowledge a joy. Shopping is usually considered a pleasurable activity, a break from routine. Some kinds of search can be pleasurable even if there is no immediate prospect of buying: consider the sales of *Jane's Fighting*

Ships, Stanley Gibbons' Stamp Catalogue, steam train magazines and so on. Sometimes, as with antiques, the satisfaction a consumer gets from the product may be increased by the length of time he has had to spend looking for it.[5] This chapter will not ask why people enjoy the search, or why some people choose to become experts in the performances of footballers, others in the price of antiques: it is enough to say that some kinds of search can be a pleasure.[6] Turning search into a pleasure, whether by making shops pleasant or by making collection fun, is a recognized form of marketing, and may be quite as important as reducing the pain of search by reducing queues, improving parking, and so on.

The fact that search can be pleasurable does not mean that any reduction in search is a bad thing. There are usually boring and unpleasant aspects that could be removed to make the rest of the search more pleasurable. For example, the existence of the *Stanley Gibbons' Stamp Catalogue* makes search a lot easier, and as a result a lot more search is done. The EEC labelling regulations make it possible for consumers to check for additives, and so get the satisfaction of searching for additive-free food: in a sense this is an added cost, as they now do something that was impossible in the past.

One important form of general knowledge is how to search. One learns how to use the yellow pages, one learns that there are stamp catalogues, and that there is a monthly guide to second-hand car prices. Sellers may educate customers in search, by wine tastings and so on.

Information processing methods are also a part of general knowledge. Some derive from our education, some from our experience, some from friends and some from advertising. They may or may not be rational or optimal and may or may not be applied in appropriate situations. The methods can be applied to a wide range of decision-making.

An equally important form of general knowledge is when to search. Buyers have perceptions, right or wrong, that with certain types of good it is worth spending time and effort searching, while with others it is not. These perceptions may exist long before the buyer is actively considering buying the product. Brand leaders may encourage the perception that it is not worth searching, while those trying to establish a new brand, possibly with novel qualities, stand to gain by persuading buyers that it is worth searching.

It is also important to learn that a product exists: most people would be perfectly happy with their LPs if they did not know that CDs existed.[7]

Negative information is at least as important as positive: more so perhaps, as one warning is more useful than a dozen lukewarm recommendations. The more negative information customers have about brands, countries of origin, and so on, the less they have to search. This is true even if the information is wrong.

Most general knowledge is never used, but it is there to be used if the occasion demands. Occasionally, decisions are made on general knowledge alone: if pipes burst, the householder uses any information available to make the decision on what plumber to employ, on the grounds that any information is better than none at all. If there is not the time for a specific search, or if the search does not seem to be worth doing, the decision will be made from whatever information is available, a rag-bag of knowledge, prejudice and guesses, even a plumber's name once seen. If a decision has to be made immediately, buyers will make it on whatever information is available, even if it is clearly inadequate. They will bet on a racehorse with a lucky name – it cannot be worse than selecting with a pin, and it might be better. Some advertising appears to be aimed at these direct decisions from general knowledge alone: emergency services, public and private, are advertised so that people know what to do in an emergency when there is no time for a specific search.

General knowledge may also be used as a tie-breaker if the consumer cannot decide between two products on their more readily identifiable characteristics. These tie-breakers are very important indeed in marketing. If a buyer is unable to decide between a Ford and a Toyota on technical grounds or on the basis of other characteristics – and how many buyers can? – he is likely to decide on a relatively trivial point. It may be the general knowledge that 'Japan produces good quality', it may be a specific feature like a beeper to warn you if you have left your lights on when you park the car. Again, marketing by features rather than fundamental characteristics is common in industries like motor cars and air travel, with the features being used as tie-breakers.

DIRECTED GENERAL KNOWLEDGE

At some stage the consumers may adopt a rather more directed search. They may decide that they want to replace their computer in a year or two, and start acquiring general knowledge about the market for computers and the quality and performance of different brands. They may discuss it with their friends, read the odd magazine, note any relevant facts that happen to turn up in the newspaper, and note what sources of information exist – how to search. At the same time they can sharpen their perception of what they need, what they are dissatisfied with in their present computer and so on. They are building up the information needed to decide to buy or not to buy, and when to make their decision. It is usually a lot cheaper to make a note of a relevant fact when it crops up in the newspaper or on television, than to try and find it at short notice.

Obviously, there can be no clear distinction drawn between this stage and the previous one, of acquiring broad general knowledge, or the next one, detailed search for the best buy. Again, this may be a preliminary to a more directed search, but in an emergency, if their computer breaks down and they have to replace it, buyers will make use of whatever information happens to be available. There is also a lot of overlap, with consumers walking round the shop, conducting their immediate search for software, but at the same time getting general knowledge about the sort of things that it sells, getting detailed general knowledge of the printers available for a future purchase, and evaluating their past purchases of computers. A similar overlap between the different searches occurs when someone is doing the weekly grocery shopping. This does make it difficult to determine empirically which kind of search the customer is doing at any one moment.

PRE-PURCHASE SEARCH

The search for Directed General Knowledge merges into pre-purchase search, as the time for purchase approaches, and as the buyer starts to get an idea of what to buy and when to buy it. In this section different routes towards the purchase will be examined, whether deciding on what product to buy and then searching for the product line with the combination of quality and price that gives the best value for money, deciding on a product line and then searching for the best price, or deciding on a shop and then looking for a product and a product line. First, however, the distinction between search and experience goods must be clarified and habitual purchase strategies described.

Search goods and experience goods

The distinction between search goods and experience goods is important to pre-purchase search. A search good is one that consumers examine and appraise before purchase. An experience good is one that they buy and evaluate afterwards by consuming. Credence goods or characteristics, are ones that the buyer has to take the seller's word for rather than experiencing, such as 'organic', 'no artificial colours', 'hand-made', 'Made in Italy', and so on.[8]

By their nature some goods cannot be evaluated until they are consumed, so they are necessarily experience goods. Other goods could be search goods but consumers choose to treat them as experience goods. Information economics suggests that it is likely to be a good strategy not to search if (a) the cost of evaluation in the shop is high relative to the cost of making a suboptimal decision, (b) the items are difficult to inspect, (c) they are cheap, (d) they are unlikely to be substandard, or (e) a guarantee of some sort (including a brand label) reduces the cost of product failure. It is more likely to be a good strategy to treat them as search goods if (a) information is cheap, or (b) the cost of a wrong decision is high. Expensive goods, goods that account for a high proportion of the consumers' expenditure, goods with a high proportion of substandard items, and variable goods are likely to be search goods.[9] In spite of the fact that it is a common situation, there are few papers in the literature covering the situation where price is easily ascertainable, and quality not.[10] A complication that does not appear to be addressed in the literature is that for most goods there are some characteristics that can be searched for, like appearance, and others that can only be experienced, like taste. The consumers' strategy will depend largely on the relative importance of taste and appearance, and on the degree to which they believe that the two are related.

Habitual purchases

Most goods are not pure search goods or pure experience goods: habitual search strategies are the norm. Rational consumers would adopt a habitual purchase strategy after comparison shopping to test the market. They buy brand X as a rule, buying other brands from time to time to test the strategy.[11] With this strategy, experience goods become search goods in a sense, and vice versa.

This explains why customers request detailed information on vitamin content, additives, and so on, when many studies[12] show that they seldom use it – it may be valuable in the initial search period and for check purposes, but not otherwise. Similarly, they say that they consider that price is a very important factor in determining what they buy, but in supermarkets it has been observed that half of them cannot remember the price of the item they put in their trolley thirty seconds previously.[13] For most products, years of experience, plus the occasional reading of labels, have given buyers a wide range of accurate knowledge, on the flavour of competing brands, on their reliability, on their relative price and so on. Any customer who has been eating breakfast cereals every morning for twenty or thirty years will have an extremely accurate idea of the eating quality of most product lines and of the preferences of each member of the house. Anyone who has spent five minutes checking cereal products for calorie and fibre content will have a very good idea of which types fall within acceptable limits. This gives a wide range of choice and the information does not have to be updated frequently.

It is surprising in the light of this that researchers should express such astonishment at how little time is spent searching in the shop. For instance de Chernatory (1989) quotes Kendall and Fenwick (1979) as showing that 25 per cent of shoppers buying rice, pasta, canned meat, canned fish and soups made a purchase decision without any time spent deliberating and 56 per cent spent *only* [my emphasis] up to 8 seconds examining which to buy. He also quotes La Scutio (1966) as saying that in 55 per cent of the observed purchases of breakfast cereals, there was no visible in-store search. In view of the amount of experience consumers have, it is surprising only that they should have taken so long.

One implication is that during the period that the seller is test-marketing a product, consumers may not be behaving normally to it. They may be test-buying it and deciding whether or not to adopt it as a habitual purchase. Accordingly, a higher than usual willingness to purchase, with fewer than usual repeat purchases, may be typical of test markets (and of course the test market period may not be long enough to record repeat purchases of infrequently-bought goods.)

If marketing can provide the buyer with the information needed to turn a product from a search good to an experience good, then the buyer sees the good as being cheaper. This necessitates identifying the product line (with a brand, perhaps) so that customers can repurchase the same line, as well as taking action to ensure consistent quality (and this may be a significant limitation on which products can be turned into habitual purchases).

This means that the information provided can have very different functions, depending on the type of good. For instance, a label may be put on an experience good to provide additional information so that the consumer can turn it into a search good. Additional information can be given on a search good to reduce the search cost, so customers are more willing to buy. A search good may be labelled with a different sort of information, such as a brand or grade, to permit easy repurchase, and so turn it into an experience good. Both brands and labels offer some implied assurance or guarantee of quality, further reducing risk.

The consumer saves a lot of time if he can switch from a search to a habitual purchase strategy, and this effectively makes the product cheaper. For this reason it pays the manufacturer to try and make the product a habitual purchase rather than a search good. The good can only become a habitual purchase if there is some way to identify it, so that customers know that the product they liked first time is the same as the one they see on the shelf. Brands, grades or labels may fulfil this function. The quality of a good with a given label or brand should be constant. No other information is needed to fulfil this function. Grade standards that fluctuate over time may be quite adequate for search goods or even experience goods, but are of little use for habitual purchases.[14] This condition means that if the manufacturers cannot measure the key quality, taste for instance, it is not possible to make the product into a habitual purchase. The condition limits the possibility of making habitual purchases of those products for which the manufacturer can only offer a higher probability of better taste, and so on arising from sampling. There is another limit to the possibility of habitual purchases, when the brand or label can be linked to one valued characteristic, but another, taste perhaps, is randomly distributed and cannot be determined except by consumption.

A grade label for an experience good performs very different functions to those of a grade label for a habitual purchase. The objective is to make it a search good instead of an experience good. If the buyer can predict the quality of the purchase in the shop, instead of having to experience it, risk is reduced. The reduction of risk, and the possibility of buying exactly the quality required must be balanced against the increased search cost.

A grade label for a search good may have the objective of making search easier and cheaper. This may result in rather more search being done, as the probable pay-off remains the same while the cost falls. Alternatively it may mean that a perfunctory search is enough to ensure that a purchase is acceptable, so less search is carried out.

The habitual purchase may be less closely defined than this, not the decision to buy Birds Eye fish fingers, but the decision to buy Birds Eye fish, or Birds Eye frozen food. Brands can perform similar functions with both search and experience goods. Essentially they are informing the customer that the product is similar to other products produced by the same manufacturer in some way, such as quality control or tastiness. Both the labels and the brands offer some implied assurance or guarantee of quality, further reducing risk.

The phenomenon of 'anchoring' is relevant here, where the goals shift in line with what has been bought in the past. For instance, if I buy a Nikon camera, I have to buy Nikon-compatible lenses. People who buy one brand after a search are likely to persuade themselves that it was a good buy, and therefore resolve to buy it in future. Mention is sometimes made of path-dependent variables, whose values depend on recent values of the variable. An obvious example is an industrial raw material, where a whole batch will be assumed to have the strength of the weakest item found in acceptance tests.

Habitual shops

Consumers may also adopt the strategy of buying at the same shop every week. This strategy is analogous to that of habitual purchase of brands or product lines. They may adopt the strategy when they believe that one shop offers better value for money or better quality control, for instance. If a shop is to get itself accepted for habitual shopping it must offer a mix of the strategies identified above. It must be identifiable, it must stock a constant quality and offer a constant value for money for each good. At the same time it must offer the assurance that all goods in stock are of similar quality and value for money, in the same way that a manufacturer has all goods bearing one brand being of the same quality and value for money. The shop can offer more convincing money-back guarantees, because the customer can complain in person.

Consumers seldom decide to buy just one product line, or to buy from only one shop. The normal strategy is more likely to be something like

> I will buy most of my groceries at the superstore on Saturday, buying extra fruit and vegetables during the week from the local greengrocer, and buying all my meat locally. If there is anything I have forgotten, I will buy it from the local grocer.

This complicated strategy reflects a complicated range of pressures. The superstore is definitely cheaper; it is easier to park there; it is easier to bring the heavy groceries home; it is easier to make an expedition there when the family car is free. On the other hand you have to buy every two days to get fresh vegetables, the local butcher happens to be good, and it is a pleasure to walk to the local shops as a break from housework.

This strategy may be varied by going to Tesco most weeks, but going to Sainsbury once a month and to Safeway every two or three months. This means that a wide range of shops is covered at no extra cost. Shopping is efficient because customers can buy whatever lines are cheap at the store they happen to be in, which is particularly important for the storable items. Equally important, it gives consumers the chance to check whether Tesco is still the best shop or whether they should switch to another shop.

Own brands

Own brands, of course, combine these two strategies, habitual shopping and habitual purchases. (The simplifying assumption that brands only convey information and do not in themselves produce utility is still in force.) Private labels now account for over 38 per cent of all UK grocery sales.[15] Taken in conjunction with meat and greengrocery, which can account for a third of turnover and a larger proportion of the profit of a supermarket, this means that the own brands are of key importance to the large British supermarket chains. Accordingly, any search theory that ignores these strategies is of limited application.

CHOICE OF SHOP

Buyers may decide what they want to buy and then search for the shop which gives the best price (the situation most often modelled). Alternatively, they may search for the best supermarket, and only after they are in it decide which product line or product group to buy. A third possibility is to search for products and for the best buy at the same time. The implications for marketing are very different.

Choosing the shop first

With food shopping it is most common for buyers to choose the shop first and use it each week, making the decision long before they decide what to buy for this week's meals. For one-off shopping, a birthday present perhaps, a customer may choose a shop offering one product group (for example, a bookshop) or one type of product (for example, a gift shop or a garden shop).

These strategies are appropriate where the consumer is engaged in a joint search for several goods, or buying a shopping basket, or doing one-stop shopping – a situation which is seldom modelled in the literature.[16] It would be hopelessly uneconomic to search for the shop which provides the cheapest salt, then the one that provides the cheapest baked beans, then the one with the best quality greengrocery or own label groceries. It is rational to search for the shop that is cheapest, that has the best quality or that offers the 'best value for money' (and value for money is specific to the individual purchaser).

This strategy means that the market basket costs rather more than it would if each item was bought at the cheapest shop for that item, but search costs within the shop are low and the overhead cost of visiting a shop (travelling there, parking, entering the shop, going round the displays, queuing at the checkout and driving home) can be spread over all purchases in the market basket.

Sometimes buyers may have decided that the chemist round the corner gives good service and has that nice Mrs Jones working there, so they should buy there when convenient. In effect, the decision is made long before the purchase is necessary, and long before they have any idea what product group they will be buying, nappies or drugs, let alone what product line. The initial search for a chemist they are happy with may take some time, but once the choice is made, search between shops is at a minimum.

The strategy is particularly appropriate where buyers cannot easily make an assessment of quality in the shop. Consumers cannot readily assess the quality of own brands, unfamiliar brands, greengrocery and meat in a strange shop. They are likely to choose a shop in the belief, right or wrong, that

- it has an effective quality control system;
- its standards are in some sense consistent over a range of products;
- all items in a shop give some consistency in value for money;
- all items in a shop are socially acceptable;
- there will be a consistent and appropriate response to consumer complaints after purchase.

Availability is important in determining how far joint search is an appropriate strategy. The probable availability may affect both the initial choice of shop and the shop where the product is finally bought. Customers may go to a distant superstore rather than to a local supermarket if they particularly want a few items for a meal and they know that these are not stocked locally. The narrower the range stocked locally and the greater the perceived probability that the local store will be out of stock, the more often they will go to the superstore, and the higher the probability that they will just stop buying locally. One study of shoppers' reactions, on an all-products basis, showed that when a product was out of stock, 39 per cent shopped elsewhere, 26 per cent intended to return later, 30 per cent bought a different brand or size and 5 per cent bought other products.[17]

This imposes pressure on retailers to keep the most important items in stock, but it is not always clear which are the most important items. They have to decide whether to sell poor quality apples rather than none at all, if there is a shortage. They have to decide how much of their capital and space to devote to providing a wide range of products, rather than doing a few in depth. They have to decide whether to sell several product lines within a product group rather than to concentrate on a single line, or, perhaps, own brand plus the market leader. The retailer incurs additional procurement costs in buying a wide range, interest costs in stocking it, the costs of inefficient use of available space if too many lines are crammed in, the costs of congestion of the aisles when consumers are pausing to choose between the many lines on offer, and so on. Often, lack of capital and lack of space make it impossible to stock all the lines a retailer would like to stock.

Choosing between shops

Customers may think for some time before deciding what shop to try for a good, and may assess the cost of going to one shop rather than another. The costs are higher if they do half their shopping in one store, and decide to do the rest elsewhere – the costs of travel, parking, in-store search, queuing at the checkout and so on, have to be repeated. However, once they enter a shop, that shop has a very considerable locational monopoly. At the least, the customers would have to make the effort of walking out and going to the shop next door. This is one of the reasons why special offers or loss leaders are used to attract people into the store.

Once the customers are in the shop, their opportunity costs change, and they are more likely to search for alternative purchases. An alternative product, which seems inferior before they enter the shop, is much more attractive when they have to leave the shop and search other shops before they can find the product which was their first choice. If they do not like the value for money of branded baked beans, they may switch to own brand. If they think that lamb chops are too expensive, they may buy pizza instead.

Once customers are in a shop, the retailers can use a range of strategies to make them perceive the costs of going elsewhere to be high. They can be told that it is difficult to reach other shops, that most other shops are out of stock, that it is extremely difficult for a non-expert to judge quality, and that some shops are unscrupulous in passing off inferior quality as best. They can be told that the risk of further search is high, as the item on display is the last one in stock, and someone will be coming back for it later in the day, so it will not be available if they do not buy it now.[18] The assurance that all shops charge the same price for a given brand makes search seem pointless, while the opposite strategy of making price and quality comparisons difficult by stocking only own brands, or special models of well-known brands, makes search seem expensive.

The pay-off from this locational monopoly may be just that the retailer sells to a high proportion of the customers who enter his shop, and that the customers, once in the shop, buy a range of goods apart from the ones that attracted them in. The retailer may be able to exploit it further, by saying that the special offer that attracted customers is over because the last one has been sold, or that the special offer is in fact an inferior product that he does not recommend. This gives him the chance to sell customers alternative goods with higher margins. He can also exploit the monopoly by revealing that the price quoted is exclusive of Value Added Tax, or that the special offer item does not carry the usual guarantee or after-sales service.

However, the degree of locational monopoly may be considerably lower than this would suggest, and considerably less than might be inferred from a model for a single, one-off purchase. In a supermarket, for example, customers who find one line expensive may buy other competing product lines or totally different products, or they may postpone the purchase until they visit another shop. They may decide to buy the bare minimum on that visit and do their main shopping elsewhere that week. On the other hand, if the customers are happy with what is in the shop, they may buy more of everything storable, and reduce or postpone purchases from other shops. They are influenced, of course, by the degree to which a product is storable, the amount of pantry, refrigerator and freezer space they have available and the amount of the good they already have stored. The response will be rather different when dealing with a product like greengrocery whose prices and quantities normally fluctuate. Male shoppers who have not made a shopping list are notoriously likely to buy far more than they meant to. The assumption of a fixed budget constraint or a fixed shopping list, which is made in most search models, ignores this dynamic effect. The concept of a budget constraint as a moving average, as total expenditure per month rather than expenditure on any one shopping expedition, seems to be more realistic. I am not aware of any search models that take into account the dynamic effects of postponing purchases or the fact that a habitual shopping strategy means that several competing shops and lines are searched automatically and costlessly.

The locational monopoly is less strong where the product is expensive, where there is known to be a wide range in prices, where the amount that can be saved is substantial, where the cost of search is low, where a single product line is involved and where it is a one-off purchase. These are conditions where comparison is normal, and where the product is normally a comparison good. In these cases, shops often facilitate comparison by opening up next door to each other, as electronics shops, shoe shops and greengrocers stalls are often confined to a small area. This is particularly important when quality varies: when price alone varies, the telephone makes search cheap and does away with much of locational advantage.[19]

Frequent price changes can also be an incentive to search, suggesting that other shops are likely to be cheaper. In volatile markets, telephone information may be obsolete by the time the buyer visits the shop. Supermarkets often react not by trying to match the prices on market stalls on a day-by-day, or hour-by-hour, basis, but by holding prices steady. They may hold prices steady for months at a time, even for products like fruit and vegetables, only changing if they consider that the average market price is going to be consistently lower for a considerable period. It can be argued that

- people do not like frequent changes in price, as it means that they have to search every time they shop, so a habitual purchase becomes a search good;[20]
- frequent changes are costly to implement;
- customers are willing to believe that the average price that a shop charges over the year is reasonable, even though it may be more expensive than other products from time to time;
- it is in the supermarket's interest that the customers treat it as a habitual shop. Frequent price changes make it more likely that customers will compare prices of competing supermarkets, and that they will spend more time within the shop comparing prices, and so cause congestion and block the aisles.

It has been shown, though, that in such circumstances, where (a) supermarkets maintain level retail prices, (b) market supply and demand fluctuate, and (c) supermarkets have preferential access to supplies, the supply to the non-supermarket sector will vary more than total supply, and prices will fluctuate violently.[21]

These possible responses to price changes within a supermarket mean that calculated elasticities must be interpreted with the greatest care. Does a special offer on potatoes mean that a month's supply is bought on one visit instead of on four, so there is a big change in the first week's sales, but none on the month's total?

Does a price rise for baked beans switch customers to other products or to other stores? Do they buy their baked beans at these other stores, or their whole weekly groceries?

Equilibrium between stores

In this competition between stores the equilibrium is not one where all stores charge the same price or even one where all charge the same for a given market basket.[22] There are many reasons for this.

People have different willingness to search, so some may be looking for the best possible bargain, while others are satisfied with a reasonably good buy or with buying where most convenient. Goldman and Johansson (1978) quote references confirming that there are major differences in the opportunity costs of time of customers: for example, working women with large families have higher opportunity costs for time.

People have different perceptions of the amount of search that will be involved. Furthermore, those who search more will change their perceptions of the degree of variability of price or quality, and so their perceptions of the optimum amount of search: if, for instance, four retailers quote exactly the same price, it seems less likely that further search will produce benefits. Contrary to the assumptions of most models, it is unlikely that the consumer knows the distributions of prices, much less where on that distribution a given shop is for a given product line. It may be desirable when modelling to differentiate between expected search and probable search.

Some consumer groups may find a high-price, high-quality purchase optimal, and others a low-price, low-quality purchase. With the many different perceptions of quality possible, this implies that an extremely large number of possible combinations could exist in equilibrium.

Chan and Leland (1982) explore the different equilibria possible when price information is cheap and quality information dear and vice versa. Models can also take into account the fact that quality uncertainty is usually greater than price uncertainty.

Nearly all stores have some degree of locational monopoly, which, again, means that different prices can rule under equilibrium. Transport costs and ease of transport of heavy and bulky items play their part in this, so some products will be affected more than others.

Supermarkets in poorer areas are likely to have higher prices because the poor tend to be less able to obtain and process information, and because the low buying power of the poor means that there may not be enough shops in a neighbourhood for competition. It is often the case that lower income, ill-educated, disadvantaged, inexperienced groups are less efficient shoppers.[23] Being less efficient, they have less incentive to search; being poorer, they have more.

People have different market baskets, so the shop that is best for one shopper may be the worst for another. Even so, poor price information makes it extremely difficult for customers to determine which store does in fact offer the best buy.[24] Differences between actual and perceived quality increase the difficulty.

Any equilibrium would in any case prove unstable. It could be upset if a consumer organization, or even a single supermarket chain, started advertising comparative prices.[25] It is important that, in practice, a substantial proportion of consumers are free-riders, relying on others to do the research and to exert the competitive pressure. If search is cheap, a lot of people will search aggressively, and will change their buying habits. This, and the fact that they tell their friends what they have found, will increase competition and reduce price dispersion. The consumer who believes that this is happening may decide that there is insufficient price dispersion to justify a search. If enough people stop searching, competition is reduced and price differences increase. When it gets bad enough, people suddenly notice that their perception is wrong, and start searching on a large scale again. As with the cobweb model, external influences, like a burst of inflation or a shortage of potatoes, may fuel the cycle.

This emphasises the point that information is a public good. It saves a lot of money for a lot of people, including those who avoid the shop or the product as a result of the information. It also helps the people who do not get the information at all: their prices fall because other people get the information and act on it.

The implication is that the marketing and advertising strategy of a supermarket chain has to be very carefully thought out if it is to attract customers without driving away too many marginal customers. Any information will necessarily drive some customers away, even if only those who prefer to buy cheap and nasty. If a toilet water is advertised as an after-shave, this immediately drives away most of the potential users (men with beards, children, women) at the same time as it attracts others.

Since buyers differ, it would be foolish for all competing super-market chains to compete on exactly the same criteria. Instead, one may offer a narrow range, with national brands at very low prices, and stores close to consumers (for example, Kwiksave), which reduces several kinds of search cost, while another offers a wide range including own brands, with a reputation for quality and a reputation for products acceptable to one social class, and with easy parking on the outskirts of town, which reduces other kinds of search cost.

CHOOSING THE PRODUCT THEN THE SHOP

Customers may decide on the product group, the product specifications and even the product line before they enter the shop. They may decide that they want an IBM compatible XT, or even that they want an Epson PCE with 20Mb hard disk, VGA colour monitor, and so on. The decision could be based on close reading of computer magazines and discussions with friends or impartial experts.

This is particularly likely to happen when

- there is plenty of cheap information like computer magazines;
- it is easy to relate the information in the magazines to the product, because of brands or labels;
- the product is expensive;
- prices vary;
- it is a one-off purchase, so habitual strategies cannot be used;
- there is a special satisfaction in being one of the 'in-group who really knows'.

This is the behaviour that has attracted most attention in the economics literature. Most of the models examine sequential search: going into one shop and deciding whether or not to go into another, the decision depending on the customer's perception of the distribution of prices in the market. Whether they buy in that shop or not depends on their perception of (a) how close the price in that shop is to what is believed to be the lowest price in the market, (b) the amount of search that can be expected to produce a better price, and (c) the cost of the extra search in relation to the probability of getting a better price. It is usual for these models to assume that buyers have perfect knowledge of the statistical distribution of the prices within the market, but that they have no idea whatsoever what the prices are in any shop until they visit it.[26] The possibility of telephoning round for the best price is almost never considered, nor the possibility of using quoted prices as a basis for bargaining.

Searching for the best price and quality

Far commoner than this in practice is the situation where the buyers have a broad idea of the product group they want and are searching for price and quality at the same time. There is not a lot in the literature on this, but those papers that do exist normally assume that

- the buyers have perfect knowledge of the statistical distribution of the prices, but not of which shops are cheap;
- the buyers have perfect knowledge of the distribution of the probable qualities, but not where to buy them;
- the value for money of the different product lines in a given shop is not uniform;
- before the customers go into a shop, all shops appear equally promising, so it is a matter of chance which shop they go into first. Once they are inside, though, it is a definite effort to walk out and go to another shop;
- their perception of the probability of getting better value for money from further search depends on their perceptions of

  (i) how close the value for money in this shop is to the optimum;
  (ii) the statistical distribution of price and quality;
  (iii) how many shops they have visited already.

Nelson (1970) expects that a store selling search goods will carry more brands, and that such stores will cluster together to make search and comparison easier. His argument is particularly relevant here. Retail markets for fruit and vegetables follow a similar pattern, with competing stalls offering the same range of produce. The consumers who choose to shop in a retail market make fruit and vegetables into a search good, a comparison good, instead of taking them as a habitual purchase.

   In this situation it is important that quality comparisons can be made from shop to shop:

- Brands alone are of limited value.
- Brand plus mark or brand plus label are of value in identifying

product lines examined in magazines. They are also of value for comparison between shops.
- Labels may be of value: 40MB, 5 expansion slots, 640K RAM, 4.77/10MHz.
- With some products, computers perhaps, brands may be of little value. It may be enough for most people to know that it is a brand they have heard of. Equally, it may be enough to know that it is sold by a shop they have heard of.
- With some products visual comparison is possible, and labels, brands, and so on are irrelevant.

THE ACTUAL PURCHASE

The actual purchase is covered in detail in the marketing literature, and aspects will be covered in later chapters, so it will not be covered here. It is emphasised that an economics of quality which covers this alone ignores most of the subject.

CONSUMPTION

Consumption provides the key input to many purchase strategies. The assumption that the buyer is the consumer and that consumption and purchase take place at the same time is convenient for mathematical modelling, but it is unrealistic. Most products are bought by one person, a home-maker or a civil servant perhaps, for another to consume, and the same product is often consumed jointly by several people. Consumption generally takes place some time after purchase, often after further processing, like cooking, or over a long period of time, like a radio. This emphasizes the point that the buyer's perception of price and quality is not the same as the consumer's. These are points that will have to be built into a realistic, dynamic model.

POST-PURCHASE SEARCH

People seldom buy a product, consume it, and forget about the transaction. They continue to search, to see if they have made the right decision. The satisfaction from the belief that one has made the right purchase can be quite as great as the satisfaction from the product itself. The knowledge that one has blundered is painful. There is some reason to believe that consumers rationalize their choice afterwards, convincing themselves that they made the right decision.[27]

Consumers do search after purchase, and they can get a lot of satisfaction from the search. This satisfaction helps determine whether they buy the same brand in future, or buy at the same shop, and it also determines whether they recommend the product to their friends.

It follows that advertising aimed at telling people how clever they were to buy the product can have a major impact on buying behaviour. There are several reasons for this:

- With habitual purchases, the pay-off is direct. If customers are constantly assured that they made the best buy, they are less likely to change their habit.
- There are some products that are bought mainly on personal recommendation, with advertising and inspection playing a relatively small role – two-thirds of US automobiles are bought on personal recommendation.[28] If the purchasers can be persuaded that they were exceptionally clever to buy the brand they did, they will recommend it to their friends. This recommendation is the most potent form of advertising.
- Manufacturers who can convince their customers that they made the best buy also benefit the retailers by reducing after-sales complaints. The retailer's reputation has to be protected. Again, it pays the manufacturer to do this even if there are no repeat purchases by customers.
- Warranties encourage consumers to complain to the manufacturers, not to their friends if anything goes wrong, which reduces the damage to the product's reputation. It is also a very valuable form of product research.
- Users' clubs, guarantees, and so on arising from this are a useful form of market research.

A good example was the unscrupulous art dealer Duveen, who supplied the foundation for the big collections in the United States. He sold pictures to multi-millionaires like Mellon who did not know anything about art. A lot of the pictures he sold were grossly overpriced or of doubtful provenance. In order to maintain his reputation, he made a point of buying back anything he had sold whenever it came on the market, at a very good price. He lost money on these pictures, but the extra price he received for everything else compensated. (And, incidentally, the collections are now valued for their quality: the fact that they were grossly overpriced is long forgotten by most people.)

OVERLAPS AND FEEDBACK LOOPS

Obviously, the searches described here overlap. Searches for different products overlap: while one is looking for a computer, one is acquiring directed general knowledge about printers and software. While one is looking for potatoes one notices in passing where the police station and the post office are situated.

For many goods search is a continuing process, with information from one purchase being fed back for use in the next purchase: it is an iterative, dynamic process.

Buyers may be doing several stages of purchase for a single good at the same time. Today's point of sale choice between competing brands of breakfast cereal is part of a habitual purchase strategy for the product and part of the strategy of choosing a shop for the weekly grocery purchase, as well as acquisition of knowledge on fibre and calorie content of breakfast cereals.

Buyers do not always do all stages of search: they may go from general knowledge to purchase, or they may not have any idea of the product's existence until they see it and buy it; they may not have any post-purchase search, or the buyers may ignore consumer satisfaction. The models in the economic literature all assume a very limited search, usually with only a single stage of search.

INDUSTRIAL BUYERS

While this framework has been described in terms of consumer marketing, it can be expected to apply, with modifications, to industrial purchasing. Indeed, given the more formal nature of industrial purchasing, it may well apply more closely. Semi-industrial services markets may be difficult to fit into the framework. It is particularly important that industrial purchasers are seldom one-off buyers, and as a result they can adopt habitual purchasing strategies. They often have significant market power as well, and this helps them build up a close relationship with their suppliers, even to the extent of imposing quality control and production specifications on them.

SEARCH BY SELLERS

The literature is silent on search by sellers, though it does appear in other guises elsewhere, in agricultural marketing, for instance. At this stage it appears likely that a theory of search by sellers will be a mirror image of search by buyers, but there is room for development of this theory.

THE FRAMEWORK

The framework set out here is intended to be more generally applicable than previous models. It shows that the search models in the literature concentrate on only one or two of the many types of search, and that, even so, the assumptions are so restrictive that the models apply to only a few situations. The breadth of the framework is an indication of how specific the models are. The importance of a dynamic approach is emphasized.

Information overload and information processing

The framework set out here does not require that consumers have perfect knowledge and minds like computers. It does, however, require that they can absorb and remember very large quantities of information. Much of this information is the outcome of previous purchases: it is the result of a choice and consumption process rather than the logic that led up to it.

It is obvious that as more and more information is used in a decision, it will take longer and longer to process it. If a decision has to be made in a given time, it can be expected that the accuracy of the final decision will rise as the first information is taken into account, that there will be declining marginal returns and eventually negative returns as the time taken to absorb the information handicaps the decision process. From these two, unexceptional, statements it was argued that there was such a thing as *information overload* and that if too much information is made available to consumers, worse decisions will be made. This hypothesis was used to call into question the pressure by legislators and consumer groups for more product information.[29] The distinction between 'using information' in the first two statements, and 'making information available' in the hypothesis is important.

There has been a substantial literature on the subject. This is based on 'laboratory experiments' – for example, asking 153 students to select an imaginary brand of detergents from information about brands A, B, C and D printed on a card. I have some reservations about the paradigm, which I will discuss in Chapter 10 on Price as an Indicator of Quality, and even within the paradigm many of these experiments were unsound.[30] Some experiments seemed to show improved decisions with more information, but since one would expect this at some levels of the curve, the hypothesis that more information availability will eventually impair decision-making was not effectively tested. Jacoby, who was one of the founders of this line of enquiry, now (1984) accepts that it was misconceived from the start, as it bore no relation at all to how people make decisions in the real world.

When considering the information used by consumers in decision-making it has to be recognized that, however much information is offered to the consumer, he will use only what he considers relevant, and he will probably only use what he considers to be most important. He may get information on only a sample of the brands available and he may use only some of the information available on these:

> it matters not if consumers can be overloaded in the laboratory (where they can be force-fed large quantities of information) if they generally will not permit themselves to be overloaded in the real world.[31]

Laboratory experiments on imaginary products tell us very little about the real world. In this case, they ignore all the general knowledge and search over time, all the habitual strategies, all the feedback loops and overlaps.

Laboratory experiments also underestimate the amount of information people can amass and store, if they can fit the information into a framework. In our normal day-to-day food consumption and shopping we have a rich framework to hang information on. Any new information can be fitted into a model, as an addition to or a modification of previous experience with that brand, that product line and that shop. We are not trying to remember imaginary prices on a card. A Fellow of the Royal Society once told me how stupid he felt as a boy because he was the only boy in the class who could not tell which teams won, lost and drew in the previous week's football matches, much less who played in the teams, and how teams' performances had varied over the season. In effect, he did not have the framework for absorbing the information, because he was not interested.

Heuristics

Heuristics may be thought of as the decision rules and methods which reduce the complex task of assessing quality and selecting purchases to a relatively simple process. The heuristic will be easier than an optimizing solution, and there is a trade-off between reduced search cost, and higher risk combined with the expectation of a poorer product. There is a large and very interesting psychological literature on the heuristics people use, suggesting that there are very serious deviations from the optimum.[32] At first sight, this evidence totally contradicts the assumption of rational man, and throws doubt on much of the economic theory on the subject. However, many of the examples and experiments they base their decisions on are one-off decisions with limited information. The model presented here shows that simple heuristics like habitual purchase which are commonly used are not irrational, and can be efficient in selecting a quality that is acceptably close to the optimum.

IMPLICATIONS

The concept of search for quality, and more particularly of sequential search for quality, have wide-ranging implications for the economics of quality. Most important, perhaps, is that it allows for an analysis that assumes that, over time, people tend to buy the quality they want to, making use of the information and experience available to them. With this assumption it is not necessary to have complex models of an individual's choice under a range of restricting assumptions such as perfect competition, or to make heroic assumptions about the possibility of aggregating the individuals' choices (the best known of these models are analysed in Chapters 15 and 16). Some other implications which are of practical importance are:

- What do short-term test market results show for habitual purchases?
- What decisions are reflected in short-run and long-run demand elasticities?

- What is the effect of a reduction in search cost on (a) apparent price, (b) apparent market demand, (c) apparent market supply? How does it vary by segment? How does it vary by type of search? How does it vary by product?
- What are the implications for advertising objectives and priorities? For targeting – general knowledge? post purchase search? point-of-sale search? How does this vary from product to product, shop to shop?
- What kinds of information are necessary to help the different types of search? When is it enough to say that the product exists? When is it necessary to say what the product does? When is it necessary to say that the product contains E254?
- What does the model suggest for the priorities of a firm? Should it concentrate on trying to persuade people to try its product? Should it be trying to persuade existing customers to buy more? Should it be trying to persuade new customers to switch to the product? Should it be trying to turn a search good into a habitual purchase?
- Should a firm be trying to reduce search or trying to make search more fun? Should it be trying to make it more difficult to compare its products with other firm's products?
- What is the optimum availability? Should there be a large range of products or a small range? Is it better to have a wide range of products each represented by a single product line, or to have a smaller range with many product lines in each? Is it better not to stock a product if you cannot get the right quality? Should you stock unknown product lines? Should you stock own brands instead of the market leaders?
- How does search affect the optimum location of the store?

These are all important strategic questions for a firm. It is not possible to generalize about the answers: they will vary by firm, by product and by market. All that can be done is raise the questions, and give an indication of where one must look to find the techniques to work out the answers. There are also questions that arise for public authorities, and for the economics profession.

- What are the regulatory implications? How should public authorities or bodies like the Consumer's Association intervene in search? What kinds of search should they try to influence? Should they aim to improve general knowledge on

obtaining and processing information, or should they concentrate on product-specific labelling regulations?
- What are the policy and welfare implications? What are the implications on the need to control monopoly? Are certain social and income groups disadvantaged in search – access to information, ability to process it, and physical access to shops?
- How does search affect the theory of brands?
- How does search affect the theory of grades?

Again, much of the value of the general model is to identify points that have to be considered in any product-specific analysis.

Chapter 5

Brands as search

This chapter explores the effect that brands have in facilitating or hindering search, and it presents broad hypotheses on how different types of brand can affect different types of search. These can be the basis of empirical work to see if these hypotheses apply to any specific product in a specific market. The chapter examines the brands within the framework established in previous chapters. It recognizes that there are many concepts of quality, it recognizes that a product is a variable, and it makes use of the search framework of Chapter 4. It aims to answer such questions as how a totally new product may find a ready market as long as it makes use of an established brand, and a brand leader may get a price 10 per cent higher than other brands even though the product is identical.

Since the chapter concentrates on the effect of brands on search, it will be assumed that a brand is information, and that the brand itself does not give satisfaction. For the purposes of this chapter, then, a Dior dress gives the same satisfaction as an identical St Michael's dress. A brand is taken to be a label on the product which may identify the manufacturer but which does not give any information on the product itself. It will also be assumed that the brand and, in some cases, previous experience of the same product are the only information available on quality. In the real world, of course, there is often further information available, like grades, classification, labelling and quality cues, and some brand names are designed to give information on the quality of the product. The impact of brands on market structure is a big subject and can only be mentioned in passing.

The following types of brand will be considered:

1 A brand specific to a single product line, like Atora suet.
2 A brand specific to a product group, like Ford cars of different types.
3 A brand covering a range of products, like Sony.
4 A brand like 'Bought in Harrods.'
5 A retailer's own brand.

These will be discussed in relation to the types of search for that product, which were discussed in Chapter 4.

A BRAND COVERING A SINGLE PRODUCT LINE

When they first set up in business, manufacturers may start with a single product line and mark that line with a brand like Fisherman's Friend cough sweets in recent years, and Ford in the days of the Model T, when you could buy any colour you wanted as long as it was black.

One-off purchase

Let us consider what effect this has on a one-off purchase, considering first the situation where there is no pre-purchase search, and then extending to where there is pre-purchase search, including amassing general knowledge, and then to the situation where there is post-purchase search.

No pre-purchase search

Where there is no pre-purchase search, and the good is a one-off purchase, the fact that the product is marked with the maker's name gives very little extra information. By definition, the consumer has not bought a product with this brand before: if the brand is one that the consumer knows already, because it covers a lot of products, like Sony or Panasonic, the situation is one of pre-purchase search, which will be examined below. Because the brand is unfamiliar, it gives only the doubtful message that someone is sufficiently confident of the product to put his brand on it. It may permit the retailer to do in-store advertising. It does facilitate comparisons between shops, as one can telephone around for quotes on Blogg's TV sets, though this implies that the consumer believes that Blogg's TV sets are of consistent quality.

It seems likely that the brand will be ignored or given very little weight if there is any reliable information available, in the form of informative labels, category labelling, and so on.

Pre-purchase search

With a pre-purchase search the buyers can collect some information about the brand before the time of purchase. They may note that it is widely stocked, which gives them some confidence in it. They may recognize that the brand has been around for some time, which gives them some confidence that the product is not made by a fly-by-night manufacturer, and that there will be after-sales service, spares and so on in the future. Information from friends, consumer magazines, and so on can be related to a specific brand, rather than to some amorphous product. (The implication throughout is that consumers believe that the product line of a single manufacturer will be more homogeneous than the product as a whole, which is usually quite a reasonable assumption. There may be less defensible assumptions on uniformity within a line, within a brand and within a sub-brand. Uniformity is examined in detail in Chapter 7.) The existence of a brand also permits comparison of quality between different product lines, provided that the quality is visible on inspection. It also facilitates price comparisons.

When a product is typically bought after pre-purchase search, manufacturers can advertise to increase brand awareness and to improve the image of the product. This means that consumers will be able to build up knowledge about the pluses of his product, and both this and the fact that the product brand is recognized will increase sales. It is not entirely irrational for consumers to believe that this puts pressure on the manufacturer to

- produce a good quality
- produce consistent quality over time
- produce consistent quality between items
- offer good value for money
- have after sales service
- offer the buyer his money back if the product fails

These are all important parts of manufacturers' sales strategies, and will be discussed later in the book.

Brands in this context do not particularly facilitate quality comparisons. Comparison is only really facilitated when the quality can be determined by inspection, and the consumer assumes that all items in one brand are of similar quality. Unlike grades and informative labels, brands do not aim to give information in ways which facilitate comparison with other products. Typically, each brand concentrates its advertising on those aspects in which it is superior, remaining silent about aspects in which its competitors are superior, and this often does nothing to help comparison. This type of advertising is not just giving information about the product: it is indirectly giving information about what is the correct way to appraise the product. Inevitably, perhaps, the buyers are told that the correct way is the way that most benefits the product advertised. Even comparative advertising, giving the specifications and price of competing brands, is done in a way which implies that a certain mix of product qualities is superior, so each manufacturer can show that his own is superior. This is one reason why branding is so popular as a marketing strategy: it makes it possible to boast about your product without making product comparisons easy, and without suggesting that serious comparisons are particularly desirable. Obviously, brand leaders do not want customers comparing the product with other more or less identical products; obviously manufacturers with inferior products do not want customers comparing quality.

What is the link between brands and grades (informational labelling), and other informational labelling? There are an infinite number of possible combinations of grade and brand for different goods, so I shall give an example. When I bought my camera, which is essentially a one-off purchase, I knew from experience exactly what features I wanted and what features I was not willing to pay for, autofocus, for instance. Over the years I had spent some days reading camera magazines, discussing cameras with friends, and so on. I had come to the conclusion that five brands of Japanese cameras were virtually indistinguishable for quality, a conclusion based on my knowledge of the brands, my knowledge that the brands had kept a good reputation over the years and on my perception of the generic brand 'Japanese'. I felt that I could be entirely neutral between these brands, and concentrate on the technical requirements, TTL spot metering, zoom lens to 200mm and at least F4. My final choice was determined by the lens. I bought a lens made by an independent manufacturer, not one of the camera companies, with a brand I knew of but did not have a very clear image of. The choice of camera to fit the lens was purely one of technical compatibility – only one of the five brands gave me a clear focusing screen with no black spot with this particular lens. Here brand, grade, and technical specifications determined the choice.

How does brand influence post-purchase search in this context? To some extent my post-purchase search will be making it clear whether I have bought a product with the specifications I need, or whether I should have paid a little more for a few added features. If I am worried about reliability, or if my camera breaks down, I am likely to blame it on the brand. If I compare it with what my friends have, I am as likely to say 'I also bought a Nikon' as 'I also chose the basic SLR with a long zoom'. In view of the rapid change in camera technology over the years and the rapid fall in prices, it may be that a brand is an easier concept to stick with than technical specifications.

Repeated purchase

Where the product line is purchased repeatedly, brands permit a range of searches not possible when there is just a one-off purchase. The first time they buy, consumers can often afford to treat the good as an experience good rather than a search good, just trying it to see what it is like. The results of this experiment are an input for the next purchase decision. They can also adopt a habitual purchase strategy, buying the same brand each time. Brands are obviously important here in linking one purchase to the next – there is always the assumption that any purchase of one brand will be of similar quality. Brands are a lot easier to remember than the detail of an informative label, and it seems probable that people who use informative labels for comparison on their first search, will decide to buy a brand, rather than a mix of characteristics. In future purchases they can be expected to buy the same brand, long after they have forgotten why it was that they made that decision. One of the reasons for special offers is that they get customers to try a new brand and decide that it is acceptable: they may then go on buying the brand long after they have forgotten that it was a 25 per cent cut in price, rather than superior quality, that made them try it in the first place. As with all such generalizations, nobody can know how widely they apply, and it takes empirical research to determine whether they apply to your particular product.

BRANDS SPECIFIC TO A PRODUCT GROUP

So far the discussion has been about a brand specific to one product line. In this section brands specific to a product group are discussed, with Ford covering a range of cars, Nikon a range of cameras and so on. This often comes about because the same technology and equipment can be used to make several models in a product group. The models can be targeted at different market segments, people with different incomes or different life-styles perhaps.

One possibility is to have a completely dominant brand name like IBM, with the different models being distinguished largely by their specifications.[1] Another possibility is to have one major brand name covering the whole product group, with a sub-brand for each model. For example, Ford brand cars include those with the sub-brands Fiesta, Grenada, and so on. Generic brands also cover a range of qualities. Sometimes the generic brand over-shadows the product brand as with Danish bacon, but sometimes it achieves almost no recognition.

Product-wide brands cover a wider share of the market than line-specific brands, so there is a greater chance of brand recognition than there would be if there was a single brand for each model.

One-off purchase

No pre-purchase search

With a one-off purchase and no pre-purchase search, the buyer may get some more confidence from the fact that several product lines in the product group carry the same brand: it suggests that there is a bigger, and therefore possibly more reliable, firm making it. It also suggests that the manufacturer has more to lose if he sells rubbish: he loses sales of all his models, not just the defective product line. When the purchase is the only purchase in the product group as a whole, the brand has the same value as for a single-line brand, except for some added confidence of this nature.[2]

However the position is rather different when the consumer has bought another item in that product group. If he has bought a low price Ford, his experience with it will influence his decision when he decides to trade it in for a higher-priced model. If he is even moderately satisfied with it, he will think twice about trying another brand which might be much better, but might be worse. He may think that the low risk if he buys the same brand next time outweighs any possibility of getting a better quality by experimenting with another brand next time. Of course this decision is strongly affected by the consumer's belief that

- a product line bearing a single brand is uniform
- the different models within a product-wide brand are in some sense uniform. This might be in engineering quality, value for money, social acceptability, availability and price of spares, after-sales service and so on.

If customers believe that the models within a product-wide brand are uniform in some or all of these senses, it may seem rational to ignore them when choosing a product line, and make the decision on features like engine size, size of the luggage compartment, quality of the trim, and so on. In this case, unimportant features become tie-breakers in the choice.

Product-wide brands may influence choice in another way. If customers compare the quality of two brands for one product line, they may, not unreasonably, assume that the brands bear that relation for all product lines. Similarly, if one shop is significantly more expensive for one product line, customers may well assume that it will be equally expensive for others. The conclusion may easily be wrong, but it seems likely that customers will still draw the conclusion when there is no better source of information available.

Pre-purchase search

When there is pre-purchase search with a product-wide brand there is a larger body of knowledge to draw on. If my friend is happy with his IBM PC, and if a computer magazine recommends the IBM AT, I am more likely to buy an IBM XT. The fact that the brands are product wide means that they are more likely to be recognized, and more likely to be used. It also means that there is more pressure on the manufacturer to keep the same quality standards over the range: if quality standards are low for the cheap cars in the range (poor reliability, poor after-sales service, non-availability of parts) customers will be disappointed with their first car, and will buy other brands for the rest of their lives. Other forms of quality like engine size, trim and comfort, are not expected to be uniform over the range, so customers will not mind if their first car is a basic, low-powered model.

Repeated purchase

When there are repeated purchases of the same product and the same product line, the single brand for a whole product range offers additional search benefits.

The customers' experience and their post-purchase search can be used to inform their search if they want to try other product lines. If the product is 'tinned soup', their experience with Campbell's will determine whether they try Campbell's or Heinz when trying a new soup. This does put a certain pressure on the manufacturer to have some uniformity over the range, not just in 'product quality' or 'reliability' but in appropriateness for one sub-market. In the case of soup, for instance, all product lines in one product group may need to have the same spiciness. Heinz has felt it necessary to have a sub-brand Weight Watchers, which are consistent in certain aspects of quality including 'slimmingness' or calorie content, but which might not appeal to their average customer. By implication, these lines have the other 'quality and reliability' aspects of other Heinz brands (see Tables 5.1, 5.2, 5.3, to illustrate one-off purchases, with pre-purchase and no pre-purchase searches and repeated searches).

BRANDS CROSSING PRODUCT GROUPS

Brands crossing product groups may imply one product line in each of several product groups, or several lines in each of several major product groups. Here there may be a common factor in that they are all food products, or that they share the same distribution system, with many Birds Eye products requiring refrigerated distribution for instance. Similarly, Panasonic has product lines in a range of electronic goods, whose only common feature is the technology used, computer printers and video recorders, for instance. Broadly speaking, the logic is similar to that for brands covering a whole product group, but there are some special features.

Table 5.1 One-off purchase, pre-purchase search

	Brand for a single line	Brand for a product group	Brand for a range of products	Shop as a brand	Own brand
Permits brand-based general knowledge	*	*	*	*	*
Permits brand-based directed general knowledge	*	*	*	*	*
Permits post-purchase search	*	*	*	*	*
Gives wide range of experience to draw on	*	*	*	–	–
Gives confidence because more hangs on it	**	**	***	****	****
Permits habitual shopping	–	–	*	***	***
Permits habitual purchases	–	–	–	–	–
Permits treating as experience good	–	–	*	**	**
Facilitates price comparison	*	*	*	–	–
Facilitates quality comparison	–	*	*	**	***

Note: The number of stars indicate the strength of the relationship.

One-off purchase

No pre-purchase search

A brand like this is particularly effective when one is making a large, one-off purchase. If I decide to buy a computer printer, I may choose a Panasonic because my Panasonic video seems to work all right. This is not necessarily a correct conclusion: indeed the fact that a firm makes good videos may suggest that they concentrate their research and development on them rather than on other products.

The fact that there is this cross-product effect means that there is pressure on the manufacturer to avoid selling any product lines

Table 5.2 One-off purchase, no pre-purchase search

	Brand for a single line	Brand for a product group	Brand for a range of products	Shop as a brand	Own brand
Permits brand-based general knowledge	–	–	*	*	*
Permits brand-based directed general knowledge	–	–	*	*	*
Permits post-purchase search	*	*	–	–	–
Gives wide range of experience to draw on	–	*	**	**	**
Gives confidence because more hangs on it	–	*	*	**	**
Permits habitual shopping	–	–	*	***	***
Permits habitual purchases	–	–	–	–	–
Permits treating as experience good	–	–	*	**	**
Facilitates price comparison	*	*	*	–	–
Facilitates quality comparison	–	*	*	**	***

Note: The number of stars indicate the strength of the relationship

that are inferior. This adds to one's confidence when using brands as a basis for pre-purchase search and general knowledge, even when the product is a one-off purchase with no pre-purchase search *for that particular product*. (The search for one product becomes the pre-purchase search for another product of the same brand.) At the least, the manufacturer might be expected to sell a product under another brand name if he knew that it did not match up to the range.

Manufacturers usually have to satisfy at least two sets of clients, consumers and retailers. When they launch a new product, a new chocolate bar for instance, they may decide that the consumer wants a totally new brand and brand image. The retailers, however,

Table 5.3 Repeated purchase

	Brand for a single line	Brand for a product group	Brand for a range of products	Shop as a brand	Own brand
Permits brand-based general knowledge	*	**	***	***	**
Permits brand-based directed general knowledge	*	**	***	***	**
Permits post-purchase search	*	**	***	***	***
Gives wide range of experience to draw on	**	**	***	***	**
Gives confidence because more hangs on it	**	****	****	***	****
Permits habitual shopping	–	–	–	****	****
Permits habitual purchases	**	**	***	****	****
Permits treating as experience good	**	**	***	****	****
Facilitates price comparison	****	**	*	**	***
Facilitates quality comparison	****	***	*	***	****

Note: The number of stars indicate the strength of the relationship.

are not interested in stocking a completely unknown brand, as they do not know how good it is, what the quality control is like, what the delivery is like and so on. To satisfy both sets of clients the product may have one brand on the wrapper, Yorkie, to appeal to the customer, and another Rowntree Mackintosh dominant on the outer case to appeal to the retailer. (In fact Rowntree Mackintosh Ltd appears in small letters on the back of the wrapper, and Societé des Produits Nestlé SA in very small letters.)

Pre-purchase search

When customers can do a pre-purchase search of that product, and there is a multiproduct brand, the advantages are much the same, with the additional advantage that the consumer can get specific information on that particular product group and product line.

Both when there is a pre-purchase search and when there is not, the producer with a multiproduct brand has an advantage over the producer with a single product brand or the producer with a single line brand. Customers are more likely to try a brand they recognize. It is obviously important that the products are of good quality.[3]

There is an implication here, though, that the product lines in the multiproduct brand all appeal to similar market segments, perhaps defined in terms of income, of life-style or of quality requirements. If the brand does not, then there may be considerably less benefit in multi-product branding.

Repeated purchase

With repeated purchase of the same product, the balance of advantage between multiproduct brands and single-line brands changes, with the single-line brands being in a better position to compete.

THE SHOP AS A BRAND

The fact that a shop agrees to stock a product line, branded or unbranded, helps reduce search in some of the ways that a multi-product brand does. Consumers may believe that the shop would only stock a product if it thought that the product was acceptable and if it was not getting complaints about it. In fact, consumers nearly always underestimate the quality control exercised by the large supermarkets, and the costs that supermarkets would incur if they sold dangerous goods. Consumers may believe that anything sold by a certain shop is

- of acceptable quality
- of acceptable value for money
- socially acceptable to a certain group
- subject to money-back guarantees

There is another, rather different, implication. Some consumers will get more satisfaction from buying a product line in Harrods, and letting it be known that it was bought in Harrods, than from buying exactly the same product line at the same price in Woolworth's. They may even get more satisfaction from paying more in Harrods.

One-off purchase

No pre-purchase search

When there is a one-off purchase with no pre-purchase search, customers can reach some conclusion on the probable quality and value for money, and so on, mainly from the fact that the product is stocked in this particular shop. For this reason, some manufacturers advertise that their products are stocked by well-known high-street shops like Boots, Dixon, Rymans and W.H.Smith, to show that they have high-street credibility. The strength, and reasonableness, of the buyers' belief is affected by the other information and quality cues available.

Sometimes the shop makes no difference at all. One would expect that all supermarkets sell all the brand leaders at the same price, or at least that a market basket costs the same in each. On the other hand the unbranded products, fish, meat, fruit and vegetables, and the own-brand products are important, and customers' perception of the price and quality of these can be largely determined by the reputation of the shop. Occasionally one is in the situation where one enters an entirely new shop, and quickly forms a perception that it is very good, very bad, or that it stocks only very good, very expensive goods. From this perception it is a small jump to drawing conclusions about any particular line.

With pre-purchase search

The meaning of pre-purchase search in this context is not the same as with brands. In effect, it must mean finding out which shops are reliable and cheap, which have good quality control and good after-sales service and so on. This does not, however, help the normal pre-purchase search, comparing the price of the good and quality. If there are no brands or labels, the only way of comparing price and quality of one supermarket's fruit and vegetables with another is by physical examination, a daunting task even for the experts.

It would be understandable if consumers compared prices on those product lines where comparison was easy, and assumed that the same relationship held throughout the range stocked. It would be understandable, too, if quality was assessed by the general ambience of the store, its location, the quality of what was stocked, the number of expensive lines on display, and so on.

Some shops do not have the reputation for selling good quality: they have a neutral reputation or the reputation for selling cheap and nasty, or just nasty. A lot of interesting questions arise with regard to these firms:

Can a bad firm get the same price for its unbranded products and own brands as the reputable firms? Probably they cannot, whatever the quality of individual lines.

Can a bad firm get the same price for brand leaders as the reputable firms can? This is difficult to answer in an environment where the reputable firms keep low prices. One possible strategy is to charge the same price as other firms, and accept slow sales, and make up the margins on other, less comparable, lines.

Can a bad firm get the same price as the reputable firms for 'good quality' fruit and vegetables? Probably not. However, in Ireland we found that firms specializing in poor quality fruit and vegetables got a relatively high price for these qualities. The lowest income groups automatically assumed that 'poor quality' fruit, and fruit from 'poor quality' shops was cheaper, so these shops could charge a high price for these qualities. The shops which catered to higher income groups would have to charge a much lower price if they ever stocked such low qualities, when produce was scarce, for instance. If the shops serving the low income groups stocked top quality produce at a very low price during glut periods, their customers would reject the produce as being too expensive: 'Those apples are too good for the likes of us'.[4]

RETAILERS' OWN BRANDS

In undeveloped economies, of course, pretty well everything is unbranded. As the economy develops, more and more is sold, first as an unbranded product in a shop, then as a manufacturer branded good, then as the own brand of a large multiple retailer. Own brands become more and more important as multiples build up the skills and bargaining power to negotiate the purchase of perishables, and then the purchase of own brands, manufactured to market leader standards, often by the same manufacturer as the brand leader.

One-off purchases

No pre-purchase search

With one-off purchases, an own brand can give considerably more information than a simple brand. I have no idea what kind of overcoat I want, or what specifications it should have, and I realize how easy it is to buy rubbish. I only know one brand for coats, Burberry, and I believe it to be expensive. However, I do know that I can go to any of two or three multiples and buy a coat with some confidence in its quality. This information is not good for price comparison, though. While Marks and Spencer, Austin Reed and Burtons may all provide acceptable quality, their prices will be different, and I do not know why: what extra quality is one offering that the other is not?

Pre-purchase search

Generally, it is harder to do quality and price searches with own brand goods, because it is so difficult to pin down what the difference is.

Repeat purchase

Own brands facilitate habitual shopping and habitual search strategies. They do, however, make it much harder to compare between shops. Hidden quality differences could explain price differences, and it is not easy to compare an own brand bought from Tesco one week with that bought from the Co-op four weeks later.

CONCLUSION

The main thrust of this chapter is to show that all types of brand are not interchangeable, producing the same results whatever the product and whatever the search method. It has been shown that some types of brand give very little information at all for one-off purchases, even if there is a pre-purchase search. Others are particularly suited to these products. Some types of brand are helpful for general knowledge or for post-purchase search, while others are totally useless for these searches.

The message comes through again and again that broad generalizations are dangerous: the branding system that suits one product or the average product may be quite useless for your product.

Chapter 6

Sorting

This chapter is concerned with the physical effects of sorting: how it determines what products, and what quality of products, are supplied to the market. It also covers the different types of cost a producer may incur from sorting, the physical costs of doing the sorting, the changed price for the output of the firm as a result of the different qualities supplied, and the less directly observed changes in market prices when a large number of firms sort in a similar fashion. This chapter will not consider how the fact that a product has been sorted alters search, nor does it consider the impact of grade labelling: these will be covered in Chapter 8.

In this chapter, and those that follow, the following questions will be asked

- Does sorting change consumer satisfaction or buyer satisfaction with the product?
- Does sorting change the value of the product to the distributor, independently of any change of value to the consumer?
- Does the fact that the product has been sorted convey any information to the buyer?
- Does the fact that one product has been sorted change the cost of search, either to those who buy or to those who choose not to buy?
- Does the fact that the product has been sorted change risk and uncertainty?
- Does sorting facilitate feedback of information to the producer?
- Does sorting influence brand position?
- What are the physical costs associated with sorting? What are the other costs?

SORTING OR PRODUCING TO A QUALITY

There are two extreme approaches to producing a product of a given quality. One extreme, which we may call the primary product approach, is to produce an extremely variable product, then sort it into several relatively uniform grades. The other extreme is the ideal factory which produces one single grade, with all its output meeting specifications. Most firms have elements of both.

Primary product approach

Sorting from a mixed product is fairly typical of a primary industry like agriculture. In the very short run the output is fixed: it is of a variable composition and there is nothing the producer can do to change that. The producer's problem is how to sort the product in such a way as to get maximum revenue in the short run and in the long run, and it may prove to be best to sell the product unsorted. A policy of only selling the best quality will mean that a relatively high proportion of total output is dumped.

In the longer term the firm can change the production process to produce a product with the same variance but a higher mean, with the same mean but a lower variance, or with a higher mean and a lower variance. This will mean that the unsorted product is itself more valuable, and that a different sorting process might prove optimal. In the longer term therefore, the firm has the options of changing the production method or changing the sorting strategy, or a mixture of both.

The firm also has the possibility of producing a new product line, either by changing grading specifications to produce a grade that is very different to existing grades, or by introducing new characteristics into the sorting process.

The perfect product

The ideal factory assumed in the literature produces items identical in all respects, so a perfectly homogeneous product can be assumed. In reality though, the most one can hope for is that a factory produces a variable product, with every item in it meeting its specifications. This outcome, 'zero defects', is rare in practice. In a trivial way it can be achieved easily enough by having very broad specifications, so it is easy to meet the specifications, but the tighter the specifications, the less probable it is. It can also be achieved, in a somewhat less trivial way, by having a process where the product is subjected to quality control inspections repeatedly throughout the production process, so there are zero defects when it leaves the factory, but this implies repeated sorting operations (quality control is sorting) with the outgrades being dumped. The ideal zero defects, where the product is built to specifications without the repeated quality control sorting and rejecting is very rare indeed.

Even such high precision products as electronic chip manufacture produces its outgrades, defective products which do not meet the specifications, and even one or two per million are worrying when a defective chip costing a few pence can immobilize a factory or send a missile to the wrong country.

This emphasizes the important distinction between specifications and tolerances. For some products like microchips, there may be very tight specifications, and very tight tolerances, with the product only being acceptable if less than three chips per million leaving the factory are not within the specifications. With light bulbs the technology is relatively crude and anything within broad specifications will meet the requirements. However, tolerances are wide: if one in twenty new light bulbs does not work, it is a nuisance, but not much more than that. A motor car's steering system, again, has very broad specifications, but, because of the disastrous effect if it fails, low tolerances.

This means that the producer of a manufactured product, like the primary producer, has to make decisions on the quality of product he wants to make, in terms of specification and tolerances. The optimum will depend on production costs and market requirements. Like the primary producer, he has the option of developing a production system which produces a very uniform product, or of having a production system which produces a relatively variable product, and having a series of quality control sorting processes throughout the manufacturing process to weed out the items that do not meet specifications. The sorting or quality control process is often integral to the manufacturing process, so it may be difficult to think of it as a separate process. This means that, formally, the major difference between the farmer and the manufacturer, is that the manufacturer ends up with a single grade for sale, and the farmer with several.

Mixed types

For many products there is an intermediate type. A considerable amount of control is exercised on what is produced, but there is still so much variation that more than one grade is needed. For example, canners may reserve certain qualities for own brands and clothing manufacturers may sell rejects under another brand name.

CHARACTERISTICS

For the purposes of this chapter we will consider only two types of characteristics out of the many that will be covered in Chapter 14. The first is assumed to be infinitely divisible along a linear scale (weight, alcohol content, and so on). The second is a simple yes/no characteristic, red or not red, leaded or unleaded. The possibility of sorting by attributes, according to the subjective perceptions of the sorter, is ignored.

TYPES OF PRODUCT

Three types of product will be considered:

Item products

Item products consist of large, discrete items, like cabbages, radio sets or frozen chickens. The product is sold by item, with a single item being a common purchase. Any one item either meets the grade specifications or it does not.

Package products

Package products are smaller, sortable items that are normally sold in a packet or by weight. A single purchase might consist of twenty Brussels sprouts or fifty Smarties. With one type of specification, the package as a whole might be considered, with the package being within specifications if the average level of characteristic lay within the specification. With another type of specifications, each item in the package should meet the grade specifications. In this case, a pack of four apples can only be 0 per cent, 25 per cent, 50 per cent, 75 per cent, or 100 per cent out of grade. The distinction is blurred if all items must be within the specification, but tolerances are permitted. In the next chapter, where uniformity is discussed, it will be shown that the distribution of qualities within a package is quite different with the two types of specification. The distinction is often not made clear when specifications are drawn up.

Bulk products

Bulk products like liquids or powders are sold by weight or volume or, indeed, in a package. They are likely to have one or more of the following

– There are very small increments in quantity sold, as with petrol.
– Any consignment, display or package of the product is seen as being perfectly homogeneous, so any purchase from a bulk container is expected to be identical.
– Any one consignment is either 0 per cent or 100 per cent out of grade.
– It is impractical to select a superior sample by selecting one item at a time.
– The product can be classified, but not sorted into its constituent grades: for example, grain or milk. True, petrol can be redistilled, or coffee beans hand sorted, but the cost makes this impractical.
– Different qualities may be blended to make a new quality, as with whisky, but this process cannot be reversed.

Distinctions

These three types of product are sometimes difficult to distinguish clearly in practice, with a bag of three oranges being not too dissimilar to three oranges bought item by item, and with a packet of raisins being not unlike a bulk good. The product may also be a bulk good at one level of the marketing chain and be sold item by item at another, as cabbages are bulk goods on the farm, package goods at wholesale and are sold item by item at retail.

There are, however, major limitations on the type of sorting that is possible or practical on the different types of good, and on the marketing and pricing system that is possible. An economic theory built round a consumer picking a used car will not have a great deal in common with one built round someone buying wheat on a commodity exchange, or someone buying cakes in a supermarket.

GRADES

The product can be classified into grades according to grade standards or specifications. The items in one grade are not necessarily identical – they might for instance vary within the size limits to that class and vary enormously in respect of characteristics not covered by the specification.[1]

The grade is normally specified in terms of the upper and lower limits of several characteristics, by the mean level of the characteristic, or by some measure of dispersion such as the range or tolerance. With yes/no characteristics, a diesel car goes into one category, a petrol car into another, and an electric car into another.

The set of grades is the list of grades that may be used at any one time. The literature has usually assumed that there is a single set of mutually exclusive grades which everybody uses, as this simplifies analysis. This is, however, rare in practice. The following sets are possible:

A mutually exclusive set

A mutually exclusive set exists when there is one single set of grades in existence and any item fits unequivocally into one of them and only one.

A cumulative set

Often the specification is cumulative: Class 1 may be not less than 60mm in diameter, Class 2 not less than 50 mm and Class 3 not less than 40mm. An item 70 mm in diameter can go into any of these classes at the producer's whim. Producers may put an item into a lower classification than its specifications justify for several reasons. First, for reasons that will be discussed below, the physical and other costs of sorting may outweigh any gains. Second, producers may prefer to mark everything as Class 3 rather than being fined for overstating the quality. Third, they may expect quality to decline between time of packing and time of sale.

Identical sets

An equivalent or identical set exists where several sets of classes are in existence when, for example, the British Standard and the American Standard are identical.

Parallel sets

Parallel sets exist where apples, for instance, have one grade for variety, another for size, another for freedom from blemish. Where there are two parallel sets, each with three grades, there are, in effect, nine possible grades, ranging from Class 1 Big, to Class 3 Small.

Overlapping sets

Overlapping sets occur when producers may choose to use Choice or Grade 1 or Class B, each having different specifications, to describe a given item. This is probably the most common in practice, with many supermarket items being subject to the EEC standards, the standards of the supermarket chains, and the standards of the country of origin, and rating differently on each.

DEGREES OF COMPULSION

It is convenient when building economic models to assume that before a grading system is introduced nobody uses the system, and afterwards everybody does. Reality is never like this. It is extremely difficult to find any product in any market which is not sorted in some way. Certainly the food in a Third World market is not sorted according to EEC regulations, but a close inspection of the marketing system reveals that all food there is sorted, to meet the requirements of different market segments. There are strong price incentives to sort. As a result, the introduction of a compulsory grading system may mean that people sort to the same grades under different names, or they change from one set they considered optimal to another. In this section the different levels of compulsion backing a grading system are set out, as a first indication of the extent to which a product is in fact sorted. Even this may be a very poor indicator of how much sorting is done: the EEC fruit and vegetable standards are compulsory for all fruit and vegetables in the EC, but in practice they are generally ignored, for the reason that they are completely unrealistic and the system would collapse if they were enforced.[2]

No fixed grades

Often there are no fixed grades, so each supplier may supply his product in whatever form he wishes. He may supply the product exactly as it is harvested or comes off the production line: alternatively, he may sort his product into more or less uniform classes.

Standard grades

The next stage is for a central authority, the government or an industry association, for instance, to lay down a set of grade specifications. There is no compulsion for anybody to use these, but anybody who does use the official grade names must label accurately. Anybody who wants to use any other grade, Smith's Superb, for instance, may do so.

Compulsory grading

The EEC approach to agricultural grading is that producers *must* sort to EEC specifications and *must* label the product with the EEC class. They may use their own brands in addition.

Compulsory unique grades

Sometimes producers are forbidden to use any grading system except that laid down by law, and are forbidden to use any other indication of quality. This has been done with some of the French labelling legislation. Similarly, those countries which successfully went metric did it by making it illegal to mark anything with imperial weights and measures.

Compulsory minimum standards

It is sometimes illegal to sell any item that does not meet certain minimum standards, possibly for public health reasons, possibly for other reasons harder to justify. This requirement may or may not be independent of other classification schemes. Compulsory minimum standards are examined in Chapter 9. Compulsory maximum standards may also exist.

Sorting forbidden

Occasionally, sorting is forbidden. For example, to get the maximum nutrition in wartime, it is forbidden to sift flour, as the white flour is produced by discarding 25-30 per cent of the nutrition of brown flour. An interesting sidelight on the relative importance of war and famine is that both Ethiopia and Malawi continued to sell white flour and high-extraction maize flour when their people were starving, with the 'brown' element going for cattle food and dog biscuits.

SORTING

It is not strictly necessary to classify a product in order to sort it into a grade. Typically a sorting procedure is sequential, first sorting by size, then by colour then by freedom from defects, and these different sorting operations may be at different levels of the production process. The product ends up in the right grade without ever having been classified as a complete product. The end result of this sequential sorting process may not be quite the same as classifying the complete product, then sorting. Indeed, classification is sometimes used in the sense of a check on the product as a whole rather than on its component characteristics – is it drinkable? does it go? It is also sometimes used to imply that the seller has processed the raw data to produce a more useful type of information, the classification.

Sorting strategies comprise a selection rule and an evaluation rule.[3] For selection it is normal to have an ALL rule, under which everything that meets the evaluation criterion is selected into a grade. Occasionally a BEST rule is found, where the best third of the crop is put into the top grade, but the quality of this grade varies over the year, depending on what is available. A FIRST strategy may be used, by which all the items meeting the evaluation criteria are put into a grade, until the requirements of that market segment is met, after which other criteria are used.

Typical evaluation rules are:

– Using compensatory evaluation, where low levels of one characteristic compensate for high levels of another, as with averaging (AVG). The weighting of the characteristics is, of course, critical. There is an element of AVG in some sorting processes, but the limitations are obvious. It would be unacceptable, for instance, to have small, sweet buns and large bread rolls sold on a supermarket shelf as a single product, on the grounds that the extra size compensated for the lack of sugar. Averaging does not fit into the ordinary sorting line or assembly line procedure very well. AVG can be used with ALL, BEST or FIRST selection strategies.

- The conjunctive rule (CONJ) sets cut-off points for some characteristics and the item is rejected if it is below the limit for any characteristic. It is appropriate for product safety and it fits well into sorting lines. It can be used with ALL but not with BEST.
- The disjunctive rule (DISJ) accepts the item if it is above a cut-off point for any characteristic, as a geologist might accept any sample with more than a certain percentage of gold or of silver. This can be used with ALL.
- A sequential elimination rule (SEQ-ELIM) uses cut-off points in the same way as CONJ or DISJ, checking the product one characteristic at a time. This fits well into assembly line manufacture or machine sorting systems. It can be used with FIRST or ALL.
- A lexicographic procedure (LEX) evaluates the product on one characteristic at a time, just as one searches a dictionary for the first letter of the word, then the second, then the third. This is certainly used for sorting filing cards. In practice, it would appear that some sequential sorting procedures have an element of this: sorting first into categories by size, and then sorting within each size group by other criteria.
- The MINIMAX strategy compares characteristics on their worst characteristics, rejecting those with the lowest levels of a characteristic or those with the most characteristics at a low level, so reducing the possibility of a disaster. This does not fit well into sorting processes.
- The MAXIMAX strategy also makes use of the BEST rule, with the purchaser selecting items on their best characteristics and choosing the ones with the highest level of characteristic, so an item may be bad in some respects.

Any of these evaluation strategies may be used sequentially and in combination with each other.

NUMBER OF GRADES

A simple form of sorting is to sort for each characteristic separately, and to specify the grade by the level of each characteristic, for example, 'Size 5, green, high heels'. Sorting this way produces a lot of grades: if a product is sorted into three grades of each of two characteristics, there are nine characteristics:

COLOUR

	1, Red	1, Green	1, Black
SIZE	2, Red	2, Green	2, Black
	3, Red	3, Green	3, Black

If a third characteristic, like width (broad, narrow, medium) is introduced, there are twenty-seven distinct grades. It is very easy to increase the number of grades to the thousands in a shoe store, and yet have none that both fits me and is of a style that I would wear.

In practice, commodities with hundreds or thousands of grades are fairly common. Apples may be described as 'Golden Delicious, Green, French, EEC Class III, 65-70mm, controlled atmosphere stored', with each of these characteristics, except perhaps the EEC Class, having commercial significance, so with the number of varieties, colours, countries of origin, size and storage methods there are thousands of possible grades.

The idea of having so many grades is frightening. It makes price reporting and administrative control difficult, and it is disturbing to people who have a rather simplistic idea of what grading systems should be trying to do. As a result there is always administrative pressure, not least from the EEC bureaucracy, to cut down the number of grades to perhaps four or five, to make choice simple, to permit easy price reporting, and to permit easy intervention for price support. They would like five grades, going from the Reject, through Class III, Class II and Class I to Class Extra, with everyone agreeing that Class Extra is better than Class I, and with everyone agreeing that all items in Class II were very close substitutes.

In order to cut the number of grades from thousands to five, it is necessary to change the specifications and sorting methods. First, it is necessary to limit the number of characteristics taken into account, because of the difficulty of combining a large number of characteristics into a single grade measure. Second, it is necessary to devise some method of combining the specifications on different characteristics.

One approach might be to have some sort of weighted average. Another might be to say that to get an apple into Class I it should be between 50 and 70mm, it should have less than 10 per cent of its surface area blemished or bruised, it should have its stalk attached, it should be of the colour appropriate to its grade and so on. The first problem that arises is that it is obviously silly to have these characteristics in a single vertical grading set if people do not all agree that more is better, that it is a vertical characteristic. One would not want a single set of quality grades for shoes, with Class Extra being sizes over 10, width of D or above, and colours at the red end of the spectrum. Even if the more obvious horizontal characteristics are eliminated, most characteristics are horizontal over some level. It is common for different market segments to value a characteristic differently and it is pretty well universal that different segments will weight characteristics differently. As a result, it is notoriously difficult to design a single grading system that gives the same ranking for all buyers. For instance, there was the situation where the French were exporting inferior cauliflowers to England, and the English at the same time were exporting inferior cauliflowers to France: what one thought inferior, the other thought superior. There was the situation where most Americans preferred a relatively lean grade of beef that the US Department of Agriculture marked down, as having too little fat.[4]

If all qualities are to be compressed into one single vertical scale, the width of the classes must be so great that the value of the grade is questionable. If the specifications on one characteristic are very tight, then the specifications on others must be very broad, or there will be virtually nothing left in the grade, and there must be a significant amount in the grade if it is to have any meaning. If for example, Class Extra apples had to be over 80mm, *all* apples meeting this specification would have to be in the grade if it were to exist at all: if one removed the bruised, the damaged, the distorted, there would be so few apples that the grade would virtually cease to exist. If, on the other hand, there were very wide specifications on all characteristics, the grade would not be uniform in any of them, and it would lose much of its information content and other value. The more characteristics are included in a specification the wider the specification must be, if the same proportion of the product is to go in the grade.

Sometimes a single, vertical, grading standard of this sort is imposed on a market which already has a grading system with hundreds or thousands of grades as with EEC standards. One approach adopted by producers is to carry on as before, but label everything with the lowest EEC grade, the disadvantage being that the uninitiated may think that this grade indicates inferior quality. If the two grading systems use similar characteristics, it may be possible to say that perhaps a hundred or two grades fall into EEC Class II, and so print grade labels which have the two sets of grade information. If the two systems do not use the same characteristics or if they give different weights to characteristics, the effect may be to require that each of the thousands of sub-grades are further divided into EEC grades. The alternative of switching from thousands of commercially meaningful grades to a single, vertical, system is seldom desirable.

COST OF SORTING

A distinction must be drawn between (a) the physical costs to the firm of sorting, (b) the costs and benefits to the firm from grading (that is the difference between the value of what goes into the sorting process and what comes out) and (c) the costs and benefits at market level from grading. It is very common for people to advocate a grading system because physical sorting costs are low, when they have not even realized that there are grading costs, either to the firm or the market.

Physical sorting costs

There are several possible cost curves associated with sorting a product into its constituent grades. At one extreme there may be an assembly line or packing line in existence, and the addition of a simple size grading or colour grading machine will mean that different grades go to each packing point. There is a capital investment but little or no added variable cost. At the other extreme the main classification may be a quality control examination of the full product, and may be essentially a variable cost.

Some sorting processes can handle almost any mix of raw materials at the same cost. A packing line with a lot of packing points is an example: if most of the raw material is of one grade, more packing points can be allocated to this grade. Sometimes, though, a limited number of packing points means that a raw material that is mainly of one quality will choke one of the packing points, while the others are hardly used, reducing the capacity of the system.

With other sorting processes it may be very cheap to remove the outgrades from a sample that is 95 per cent Class 1, but it is expensive to remove the outgrades if it is only 85 per cent Class 1. This may be the case where visual inspection is the evaluation procedure.

Sometimes the mixed raw material may be saleable as, say, Grade C (that is, there could be some averaging, or tolerances, or cumulative sets). The Grade B could be sorted out, at a cost, and the Grade A could be sorted out at a greater cost. This is common with commodities.

Increased cost of sorting may be offset by reduced costs later in the production or distribution process. It is often argued, for example, that increased expenditures in quality control at manu-facturing level saves a far greater amount in after-sales service. The question is who gets the benefit. In a vertically-integrated oper-ation, increased costs to the manufacturing division can reduce the costs of the marketing or service division. In other cases the distributor reaps the benefit of the manufacturer's extra costs, but may not pay for it.

Changes in uniformity may be a simple matter of different grids or riddle sizes in the size grade, or they may be a matter of tightened control throughout the production process. Broadly speaking, the fewer the grades, the less the uniformity.

Producers with new technology or more time may be able to sort to a higher accuracy than was envisaged when the tolerances were set. It may have been envisaged that if 10 per cent tolerances were set, producers would have to keep outgrades below 5 per cent on average, because of the limits of technology. With better machinery, capable of sorting to tighter tolerances, they may be able to get away with 7.5 per cent outgrades with the same prob-ability of exceeding the tolerances.[5]

The grading costs to the firm

The grading costs and benefits to the firm are the difference between the value of the raw product entering the sorting process and the product leaving it.[6] The rational producer will not sort unless the total revenue from the sorted grades is greater than the total revenue from the unsorted product plus the cost of sorting.

In the following cases there will be a *reduction* in the value of the product through sorting:

Case 1

When a proportion of the output is of a lower grade than the input, that proportion will have a lower value. This may happen when, for instance, a mixed lot of A, B and C Grades is classified as Grade B before sorting. After sorting, the Grade C has a lower value and the Grade A a higher value.

Whether the total revenue is higher will depend on such factors as whether all Grade B gets the same price whether mixed or uniform, or whether the price depends on average level and uniformity within the grade, or whether each item gets the price appropriate for its quality whether it is sorted or not. Very different products and marketing systems are implied by these alternatives – for example, a customer buying fruit off a supermarket shelf, or an industrial buyer will inspect before purchase and pay according to the actual quality, while in other markets purchase on description may be the norm.

The total revenue depends partly on the ratio of price to level of characteristic. The drop in price from sorting an item into Grade C may be bigger than the rise from sorting an item into Grade A: a linear relationship between price and level of characteristic cannot be assumed to be normal.

The proportion of the final product going into Class A compared with that going into Class C is also important. Grading is less likely to be profitable if 10 per cent moves up a grade and 30 per cent moves down a grade. (Note the assumption here that the price received for Grade B is not altered when the Grade C and A are removed.)

This is extremely important in practice. Businessmen and economists often get dazzled by the high prices for Grade A and put up expensive sorting plants, without taking into account the increased waste, the difficulty they will have in selling Grade C and a possible fall in the price of Grade B when the Grade A is sorted out.

Case 2

The price of a given grade may fall as a result of sorting. When there are cumulative grades, for instance, Grade B may include Grade A, and as the Grade A is removed, the average level of the Grade B declines. In a market where the price depends on the average level of characteristic, the price declines accordingly. This may happen where the product is inspected before purchase or where there is a habitual purchase strategy. In practice it is often found that if the lowest grade is sorted so that all the better items are removed, the price for the remainder is so low that it is not worth selling it.

Case 3

A proportion of the output may become unsaleable as a result of tighter tolerances in the higher grades. If instead of everything being sold at a grade with 10 per cent tolerance, half is sold in grades with 5 per cent tolerance, total sales may be 2.5 per cent lower.

Case 4

A proportion of the output may be physically damaged during sorting. With some products the only possible way of evaluation is by destructive testing. This may be cheap with a uniform bulk good, drinking the odd glass of wine, or expensive with a variable unit product.

Grading the product produces net benefits when the output is worth more than the input – and why else should anybody grade? This implies the weighted average price of the output being greater than that of the mixed product. The higher prices may arise from any of the following:

- Reduced search (discussed in Chapters 4, 5 and 8)
- Increased uniformity (discussed in the next chapter)
- Reduced production or distribution cost

Market level sorting costs

The costs and benefits of sorting at market level are, again, the difference between the value of the product going in and the value of the product coming out. One set of costs and benefits are analogous to the costs and benefits to the individual firm. The other are the costs and benefits arising from changed supply and demand at market level. If, for example, a grading scheme results in a great reduction in the quantity of mixed Grade B on the market, and a corresponding increase in the quantity of Grade A and Grade C, then one can expect that there will be a fall in the price of Grade A and Grade C and a rise in the price of Grade B. (There is an implicit assumption here that the product is not sold on inspection, with each item getting the price its level of characteristic justifies. Similarly, there is an assumption that the change in the average composition of Grade A does not itself alter the price. There is also an assumption of averaging, so that the A and C can be averaged to produce a true B.)

The implication is that it will pay the first firms who experiment with sorting, as they will get a high premium for their Grade A and a price for Grade C which is not too low. As more and more firms adopt sorting the premium will fall and the price for Grade C will also fall. A similar progression in prices can be expected when one firm introduces an expensive new process which produces mostly Grade A. The initial profits are high, but they fall as other firms adopt the process.

These market level changes are generally ignored by those wishing to impose industry-wide grading and sorting schemes; they do not appreciate that the price structure before the system is imposed will be very different from that after the system is adopted. They calculate the advantages on the assumption that everyone will get the Class A prices instead of the current Class B prices, and do not allow for the fall in prices as Class A supplies increase, or the rise as Class B supplies fall. Accordingly, if the system is based on the original price levels and a compulsory system is imposed, a proportion of producers will be worse off. The situation is worsened by the fact that a significant number of producers find it uneconomic to produce Class A even at current prices.

EFFECT OF A CHANGE IN GRADE SPECIFICATIONS

Any change in sorting specifications changes all supply and demand functions, for the product as a whole, for the grades, and for individual items, unless, of course, both the old and the new sorting specifications are irrelevant. One cannot use *ex ante* data, however complete, to describe what will be the effect of introducing a grading system throughout a market: any prediction will be a guess. Still less can one predict the effect of introducing grading systems for several competing products simultaneously.

Any change in specifications that results in a different quantity being put into a grade changes the supply and demand function of the firm and the individual. If, for example, a product is bought entirely on description, and the borderline is shifted so that more items go into Class 2 and less into Class I, then, in the market period:

1 There is more Class 2 available, and prices for this Class will tend to fall.
2 The average quality of Class 2 will rise, and so its price will tend to rise.
3 Some people who would have been satisfied with the poorer Class 1 will now buy Class 2, raising the demand for Class 2 and lowering that for Class 1 (that is, the probable quality of a purchase of Class 2 has risen).
4 The quantity in Class 1 will fall, so price will tend to rise.
5 The probable quality of a purchase of Class 1 will rise, so price will tend to rise.
6 Classes 1 and 2 will become closer or less close substitutes, so the cross-elasticity will change.
7 The ratio of prices between the two grades will change, and this will change the cross-elasticity at the margin.
8 Class 1 and Class 2 will become closer or less close substitutes for other goods, and the cross-elasticity will change.
9 The ratio between the prices of Class 1, Class 2 and alternative goods will change and this will change the cross-elasticity at the margin.
10 The changed quality may make Class 2 more or less suitable for some use.
11 The search cost and risk for Class 1 falls, as it is more uniform, but it rises for Class 2.
12 Some items are considered to be worse just because they are now labelled as Class 2 rather than Class 1 as before.
13 The quantity of waste may change.
14 Production and handling costs may change.

The overall effect may be an increase or a decrease in the price paid or the total revenue. The effect is greatest when the good is being bought on description. This is an extremely simple example as changes normally involve changes in several limits or in the number of grades. There could also be a change in the sorting strategy, with more going into the top and bottom grades and less into the mixed grade. A change in production processes changes the proportion in each grade. Labelling may change. It is impossible to predict the price effects of these changes as there is literally an infinite number of possible grading systems for a single good, even when there is only a single, vertical, set of grades. If one allows separate scales for each characteristic, the complexities increase.

SEGMENTATION

One of the benefits expected from sorting is market segmentation, where it is accepted that the demand for quality is not the same in each segment of the market, and production, sorting and distribution are changed so that the product going to each segment matches the demand.[7] With product differentiation, and more particularly with product variation, each producer has a different good which he brands and advertises to bring a convergence of demand on to the good, and so reduce cross-elasticity.

Segmentation may be achieved by sorting the product so that each grade meets the needs of one segment of the market. As a general rule, total demand will be greater when there are many grades, than where the product is mixed in one heterogeneous mass. It is obvious that, if production, search and distribution costs are ignored, the more grades there are, the more chance there is that a grade will exist that will closely match each individual's preferences, so customers will make optimal choices and welfare and sales will be maximized.[8] As the number of grades increases, the marginal increase in welfare from adding a further grade falls. In calculating the optimum number of grades one would have to take into account the impact on search costs, on production costs and on distribution costs of an increase in the number, as well as the impact on demand discussed in the previous section.

Vertical segmentation exists when everyone agrees that one grade is better than another, but some choose to buy the cheaper grade. Horizontal segmentation separates out and identifies grades that are not better or worse, but different, due to differences in end use or in consumer tastes, for example, red and green apples. The location of grade boundaries is critical. Variants of the

Hotelling (1929) model are often used to analyse the optimum number and position of new products, homogeneous in quality, along the quality spectrum.[9] It can be shown, for example, that it could be disastrous for a producer to base his specification on the quality demanded by the majority of the population. If two-thirds of the population prefer type A and one-third prefers type B, and there are ten firms in the market supplying type A, what does a newcomer do? If he also produces type A, he will have to fight hard to get one-eleventh of the market. If he produces type B, he might get one-third of the market.

As well as increasing effective demand in this way, segmentation can earn monopoly profits, for example, by changing the boundary to reduce the supply of a Class 1 with an inelastic demand and to increase that of other classes. This is most likely to be done by a national marketing board, which can enforce standards, and can adopt a strategy that benefits the industry as a whole, though not necessarily all sellers. In the long run, changes in production, and the introduction of brands, advertising and alternative market channels will erode this monopoly profit. Supply control is needed to make monopoly profits from segmentation in the long run (though conceivably some profits could be made if the segmentation changed in each market period according to fluctuations in supply and demand).

A firm may advertise to and supply only one segment, reducing the costs and increasing the effectiveness of the advertising. Supermarkets stock qualities appealing to several segments, because they sell to a wider range of customers than most retailers do, and because they do not have counter assistants who can persuade a customer that the quality in stock is, in fact, the one best suited to the customer's needs. Increasing affluence also leads to more demand for variety (new goods, more goods or more variety within a good). It appears to be more difficult to segment when the market is small, is dominated by heavy users, or has a dominant brand.[10] The use of segmentation by industrial and agribusiness buyers is important.

Techniques to identify those customers who have similar demand functions and can be thought of as being a segment of the market have not been widely successful because they are too refined for the data[11] and because researchers have 'failed to analyse the marketing environment before applying their favourite methodological approach'.[12] In practice, research identifies segments by factors like the age, income and family size of customers with certain preferences, which makes calculation of the true elasticities difficult, and hides the existence of segments which are not related to these socio-economic indicators, and of segments arising from the fact that all consumers usually prefer Grade X, but sometimes prefer Grade Y.

CONCLUSION

This chapter showed that there was an element of sorting in most manufacturing processes as well as in primary product production. It showed that there are different kinds of product, so a sorting procedure for chickens, for instance, would not be the same as that for milk. A discussion of the many types of grade set that are commonly in operation and of the degree of compulsion that may be expected showed that a straightforward sorting model of the type often assumed in economic analysis is of limited application, even for a single firm. The sorting process itself was examined, in its ideal form as a classification procedure followed by a selection rule, and in its more realistic forms. It was shown that the different sorting strategies could affect the output.

The cost of sorting was shown to be a lot more than the cost of putting a product over the sorting line: the firm has to take into account the level of waste, and the price achieved for each grade produced. There can be very substantial variations in this depending on the market in which the product is sold, whether it is sold by description or on inspection, for instance. The market effects are also substantial: if all producers change their sorting strategy at the same time, market prices will change.

Changes in the grade specifications change the quality and quantity of the product lines on offer, and change the producers' cost curves. At the same time demand functions change. These changes in quality can result in product lines that more nearly meet the requirements of the market segments than the unsorted product does, so increasing total demand for the product.

Chapter 7

Uniformity

Nearly all the formal economic models of quality are based on consumers' evaluation of a single item, and are based on the assumption that each product line is homogeneous, with each item produced being exactly the same as every other item. In this chapter it is recognized that in the real world people do not buy or consume all products one by one: some are bought in packets and some are consumed several items at a time. This means that the degree of uniformity affects the value of the product. A consignment of nuts and bolts of assorted sizes is not of the same value on an assembly line as several packets, each having one size: with a mixed consignment the assembly workers would have to spend a significant amount of their time searching for the right nut for each bolt and the right nut and bolt for each hole. Similarly, if the nuts and bolts supplied were of different sizes each week, it would be very difficult to run an assembly line. The degree of uniformity also affects search costs: if all ball-point pens are obviously much the same, there is no point in searching for the best. Generally, people are not offered a single item of a product line, but they either get a random selection from a more or less uniform consignment, or they can select from a display of several items.

This chapter also recognizes that products are never perfectly homogeneous in the real world. To some extent the variation is deliberate: as a matter of marketing strategy a box of chocolates contains several varieties of chocolate; the quality and content of a packet of detergent changes constantly as technology develops, so today's product may bear little relation to the washing powder sold under the same brand and in a similar cardboard box in the 1930s and 1940s; a tea manufacturer sends different blends to towns in

Britain, according to the type of water, so that the final brew is the same (an interesting example of different quality characteristics making an identical product).

There is also a lack of uniformity arising from imperfections in the production process. Any process produces a variable product, and any quality control process lets a variable product leave the factory. It is possible to reduce the variability *at a cost* by (a) changing the production process or (b) tightening up on quality control and sorting.[1]

WHY IS UNIFORMITY IMPORTANT?

Sorting procedures have two effects: one is to produce a consignment where the mean level of characteristics conforms to the grade standards; the other is the more subtle one of providing a uniform product. The more uniform product which comes out of a sorting process may mean that

- a customer gets a more uniform purchase, which may have a greater value in use;
- the product is more attractive on display, so more are bought;
- search costs are changed;
- distribution costs are changed;
- distributors sell more;
- the cost of manufacturing using that product as raw material changes;
- the more uniform product more nearly matches the requirements of one market segment;

Similar changes occur as the result of changing production techniques to produce a more uniform quality. Industry has long recognized the importance of uniformity and enormous sums are spent on quality control in order to get a product that is uniform, rather than one that has the right average level of quality. Marketing has also recognized its importance. It is almost completely ignored in the economic literature though: it is nearly always assumed, for instance, that a given item gives the same satisfaction if it is bought in a sorted or an unsorted lot, and that the consumer gets the same satisfaction from one tough steak and one very tender steak as from two ordinary ones.

In this chapter the relationship between sorting for average level of characteristic and sorting for uniformity will be looked at further. The different types of uniformity will be separated out, and the benefits that can be obtained from each will be looked at.

DEFINING UNIFORMITY

Objective definitions for uniformity

For sorting and quality control purposes, a single-characteristic product may have its uniformity defined in all the classic ways: standard deviation, range or tolerance (if the tolerance permits 10 per cent of the product to be out of grade an interdecile range is being set). The grade specification may indicate that a product which is half Grade A and half Grade C must be sold as Grade D because it is not uniform.[2] The specifications are often defined so that some combination of the statistical measures is appropriate.

A point nearly always overlooked is that the uniformity should be specified differently at different levels of the distribution chain. This is not just because manufacturers, distributors and consumers want different types and degrees of uniformity for different reasons. Statistically, the range and standard deviation vary with the size of the population,[3] and there is a different population size when we consider all the apples in an orchard, all the apples in a consignment to a supermarket, the apples in a box, and the apples in a purchase. If, for instance, a 10 per cent tolerance is permitted, a box of apples may have 10 per cent out of grade and still meet the grade specifications. If, however, this same box is repacked into plastic bags, each containing nine apples, then any bag having one apple out of grade (11.1 per cent) is itself out of grade. It is possible to have between 11 per cent and 89 per cent of the packs not meeting specifications when the box itself does. This emphasizes the point that a single set of standards cannot be expected to be suitable for all levels of the marketing chain.

Care must be taken in specifying uniformity when the size of the product is itself a quality characteristic. For example, large cashew nuts get a better price so they are classified by size, as well as having parallel grades for splits, brokens, colour and so on. The grades are defined by number per pound and

> The range between the maximum and the minimum number per count becomes narrower as the number of kernels per pound becomes fewer and, of course, the fewer the number of kernels per pound, the larger the size of the individual kernels.[4]

With a multi-attribute product, uniformity can be defined for sorting and quality control purposes in terms of the standard deviation or range of each characteristic separately. However, sorting in respect of one characteristic makes the product more uniform in terms of that characteristic, but less uniform in terms of the other characteristics – again, there is a smaller population, and nothing has been done to reduce the scatter of other characteristics. The only way of producing grades that are uniform in all characteristics is to have more grades: it has been shown in the previous chapter that nine grades are required to sort a product so that there are three uniform grades for two characteristics, and twenty-seven grades are needed if there are three characteristics.

Subjective uniformity

Even with a single characteristic, customers' perception of uniformity is subjective. One customer may have a perception related to the standard deviation, one related to the range, one related to the tolerance. One customer will consider a given sample to be uniform, another not.

The perception is likely to relate to the end use of the product: if uniformity is irrelevant it may not be noticed.

With a multicharacteristic product, perception of uniformity must be even more variable. What degree of uniformity in size is equivalent to a given uniformity in shape? Is a consignment of soap packets with varying colours of packet uniform, if all other characteristics are identical? (A conjunctive approach may approximate to the retailer's evaluation strategy here: reject the product if any one of its characteristics is not uniform.) Is a packet of Smarties uniform, where all the sweets are identical except for their colour?

There is often the tendency to extrapolate from what one can see to what one cannot. It is easy to assume that a product that is obviously perfectly uniform in one characteristic must be equally uniform in others, though for the reasons mentioned, the opposite may be the case in fact. Often, indeed, customers and retailers confuse neatness, tidiness and presentation with uniformity. In an Australian supermarket I heard the greengrocery supervisor telling his assistant to have all the apples on display stalk end up – 'That is how apples grow'. The resulting display was superb and the apples were perfectly uniform, in yet another characteristic, one which did not affect the consumption characteristics, but which nevertheless increased sales.

TYPES OF UNIFORMITY

Uniformity may be valued by the manufacturer, distributor, buyer or final consumer, but it may also be disliked – where would the fashion market be without diversity.[5] It can also be completely irrelevant: traditionally a chain is valued according to the strength of its weakest link.

There are two main benefits which can come from uniformity, increased value in use (approximating to the traditional concept of utility perhaps) and improved search.

Utility

In Chapter 1 it was shown that improved quality benefited distributors directly, by reducing distribution cost, and indirectly, by increasing sales to the consumer. Similarly there were direct and indirect benefits to the manufacturer and buyer. The same applies with uniformity: there are both direct and indirect benefits.

Uniformity within a purchase

A uniform purchase may have a higher value in use than a variable purchase with the identical average value of characteristic. This may be because the purchaser values it higher for purely aesthetic reasons, because it is easier to use, with uniformly-sized potatoes all cooking in the same time for instance, or because the end product is preferred.

Similar considerations can apply in industrial use, though in some processes uniformity is irrelevant and only average level of characteristic matters.

Buyers may get an increased aesthetic pleasure from making a uniform purchase or from selecting from a uniform display, or even from shopping in a store with uniform displays, getting a pleasure which is not related to the final satisfaction from consumption. This phenomenon also affects industrial purchases, with industrial buyers paying over the odds for a well-presented product. It is not easy to disentangle these effects from increased value in consumption or reduced search, as all result in increased sales.

Distributors have lower distribution costs if they purchase a uniform product. They do not have to spend as much time inspecting and resorting at reception; they do not have to spend time policing the display and they do not have the enormous drop in margin that arises from waste. The effect of waste on the final retail margin may be shown by the following:

To get 25 per cent margin with zero waste, one charges 33 per cent mark-up.
To get 25 per cent margin with 10 per cent waste one charges 48 per cent mark-up.
To get 25 per cent margin with 20 per cent waste one charges 66 per cent mark-up.
To get 25 per cent margin with 30 per cent waste one charges 90 per cent mark-up.
To get 25 per cent margin with 40 per cent waste one charges 122 per cent mark-up.
To get 25 per cent margin with 50 per cent waste one charges 166 per cent mark-up.
To get 25 per cent margin with 60 per cent waste one charges 233 per cent mark-up.

The margin is the return from all items sold minus the cost of all items bought, expressed as a percentage of the return from all items sold. A 25 per cent margin implies total sales of £133.3 from purchases of £100.

It goes further than that, though; a supermarket may buy cauliflowers sorted and packed to Class II standards and sell them by self-selection on a supermarket shelf at a single fixed price per cauliflower. Customers select out those cauliflowers that are nearly Class I and when these are sold they work their way down the quality scale. The shelf is filled up whenever it is half full, whenever the best half of the grade has been sold in fact. By the time the shelf has been restocked three or four times most of what is on display is in the bottom half of the grade. At the end of a busy day it is all near the bottom limit. What is on offer is definitely worse value for money than it was when the display was first stocked, and sales slow down accordingly.[6]

If, in addition, 10 per cent of the cauliflowers are out of grade, as the tolerances permit, it is not long before the display as a whole is Class III or worse, even though all the cauliflowers put on display were from boxes which met the Class II specifications. This can bring sales to a halt, as well as exposing the retailer to risk of prosecution. For this reason, retailers usually demand produce sorted to closer tolerances than those laid down in the regulations.

A similar phenomenon arises lower down the distribution chain. For example, when Rhodesia was selling tobacco illegally during Unilateral Declaration of Independence, it set the grade price and let customers pick what they wanted. The first buyers could take the pick of the grade at a price related to the run of the grade, leaving later customers with an overpriced product. To reduce this effect to the minimum, the sellers subdivided the grades into 5,000 categories to keep a very small difference between the top and the bottom of the grade. Something similar was found with beef marketing in the USA: the customers who inspected the product at the point of slaughter bought the best sides of beef in the grade, leaving a below-average sample to be sold on description at the same price to more distant buyers.

Supermarket chains find that it makes management and accounting much easier if every shop in a chain is selling exactly the same quality at the same price. If a uniform product and a uniform display increases sales, or increases the possible price, the distributors get an indirect benefit, not related to any reduction in cost.

Manufacturers incur obvious costs in handling non-uniform raw materials, and they may also end up producing non-uniform outputs, including defective items, even when their own operations are perfect.

Uniformity within packages and between packages

To an ever greater degree goods are sold in packages. The grocer who weighs out half a kilo of sugar or fifteen shillings' worth of flour exists only in the Third World today. Modern retailers weigh out purchases in the fish and delicatessen departments, and possibly the meat and greengrocery as well, partly to give the image of personal service and freshness (though why this should give the image is not clear). Greengrocery is often sold by self-selection, with the customer either buying pre-packaged goods, or assembling items for his own package.

Customers' perceptions of a product and their purchasing patterns change when the product is packed rather than being sold loose. In fact the plastic bag was invented in the 1940s for a marketing experiment which showed that if apples were put into a package, customers would buy more, and they would buy a size (small) and a quality (bruised) which they would otherwise reject.[7] It is not necessary for us to speculate why this might be, merely to note that it is so.

When commodities are sold in packages, supply is not linear, but discontinuous. A customer can buy 5lb of potatoes or 10lb, but not 7lb. This must have some effect on the amount purchased on a given occasion, but customers may balance out their purchases over time as the extra purchase today can be stored until next week. With a more perishable product, the size of package can have a significant effect on sales in the longer run.

It is not just the final consumer who buys packages. The retailer buys consignments consisting of boxes (outers) and the factory may buy a consignment consisting of twelve container loads.

Two different types of uniformity will determine utility and the prospect of the consumer getting a uniform purchase: uniformity within packages and uniformity between packages. A package of one item (a car, perhaps) is necessarily uniform, and so is a package of a bulk good (a bottle of whisky) To the extent that people tend to buy a single package as a single purchase, uniformity within package is the same as uniformity within a purchase. However, for some products, consumers buy two or more packages as a single purchase. Several possibilities arise here, for example:

- The product is consumed one packet at a time (cornflakes) so some benefits of uniformity are realized if there is uniformity within a package, even if there is little uniformity between packages. Costs could still occur in resetting an industrial process between runs, relabelling supermarket shelves or changing cooking times.
- The packages bought in one purchase are unpacked and mixed before use. A bag of perfectly uniform and small potatoes plus a bag of perfectly uniform and large potatoes means a mixed purchase. A fleet consisting of fifty perfectly uniform Fiestas and of fifty perfectly uniform Golfs, is not uniform and is not easy to manage. On the other hand, blending 2-Star and 4-Star petrol does produce a uniform product.

The sequence in which sorting operations are carried out can affect the product in ways not usually foreseen. Consider, for example, a good with a single characteristic whose constituent items are distributed uniformly along the level of the characteristic axis (an unlikely situation, but the assumption is often made in economic analyses). If the product is sorted into packages so that every item in the package meets the category specifications, there is, in effect, a sample from all items in the grade, and the mean level of characteristic of a package will be distributed as in Figure 7.1. Packages with a mean level of characteristic near the top or bottom of the grade will necessarily be uniform and will be uncommon. If, on the other hand, the items are sorted into packages which are classified afterwards according to the average level of characteristic, the mean will be distributed as in Figure 7.2. With the distribution in Figure 7.1, packages with a mean level near the top and bottom are necessarily uniform, but this is not so with the distribution in Figure 7.2, where it only applies to the top of the top grade and to the bottom of the bottom grade, and, even so, to a lesser extent. There are obviously very significant marketing implications, whether the product is sold on description or by self-selection. Similar effects arise, usually unintentionally, from the ordering of a series of sorting or quality control processes.

The degree of variation within the package can be derived from sampling theory, assuming random selection of items into a package. For example, the range might be taken as a measure of the uniformity of the sample. The range is related to the size of sample and to the size of the bulk consignment. For small samples, such as prepacks, the range is subject to very little more sampling variability than the standard deviations.[8] Whatever the sampling distribution, there will be an appreciable proportion of the packages with a higher variance than the parent population. In so far as the uniformity is measured by the range, therefore:

- With small packages (under ten items) the range is subject to very little more sampling variability than the standard deviation.
- With small packages, range is probably as meaningful as standard deviation.
- The larger the package size, the larger the expected range within that package.

Packages selected out of a uniformly-distributed population are not uniformly uniform. That is to say, some packages with a given average level of characteristic may have all items with that level,

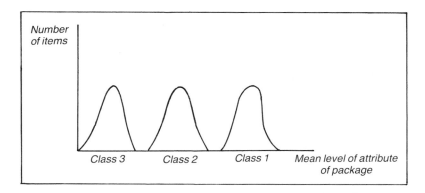

Figure 7.1 Distribution of packages in different grades with all items meeting category specifications

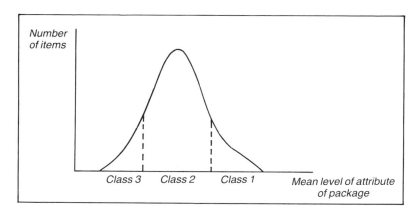

Figure 7.2 Distribution of packages in grades, when mean level of characteristic determines grade

while others may have none, with all being very good or very bad. The statistical distribution of the standard deviation of samples of a given size from a given population can be calculated. As in the figures, the distribution will be very different if the packages are selected from items all of which meet the specifications.

The practical implications of uniformity and variance around the mean in manufacturing are many and various. For example, it has been found that it is better to have components with the characteristics loosely distributed around the midpoint of the permitted range than to have them closely distributed around a point that is not the midpoint. The benefit comes when stacking components for bolting together for assembly: when the holes are loosely distributed about the midpoint, a bolt can usually be slipped in: when they are tightly distributed about another point, the bolt often sticks. This is known as tolerance stacking.[9]

Uniformity over time

There may be an added utility arising from uniformity over time which, again, is not related to average level of characteristic. Obviously, a manufacturer saves money from not having to change his recipes and techniques every time a new consignment arrives, and he benefits from being able to treat successive consignments as an identical product in store.

It is not quite so clear that the final consumer gets the same added value in use from uniformity over time. Certainly the buyer, the home-maker, is often in the position of buying inputs that are uniform over time, to produce meals that vary consistently for the end users, the family. Consumers do value novelty and variation in the end product. On the other hand there is a pleasure from having an old favourite. With Black Magic chocolates consumers value the variation within a package, the uniformity between packages, and the uniformity over time.

Quality variation within grades

One can rank hotels from a one-star hotel to a five-star hotel, and still have an excellent one-star hotel and a very bad five-star hotel.[10] What is happening here is:

1 The grade standards are specified according to a limited range

of characteristics, like the size of bedroom, en suite bathrooms, decor, swimming bath, and so on. The set of standards ranks hotels into five grades.

2 If a hotel is intended to be a four-star hotel, but does not meet the standards on any one of these characteristics, it is not a four-star hotel. It is given a ranking according to the level of its worst characteristic.

3 Hotels classified as two-star can vary from those which barely meet the standard on all the characteristics specified, to those which are five-star on all characteristics except one.

4 There are a lot of other characteristics which are not included in the grade specifications. These might include service, quality of food, view, accessibility to the business district, and so on. It is possible for a hotel to meet five-star requirements on all the characteristics specified for the grade, but to be very bad on the other characteristics.

COSTS OF UNIFORMITY

It is easy to say that everything should be uniform, but every increase in uniformity, of any type, costs money. Manufacturing problems are reduced if the product can be changed slightly when the normal quality of raw material cannot be obtained, and costs of procurement are reduced if the recipes can be changed as the raw material costs change, substituting palm-oil for groundnut oil as the relative prices change. Before spending money on a quality and sorting scheme, one should spend some time finding out what forms of uniformity the buyers do value, if any. It is worth being clear when talking of uniformity over time whether we are talking of

- constant average level of characteristic in a purchase;
- constant uniformity of a purchase;
- constant level of characteristic and degree of uniformity of a purchase over time.

Or even

- constant average level of characteristic within a package over time;
- constant uniformity within a package;
- constant level and uniformity of a characteristic within a package;

- constant average level of characteristics of packages on offer over time
- constant uniformity of average level between packages;
- constant uniformity of level and uniformity of characteristics on offer.

Having uniform products over time saves the supermarkets from having to change price tags and labels every time a new consignment comes in, which is time consuming and easy to forget – and failure may lead to prosecution.

SEARCH

The uniform product may also have a value different to that of a variable product with the same average level of characteristics for reasons other than value in use, namely search cost. The importance of search has been shown in previous chapters and the relationship between sorting generally and search will be discussed below.

Here I will set out, very briefly, the types of saving in search that may arise from uniformity, whether uniformity of what is on offer, uniformity between shops, uniformity within and between packages or uniformity over time.

Consumer search

If the product on offer, in a supermarket display, for instance, is uniform, then consumer search is easier. To the extent that the buyer believes that it is uniform he may be willing to make a random choice rather than inspecting before choosing. Because there are fewer items that are very good or very bad, he will have little incentive to search within a given display even if it is cheap to do so. This uniformity makes search within a shop less profitable and at the same time makes it a big jump in search costs if he moves to another shop.

Risk is reduced. While people enjoy shopping and they enjoy the possibility of getting a bargain, they do not enjoy the feeling that if they do not search they will be landed with a bad bargain. This suggests that they might be happier with a product with a strict lower limit, but which may vary upwards.

There are costs of course. The reduced search has been obtained at the cost of a significant reduction in choice. The reduced risk of a disaster has been achieved at the cost of a reduced possibility of a bargain. Those people with low opportunity costs of time and those to whom search is a pleasure will be worse off.

Distributors

Search by distributors can also be reduced by increased uniformity. This is most obvious in procurement. Quality control at purchase is cheaper because fewer samples have to be taken.

Another form of search, search for customers willing to buy the product, is also simpler if you have a uniform well-defined product. It is not a matter of hawking a mixed product round until somebody is willing to take it; instead, a defined quality can be taken to the customer most likely to buy it. The possibility of selling on description also arises.

The distributors also get some benefits indirectly from the fact that there is reduced consumer search. First, improved sales mean a greater turnover per square foot. This may benefit the firm whose speed of turnover rises, against the firm whose speed of turnover falls, leading to no net benefit at market level, but the reduced search could also lead to a bigger sale for the product as a whole, benefiting all distributors. (Speed of turnover is an extremely important concept in marketing, where retailers' total margin is determined by percentage margin and speed of turnover. Retailers are constantly making the choice between a high percentage margin and slow sales and the strategy of 'pile it high, sell it cheap'. If the low margin leads to much faster sales it can be by far the most profitable strategy. In production economics the two are usually compounded into a gross margin which hides the time element, and in mainstream economics the concepts tend to get lost behind marginal revenue and marginal costs, while constraints of storage and selling space, and interest on stocks are ignored.)

If the product on display is not uniform, consumers will stop and examine it trying to find the best buy. In a supermarket greengrocery department this means that people abandon their trolleys, while they hunt for the best pineapple, so aisles have to be wider to avoid congestion. This reduces sales per square foot. Again, increased search by the consumer indirectly changes distributors' profits.

Supermarket chains try to keep uniform products and uniform prices throughout the chain, partly as a matter of image, partly so that buyers will be confident that they will get a good deal wherever they see the supermarket name. They feel that consumers will be disturbed if they do not know what will be in store and that this uncertainty harms the shop's reputation. (The degree to which these beliefs are well founded is important to the shop, but not, perhaps, to the manufacturer.)

Producers

Producers benefit directly from uniformity when they are procuring raw materials. Uniformity of the finished product makes it easier for them to match a given product to a given market. (This is not the benefit from segmentation, rather a reduced cost of supplying segments.)

Increased profits arising from increased sales are a secondary benefit.

ON THE OPTIMUM NUMBER OF GRADES

There are frequent complaints by consumer groups, either that there are too many brands, grades or varieties on the market, which they say increases production and marketing costs and increases search cost, or else that there are too few choices available because of restrictions by monopolists. Producers and distributors also agonize over whether the market can take another brand or whether they should reduce or increase their number of lines.

If each consumer has a different set of preferences at a given price structure, and if there are no search costs or added production and distribution costs from increasing the number of grades, then the optimum number of grades will be very large indeed. As a first approximation, it might be suggested that there should be a different quality for each consumer, and more if there are more than one use per consumer. If, in addition, consumers want variety over time, more grades would be desirable. This would apply whether each grade was produced to order or grades were sorted out of a bulk product. The number of grades could be so big that each item was a grade on its own, in which case many grades approximate to no grades. It is implied here that each buyer buys by grade description: if the buyer is in a position to select the best item out of the grade or display on offer, the situation is more complex.

The optimum number of grades to maximize consumer satisfaction falls if several grades can give equivalent satisfaction. This may happen where the mix of characteristics is different, but the two are valued equally (which is more likely to occur with grades that are suboptimal than with the combination that maximizes a consumer's satisfaction). It may also happen when the ratio between the prices of two grades is such that a consumer is indifferent between the optimum grade and a cheaper but less satisfying grade. Obviously price effects are very strange indeed if one assumes that each buyer buys one and only one grade, that nobody else buys that grade, and the buyer is indifferent between several grades, and especially if there is a variation in the grade purchased over time, so it is important to move to more realistic market assumptions.

The optimum number of grades to maximize consumer satisfaction is reduced if many consumers share the same tastes. While it would be very convenient to assume that there was considerable overlap, with only twenty different grades representing the optima for the population as a whole, this is quite unrealistic. Theory suggests that there will be very little overlap at all, when there are many characteristics and attributes to be taken into account, and each consumer weights and values each separately. Practice suggests that there would be a very wide range of selections, indeed, if consumers had a choice. If one looks at the number of brands of motor car on sale in this country, the number of different sub-brands, the number of lines within each sub-brand, and the optional features chosen, one may be excused for believing that the only reason any two consumers buy identical cars is that there are not quite enough options available. Similarly, one may believe that no two people would design the same house and no two consumers would buy the same wardrobe.

It seems more realistic to argue that the high search cost of finding the one and only optimum purchase for each consumer is a major constraint. The cost of searching many retailers to find the one and only optimum purchase, taking price and quality into account, is prohibitive, even when making a major purchase like a house. Consumers are willing to accept suboptimal purchases if the search cost can be reduced. A large reduction in the number of options will reduce the search cost, and for many products this may not result in a serious reduction in the satisfaction gained when consuming the product. There is a trade-off between search cost and the satisfaction obtained from consuming the product This is true, in different ways, when one is talking of the optimum number of homogeneous product lines to manufacture for a market, and when one is talking of the optimum number of grades into which to sort a heterogeneous product.

Production costs

If the number of options available is the major limitation on the qualities available, why is the number limited? One reason, clearly, is that it is costly to produce a large number of unique qualities. There are economies of scale in concentrating on one quality, so the first manufacturer to produce in quantity can chose to produce at any level of quality, and sell at a lower price than a manufacturer producing a one-off product. The new product is of a quality which is exactly what one consumer wants, and rather like what other consumers want, and if it is significantly cheaper they may buy it. Once the market is established, the decision facing the manufacturer who is considering producing a new quality is based on a range of factors:

- What is the cost curve for producing at each level of quality?
- How many items will have to be produced to sell at a price low enough to attract sufficient customers from other producers?
- How will competitors react to the new product? Will they cut their price to maintain market share? Will they introduce a 'spoiler' of the same quality so that it is uneconomic to produce, and the interloper has to drop the product?
- How will consumers assess a different quality at a different price? Some, no doubt, will find the new quality closer to their optimum choice, and if the price is low enough, some may find it less close, but cheaper. The reaction will depend, in part, on what proportion of customers have preferences around that level of quality, and how close competing qualities are.[11] It will also depend on elasticities and cross-elasticities, which must be unknown at the time the decision is made.
- How will the new product fit into the consumers' search pattern? Many will, no doubt, have chosen one quality as a habitual purchase, and will not even try the new product in the

short run. The interloper may go bankrupt before the new product attracts its new customers. This is especially likely to happen with branded goods.

Distribution costs are also a constraint. It is difficult and expensive to supply a large number of competing qualities. In practice, if one wants to buy organic bread or a carob-based chocolate substitute, one must go to a specialist health food shop and pay a high price for the product. High distribution costs and low turnover mean that the seller has to charge more than a supermarket would for an equivalent product. The manufacturer has to convince a supermarket chain that the product will sell in volume before it becomes possible to offer it at a low enough price to attract that volume.

One example of this is the market for petrol. At one time five grades were sold. It cost a certain amount more to produce five star, and the cost of distributing this small-volume line was high, so the companies were eager to cut out this quality, even though it would reduce the satisfaction of some consumers. A game situation arose, where the last firm to withdraw the grade would get all the trade for this grade, in which case distribution could well be profitable. Once this grade was withdrawn, with no very big effect on sales, other grades were removed, cutting the range on offer still further. When unleaded petrol was introduced, some companies reacted by selling only four-star leaded and four-star unleaded, and gave no choice on octane.

Producers face a different choice when they produce a heterogeneous product, and have to determine how many grades (and how much uniformity therefore) to sort it into.

One may expect that total demand for a product increases as more qualities are available, other things being equal. This means that there is more possibility that a quality will exactly match a consumer's preferences, and at the same time, that alternative products are less close substitutes.

The conclusion is that there is no easy answer to the question 'What is the optimum number of qualities?' or 'Should I introduce a new product line with a different quality?' The answer to these questions must be specific to that product and that market. A substantial economic analysis is required, not an off-the-shelf recipe.

CONCLUSION

This chapter has addressed an area of quality which is almost entirely ignored in the economic literature, but which is of the greatest practical importance in manufacturing and in distribution.

It has been shown that variation in quality of a product line is inevitable, and that manufacturers may choose to vary the quality. The importance of the distinction between uniformity of quality between bulk consignments and uniformity within small packages has been emphasized and so has the importance of the distinction between uniformity within packages, between packages and over time.

It has been shown how changed uniformity can change the utility of the product when consumed, the cost of production and distribution and the attractiveness of the product at the point of purchase, and the search costs. All these mean that market segmentation can increase total demand.

Chapter 8

Grades and search

INTRODUCTION

This chapter explores ways in which consumer search can be changed by the fact that the product is graded, whether by classification, sorting, grade labelling or price labelling. Even if the objective characteristics of a product are unchanged by a grading process, the fact that it has been graded will change the choice consumers have and the final selection they make. In the last chapter it was shown that sorting could also change the value in use of the product and the attractiveness of a display.

This chapter will start with an introduction to the type of information that a grade can give. This will be followed by an examination of the effect of grades in a market where there are no brands or other quality cues. The situation where all producers use the same grading system will be examined, and the situation where each uses his own.

A major objective is to identify those facets of a grading scheme that *can* affect demand. There is an infinite variety of possible grading schemes, so it is not possible to generalize for all, saying that grading has X, Y and Z effects in all cases. It is possible, though, to give a broad idea of how some aspects work in some situations.

WHAT INFORMATION CAN GRADES GIVE?

A grade or grade label is not a method of giving the *maximum* amount of information to the consumer, or of giving all the information needed to make an optimum decision. On the contrary, it may be a way of *reducing* the information available so that consumers can make a satisfactory decision, with very little cost in assembling or processing information, rather than making the best possible choice after a great deal of search. An effective grading system may filter out useless information, noise, and give information only on meaningful characteristics, and on characteristics that are not obvious to the consumer.

A grade is also a way of packaging the information more compactly. 'Class 2', for example, may give only broad indications of what a product is – how can you give precise description of a heterogeneous product in two words? – but it gives precise information on *what it is not*. For example, it means that the product meets certain minimum specifications on, say, ten characteristics. One of the most valuable uses of a grade label is to help customers avoid it. If a product is labelled 'Grade 3' a lot of customers know that it is not worth their while to look at it, while if it is labelled 'Grade 1' another range of customers will avoid it. This does raise the possibility that there are markets and products where it does not pay the seller to label the product, because this drives away more potential customers than it attracts. Certainly with dangerous or inferior products, it is not in the seller's interest to label the product.

Grades may also be a way of processing information, so that the buyer is not just given the bare facts but is given some interpretation of them. The grade label 'Poison' is more valuable to the buyer than the words 'Arsenic 2.5 per cent' in the list of contents. This information-processing component may be an important part of a classification scheme.

Grade labelling

The information that is given by grading varies enormously. The following levels were set out in Chapter 3.

1 The product may not be labelled at all.
2 The product may not be labelled, but it may be obvious to the shopper that it has been sorted or classified according to some unstated specifications.
3 The grade may indicate no more than that the product has been sorted or classified to, say, 'Choice', or 'Export Grade', where the buyer does not know the specifications.
4 The grading system may be one that the consumer does not

know about, but could, in principle, find out about if he put enough effort into it, writing to the EEC in Brussels for instance.

5 The grade label may itself indicate the ranking of the grades, with the implication that Class 3 is, in some unspecified way, inferior to Class 1.

6 Exact specifications in some or all relevant characteristics may be marked.

7 The seller may label his better grades, but leave the cheaper grades unlabelled.

8 Any of the above may be combined with a brand label.

Combinations of the above exist: the label 'English apples, Cox's Orange Pippins, EEC Class 1, 60-65 mm, Organic' gives precise information on size, variety and country of origin, with less precise information on the use of insecticides, and very vague information about the characteristics covered by the EEC standards.

Price labels can be interpreted by the consumer, rightly or wrongly, as giving an indication of what the seller thinks is the best quality.

The different methods listed here seldom appear in isolation. A product may be obviously sorted as well as branded. It may have a grade label and be sold by a retailer with a reputation for poor quality. It may be labelled EEC Grade III, but be sold in a shop with the reputation for selling the highest quality, indicating that the retailer and the consumers think that the EEC grade is irrelevant.

Parallel grades can give a great deal more precision than a single grading system like Class I, Class II, Class III. A grade label 'Irish, Cox's Orange Pippins, Class I, 70-80 mm' combined with the brand label 'Jones's', can identify the product with the greatest precision, perhaps down to a single box, as there is not much Cox grown in Ireland, Jones is not a common name there and the size is an uncommon one for Cox. This raises the point, though, that it is not the objective of the grading scheme to identify a particular box uniquely. It is not even the objective to describe the quality as exactly as possible.[1]

No brands or cues

The analysis that follows explores markets where there are no brands or other quality cues. The only sources of information for the buyer are inspection of the product or information derived from grading. If there were no grading at all, no classification, sorting, grade labelling or price labelling, the buyer in a shop would be presented with a jumble of qualities just as they came from the end of the production line. However, markets where this happens are very rare indeed: there are nearly always several grading systems in operation. This means that we are concerned with the information provided by different grading schemes, rather than with a comparison between a given scheme and an imaginary no-grading situation.

It is also assumed here that grade labels are correct, though in practice mislabelling seems to be very common indeed. It is particularly common where the product is perishable and the quality declines during distribution. It may be common where the grading system is irrelevant and people ignore the labels.

SINGLE GRADING SYSTEM FOR THE WHOLE MARKET

This section considers a market where there is a single, unique, grading system covering the entire market. All sellers grade according to the same grade specification. There is only one characteristic of importance, and the grade specification covers only this. They do not have any other grading system of their own operating in parallel and nor do they have their own brands. Everything is sorted.

Physical implications

The fact that a product has undergone a grading process and particularly a sorting process is likely to have implications on the physical nature of the product and on the choices available to the consumer.

One example of a grading scheme is one where:

1 The whole output is sorted according to a single grading scheme. This scheme has no tolerances.
2 Items that are unsaleable are dumped.
3 Items that will fetch a very low price are dumped or diverted to alternative markets. For many products there is a distinction between substandard and defective items, with the defective having no value.

4 The product is sorted into three grades which are relatively uniform in a small number of key characteristics.
5 Each wholesaler handles all grades. In many markets they would specialize in one or two. The produce is not identified by the producer's name.
6 Retailers buying one grade get a random sample of what is available in that grade. They are not in a position to select out the best of that grade, or to relate purchases to previous purchases from the same producer.
7 Each retailer buys one grade and only one at any one time.
8 Each retailer buys the same grade every time he purchases.
9 The product is labelled with its grade and price, and nothing else, at retail and at wholesale.
10 All items in a grade in one shop have the same price. Items from the top of the grade have the same price as items from the bottom.
11 The quality is evident to the buyer at the point of purchase.
12 There is self-selection. The buyer can select out the better items in a grade.
13 Prices vary between shops. The price may vary over time, but it is not related to changes in the average quality on display; it does not fall when all the best items have been sold, and the average quality remaining is low.
14 The quality on offer does not vary systematically. It is not possible to say, as one might with fresh produce, that the quality on offer is best just after the morning delivery, and worst when the stocks are at a minimum at the end of the day.

This is, of course, a very simple model of a very complex market, and many of the assumptions would not apply in a supermarket chain: for example, different shops in one supermarket chain often have different acceptance standards, so their quality is not identical on delivery, and some producers consistently produce above-average Grade 2 and consistently supply the same wholesalers and retailers. It is important, though, to be clear how many assumptions have to be made even for a simple model.

The physical implications of this simple sorting procedure are wide ranging:

– With perfect sorting and no deterioration in the shop, the buyer cannot buy a defective, or perfectly useless, item, so the risk of disaster is reduced.

- The buyer cannot buy a substandard item in this market. To the extent that substandard items are diverted to other markets, they may still be available and part of aggregate supply.
- The product on offer in a store is relatively uniform, so the consumer has less incentive to search within the store than with unsorted produce. This implies, of course, a retailing system like self-selection where the customer can search. With counter service or buying on description the customer takes what is offered, but the sorting means that there is a reduced risk that the item will be defective or substandard.
- Once a consumer has entered a store, he has only one grade available: it is a big decision to go to another shop to compare. This has important implications on locational monopoly, on the range that should be stocked by a store, and on its policy on availability.
- The grade in one shop is not just uniform in one purchase, it is uniform over time. This makes pre-purchase search and habitual purchase strategies feasible.

Comparisons of quality between shops in the long run becomes feasible. It is at least feasible to divide all shops into three broad levels of quality. By assumption, all shops selling Grade A sell the same quality, on average, but at any one time they may be offering a different level of quality. For example, a shop which has just recently had a delivery will have items from the top of the grade available, as well as items from the average and bottom of the grade. A shop which has nearly cleared out the last delivery will have sold the best items and have only the bottom of the grade available. Because the average level of quality varies over time, search to compare prices and qualities may not be terribly useful: by the time the search has been carried out, the quality in the first shop has changed. This arises out of the assumptions that there is self-selection, and that all items in a grade are priced the same; if each item is priced according to the level of quality, using the seller's perception of the price consumers are willing to pay, then one might expect all qualities to sell at the same rate. The average consumer could then buy at random, knowing that he would get the same value for money anywhere. Consumers with expensive tastes would get better value for money buying expensive items, and consumers who were not particularly interested in frills would get better value for money by buying cheap. As with many of the conclusions here, the situation is far more complex if a grade with several important characteristics exists, with varying consumer demands for each characteristic.

Comparison of prices between shops in the long run is possible. Shop A usually has a lower price for a grade than Shop B. However, at any one time comparison is more difficult: Shop A may happen to have a higher price for Grade 1 than Shop B, but to have a higher quality available. Shop C may sell only Grade 2 at a lower price, but since this Grade 2 is freshly delivered there are some items which are virtually Grade 1, at Grade 2 prices, while Shop B has some items which are virtually Grade 2 at Grade 1 prices. Indeed, if there are tolerances in the specifications, Shop C may have some items labelled Class 2 which are well into Grade 1, while Shop B may have some items labelled Class 1 which are a low Class 2. In the last chapter it was shown how the quality on display could fall quickly from self-selection.

It is possible that consumers could carry out a two-stage search, perhaps telephoning round to check which stores have the required grade available, and which stores are cheaper for that grade, and only then visiting a few shops to search for the best item in the grade.

By assumption, we do not have the situation where the keener buyers always visit a shop at the same time each day, just after delivery, to get the best product, while others visit whenever it is convenient. An example of a very different product, typical of industrial raw materials, is cotton, whose quality can be described simply as follows. Cotton is classified as it is picked, and seed cotton of different grades is put in different sacks. All seed cotton of one grade from one area is ginned together to produce a homogeneous classification, like Sudan Gezira, Barakat Class B, for instance. This is kept physically separate from other grades, even Barakat Class B from other areas of the Sudan, until it reaches the spinning mill in England. The spinner makes a blend of different grades of cotton, based on their spinning characteristics, staple length, strength, and so on and the quality of the yarn he wants to produce. The degree of separation required to produce good yarn is indicated by the fact that the Liverpool Cotton Exchange used to know the names of each manager of a small ginnery in East Africa, and pay a premium related to the quality of output he produced from a given quality of seed cotton, a premium that followed the manager when he was transferred to another ginnery.

In the absence of such a grading system, mixed grades would be picked, mixed grades would be ginned and mixed types would be put into the spinning mill, so it would not be possible to produce special qualities like Sea Island Cotton. It would be a matter of chance whether the spinner had American or Sudanese, long or short staple, high or low Pressley, and so on on any one day. Quality of yarn would be very variable, top quality cottons would not exist, and low quality cottons would be very expensive because they would be made with average quality lint. All this would happen because of the different physical distribution arising from a different grading system.

This product differs from the one previously described in that:

- The process keeps grades separate from the start, rather than sorting a mixed product to produce different grades.
- Once the product has been blended, in the ginnery or in the spinning mill, it cannot be unblended, like whisky, milk, wheat and petrol.
- The different qualities are kept separate as long as possible, to give as much flexibility as possible in spinning. This means that the maximum number of spinners are interested in the product at any one time; if it was mixed together into a blend at an early stage, at ginning for instance, only those spinners who were interested in that particular blend would be in the market. The situation is very different with tobacco, where the world market is dominated by seven large companies. Here the companies buy the qualities they want at an early stage in the distribution chain, as soon as they leave the farm, and the blending operations start immediately afterwards, with further blending operations later in the chain combining the product of different countries. With condiments, there is no blending until the product reaches the final consumer.
- The product is typically bought on description. However, the cotton exchanges have systems of arbitration using standard samples for each country, which mean that a seller who over-states his quality gains nothing in the short run, and may suffer a loss of reputation in the long run.

Buying on description

Obvious quality

With some products, quality is obvious. An experienced industrial buyer, for instance, can often form an instant judgement of the quality of bulk raw materials merely from a cursory inspection. With products like fruit and vegetables, a quick glance is enough to give the buyer all the information that would be available from a grade label and to assess how uniform the product is. The realities of retailing with self-selection, with tolerances in the grading specifications, and with a perishable product, mean that the product on display seldom corresponds to the quality of the bulk product meeting the grade specifications (see Chapter 7).

There may or may not be a cost incurred in assessing this obvious quality, with the industrial buyer visiting the producer to inspect, rather than ordering on the telephone, or carrying out a laboratory test on samples. To the extent that this is so, there will be a trade-off between the cost of perfect knowledge and the cost of suboptimal choice. On the other hand, where there is obvious quality, the customer in a supermarket can instantly and adequately compare the quality of all items of the same product available in this shop, and select the best, or at least a satisfactory, item. He is not affected by any deliberate or accidental mislabelling. Errors in recall make this less reliable when comparing the quality in one shop with that in another when there is a time difference, when trying to visualize quality independent of cues like shop ambience, smartness of display and shop reputation, when trying to visualize the quality of the best on offer in each shop rather than the average quality on offer, and when adopting long-term search and habitual search strategies. The fact that the relative quality of the best items on offer keeps fluctuating with self-selection makes recall difficult, and would make comparisons difficult even with perfect recall.

Labelling when quality is obvious

Would labelling reduce search costs for products whose quality is obvious? Certainly there are products for which this would be the case, where travelling to inspect is more expensive than buying on description, for instance. However, much of the saving in search from grading described above comes from a physical separation of the product rather than from labelling.

Labelling is expensive: quite apart from the physical labelling operations, retailers have to set up a policing operation to check that the labels relate to the actual quality of the product, which is particularly expensive with perishable products whose quality may decline over the course of a day, and with the decline in quality from self-selection which was described in the last chapter. There is also the possibility of a prosecution under the Trades Description Act, with the accompanying bad publicity.

If labels perfectly duplicate the evidence of peoples' own eyes, then people are not going to use them, as they will be looking at the product before making a choice anyway. There may, perhaps, be the possibility that the label will change their perception of what they see. If the labels do not perfectly duplicate peoples' perceptions, this could arouse uncertainty about the product or the labelling system.

Grade labels may not be intended to duplicate the evidence of peoples' eyes, but to take this evidence and process it. One example is turning a mass of information into the label Grade A. Generally, these labels are very imperfectly related to consumer perceptions, because the weightings given to the characteristics naturally vary from consumer to consumer. Quite often too, these grading specifications are drawn up by committees based on their perception of what the consumer ought to want. As a result, there are plenty of examples in the literature of consumers absolutely preferring Grade 2 to Grade 1, when it is supposed to be a vertical scale. Conceivably, though, the label could process the information available in a way not every consumer could process it, pointing out which items were dangerous, for instance. It might also be used as education, showing that there was another way of processing the information.

Quality partly hidden

Generally, some quality characteristics are open to inspection, at a cost, but others are hidden, in the sense that they cannot be assessed in a normal point-of-sale inspection. These may be characteristics that are evident on consumption, like the worm in the apple, or characteristics like Halal or organic which cannot be identified in consumption, and must be taken on trust.

Characteristics hidden from both manufacturer and consumer

Some characteristics may be hidden from both manufacturer and consumer. If grade specifications are based on the same evident characteristics that the customer can see for himself, and the others are ignored, the position is basically the same as when all characteristics are evident, as in the last section. The consumer will make a decision, suboptimal, on those characteristics he can identify, and bear the risk of the others. Labelling is unlikely to affect the decision.

Hidden characteristics known but not in specifications

If the hidden characteristics can be identified at a cost there is a trade-off between increased search cost and improved decision-making. With most goods, it is possible for the manufacturer to measure characteristics as a part of the manufacturing process at little extra cost, while it is impractical for the consumer to do so. The manufacturer may be able to do the increased search, but not be willing to do so: how does he benefit from knowing, and telling the consumer, that some items in a grade are better than others? The fall in the price of items identified as inferior may not be compensated for by the rise in the price of items identified as superior, even if the costs of identifying the items and sorting them is ignored.

If consumers believe that the manufacturers could sort by hidden characteristics, but choose not to do so, they will act as though neither consumer nor producer knew, as in the previous section.

If they believe that manufacturers can deliberately alter the quantity of the hidden characteristics by a change in manufacturing specification and that manufacturers can save money by doing so, then consumer perception of probable quality will fall. Habitual purchase strategies may improve the situation, where the characteristic is one that can be identified on consumption.

If they believe that producers or retailers can remove the best of each grade and sell it to special markets at a higher price, their perception of the average quality that is left, will fall. In some special cases, where the low level of the hidden attribute means that the product is useless, this can lead to the market collapse described in the Akerlof (1970) model.

This fall in consumer confidence cannot be reversed by labelling the product, as the grade gives only the information that the consumer has already. A change in the grade specifications, branding, or guarantees may help.

If important characteristics are hidden, it will be impossible for consumers to find the optimum product by searching on obvious characteristics. Indeed if the characteristics are negatively correlated (organic and perfect appearance, for instance) search may seem pointless. Sometimes, of course, it will not pay manufacturers to identify the hidden characteristics, but consumers may do so at a cost. This is a trade-off between increased search costs and increased benefit.

Increasingly important in marketing are assurances that certain processes have been carried out, like method of slaughter (Halal), method of manufacture (for example, Champagne), method of production (hygienic, organic), storing (wine, cheese). Similarly, consumers want assurances of safety of the end product, and assurances that it contains the right vitamins. A disinterested observer *could* have observed that these processes were carried out and that the end product is free from dangerous additives, but the consumer is not in a position to verify this either at the time of purchase or at the time of consumption. Clearly, rational consumers will only believe claims about these if they have some reason to believe that there are sanctions on sellers who make false claims. This may mean that the grading scheme is backed by an obvious checking and control system. It may mean that there is branding, and that the consumer believes that a major manufacturer or retailer who sold mislabelled products would suffer a serious loss of sales if he was exposed.

Grades specify all relevant characteristics

If the grading standards cover all hidden and open characteristics, then the consumer has the choice of

1 making a decision on the evidence of his eyes only, an inferior decision because it ignores some of the evidence;
2 making a decision on the evidence of his own eyes plus the grade label;
3 making a decision on the grade label alone.

If inspection is costless it seems reasonable to use 2, making a decision on the evidence of his own eyes plus the grade label. If the label gives information on hidden and open characteristics separately, a buyer may ignore the information on open characteristics, preferring to use his own eyes, but take information on hidden characteristics separately. He may compare his own evaluation of the open characteristics with that of the label, and have a greater confidence in its assessment of the hidden characteristics the more the two tally. If, however, the grade label gives a single score, Grade B, to cover hidden and open characteristics, the buyer may attempt to find out the probable level of the hidden characteristics on the basis of his observation of the open characteristics.

The value of the other two choices, 1 and 3, depends on the labelling system used. If it is merely 'Grade 1' and several characteristics are covered, the quality of the information on any item is poor, and in many or even most circumstances the label will not help any buyer but one whose values exactly correspond with the grading system.

In the case where some of the characteristics are obvious and some hidden, the buyer is best served by a label which covers only the hidden characteristics. Even if this is just 'Grade 1', it gives a better quality of information, because it covers fewer characteristics, and its weighting is less complicated.

All quality hidden

If all quality characteristics are effectively hidden at the time of purchase, the consumer has no choice but to base the choice on the information given, however bad it is. The buyer has to buy a random sample of what is offered, and does not have the option of picking out the best items in the grade.

If the grade standards cover only some of these hidden characteristics, the decision will necessarily be imperfect. If, in addition, the seller has information about the quality of the product that the buyer has not, buyers' perceptions of the probable quality may be low.

If all quality characteristics are covered by the specifications, the consumer may still get very limited information. If, for example, there are only three grades to cover a broad range of characteristics and qualities, the grade labels are likely to be of very little informational value. Generally, more grades, possibly parallel grades, are needed to give useful information when an attempt is made to give adequate information for buying and selling on description alone. In the commodity markets it is common to have thousands of grades, arising out of parallel grading systems.

Even if there is a large number of grades, the amount of useful information communicated is small. The grades may reflect the order of preferences of a consumer, but this is not enough to determine the optimum purchase, whether to buy a cheap Class 3 or an expensive Class 1. More often, though, the grades will be a very imperfect reflection of consumers' preferences. This is particularly likely to be the case when there are a lot of meaningful characteristics, when the product has several end uses and when there is a wide range of qualities.

If, therefore, buying on description is to be of any real value in the circumstances described, when there are no brands or quality cues and when sellers are not identifiable, market level grades with sanctions and enforcement are needed. Such schemes are complex and expensive. As a result, these pure grading systems, buying and selling on description using market grades, are very rare indeed. They are approximated in some commodity markets, but a close examination of the markets usually reveals some element of repeat purchases, as well as a well-organized arbitration system. Wherever possible sellers are identified, by country or marketing organization if not by individual producer – I have mentioned the Liverpool Cotton Exchange knowing the names of individual ginnery managers in Africa. Sometimes buyers will set up their own buying organization to examine crops in the field and products in the factory, so that they get better information than a grade description. Vertical integration is used as a very powerful way of reducing risk when buying on description: the company does the quality determination as early as possible in the production or distribution chain, and saves on the risk and inspection costs that otherwise arise every time the product changes hands.

EACH SELLER WITH A UNIQUE GRADING SYSTEM

In this section the situation is considered where each seller has a unique grading system. There is no market level grading system used by everybody: instead, each retailer adopts his own system with one, two or ten grades, divided according to grade specifications of his own. By assumption there are no brands.[2]

Physical limitations

This does mean that there are many more possible combinations of quality on the market. No two retailers need sell grades with the same specifications. If we take the grade as a mixture which cannot be separated, so the buyer is not able to select out the items he wants, this gives the buyer far more possible choices than with market grades. By searching, he can find a grade that closely approximates to his preferences. If, however, the product is one where it is possible to select the item he wants from a display, the possible choices are the same, but search cost is different.

Other things being equal, the fact that there are many different grading systems means that there is more choice, when buying the product as offered. It is possible, of course that 100 traders, each with three grades, may offer less discrimination than a market-level system with fifteen grades.

Search

The more grades, the more uniform the product is within that grade. With a multitude of grading systems, some may have a product uniform in terms of colour, some in size, some in shape. If the buyer can find a grade uniform in terms of the characteristics he values, it may not pay him to search within the grade to find the best item, assuming that this is possible.

There is a trade-off in the welfare gains obtained. The multitude of grades makes it more possible to obtain a quality near to optimum, assuming no selection of the best item within a grade. Where selection is possible, it makes it easier to select the best, and possibly justifies taking a random selection as being satisfactory. Against this must be set the cost of finding the seller who has the right grade, and identifying the grading specifications. If it is a one-off purchase in a crowded market, the situation with this grading system may approximate to one where there is no grading, but an unsorted product. Where sellers are identified and there is repeated purchase, there may be a considerable cost in finding the appropriate seller, but little search cost in buying after this. This makes market segmentation possible. This is very close to the branded product situation.

Where most customers inspect before buying, an equilibrium may be expected where each grade (or indeed each quality) offers similar value for money. Any one customer who believes that he has average tastes may buy at random, saving search costs and getting the same value for money. Anyone with unusual tastes may have found that he gets exceptional value for money by always buying, say, the highest grade, and therefore may adopt the policy of always buying this grade without inspection. However, the more customers who stop inspecting and buy at random, the less prices can be expected to conform to equilibrium levels, the less reliable price will be as a cue, and the less uniform will be value for money.[3] The optimum amount of search is cyclical: high when a grade is introduced, low when it is established, and higher when the price: quality relationship breaks down. Salop (1977) suggests that cynical consumers, or those who have read Akerlof (1970) will inspect, and will drop out of the market rather than buy on description. It is these cynics who inspect that keep prices related to quality, and indeed who keep labels related to actual quality.

CONCLUSION

This chapter has shown that sorting physically changes the choices open to the consumer, and this change in choices changes the optimum search pattern. The change in the physical availability also changes the information available to the consumer, and the use that can be made of information.

The situation where everything is bought on description is virtually the only one described in the literature. It has been shown here, and in previous chapters on search, that there are almost no markets in the real world where sales are entirely on description. Instead, repeated purchase, inspection, partial inspection, warranties and so on are used to reduce the risk of a purchase entirely on description.

The value of information, including grades, depends on the information that can be obtained from an inspection. If the product's quality is immediately apparent to the buyer, then the benefit from a label is limited. Generally speaking, the benefit is greater when the label covers characteristics that are hidden from the buyer. However, the more that the label is meant to describe, the less adequate a simple, vertical, grading scheme is: the more likely a parallel system with many possible grades will be needed. Because of the difficulty of working with, monitoring and enforcing such a system, all markets try to avoid sales on description alone.

A key conclusion is that it is not possible to generalize. Grades have very different importance depending on whether or not the product is sold on description, whether or not all characteristics are hidden, whether or not it is possible for the buyer to select out the best items on offer, whether or not there are repeat purchases. The appropriate search pattern is altered by pricing, whether each item is priced individually or there is a single price for a grade.

Chapter 9

Compulsory minimum standards: good or bad?

WHAT ARE COMPULSORY MINIMUM STANDARDS?

Governments are frequently put under heavy pressure to impose compulsory minimum standards for a product, banning the sale of any item that does not meet certain minimum criteria. In this chapter I will examine the case for and against the minimum standards. First I will look at some cases in which nearly everybody would agree that minimum standards are desirable, and then identify those factors which are most important in reaching the conclusion. I shall then examine a very common case where these special factors do not hold and where compulsory minimum standards are definitely not desirable.[1]

Governments have had compulsory minimum standards for centuries on matters of food safety, weights and measures and so on. The Victorians accompanied the industrial revolution with what they saw to be the basic minimum standards for effective trade and to provide a minimum of personal security to the public. By the 1970s the EEC in particular was engaged in a programme of setting out minimum standards for any products they could think of, and there are even OECD standards for 'products for which there are no standards'.[2] It was never made clear what this burst of standards was intended to achieve. Today the EEC, or at least the non-agricultural directorates, seem to be working on a different approach to consumer protection. The British government in the 1980s reduced enforcement of legislation on food hygiene, food safety, safety of ships and so on, apparently in the belief that 'market forces' will exercise any control that is necessary, and in the belief that anything that benefits the consumer must harm the producer.

It is usually not possible to get a definitive official statement of what a given set of minimum standards is intended to achieve, and if one talks to the officials concerned, one gets a range of different, and often contradictory, objectives, with no explanation of how this particular set of standards can achieve this object. Sometimes identical objectives are set out for systems which must have entirely different effects when implemented. A typical statement made by an influential manufacturer/distributor welcoming a set of minimum standards is

> As I see it, we shall be able to pick and choose and get a better grade of article. Our leakage in waste will not be so great, and we shall be in better competition, offering a good article, and when the market has to pay top prices the sub-standard stuff will eventually disappear from the market.[3]

It is an achievement to combine as many conflicting aims and begged questions in two sentences. The following justifications are often implicit in arguments in favour of minimum standards:

- Helping the consumer by:
    (a) Action to reduce the probability of a defective or inferior product being bought.
    (b) Action to reduce the cost to the consumer when a defective or inferior item is purchased.
    (c) Action to reduce search cost, so that the consumers can themselves avoid defective or inferior items.
- Increasing sales to consumers, to the benefit of producers and traders.
- Facilitating trade, to the benefit of producers and traders.
- Restricting supply, so that producers can earn a monopoly profit. A minimum standard may be the easiest way to administer a quota.[4] Politically, it is more acceptable to say that action is taken to raise the quality of the product the consumer gets, than to say it is to raise the income of producers by restricting production or by restricting imports.
- Giving special advantages to certain groups of producer, those producing certain qualities or those producing a quality that cannot be produced by foreign producers, for instance.
- Helping control monopolies. In the USA in particular monopolies, especially public utilities, may be subject to price controls. There is always a danger that they will circumvent

these controls by keeping the same price and reducing quality, so minimum standards are included in the price controls.[5]

Hidden characteristics

Let us consider first a product with characteristics that the consumer cannot inspect before purchase. The consumer faces the risk that his purchase will have a hidden imperfection or defect which is not apparent until the product is consumed, or, indeed until long afterwards, as is the case with drugs. An almost identical situation arises when the imperfection or defect is detectable, but only at a cost that is quite unreasonable – the imperfection might only be a marginally lower level of characteristic than the minimum standard permits, or the loss from product failure might be negligible.

If the manufacturer cannot identify the hidden level of characteristic or cannot do so at a reasonable cost, then minimum standards in the form of stopping the sale of goods with a low level of characteristic are impossible. Equally, it is not possible to label each item that does not meet the standard, so that the consumer can himself avoid buying it. If the manufacturer can measure the characteristic, he can separate out Class III. The question is, then, whether it would be better to take the Class III off the market, or to label it and sell it separately.

In some circumstances there can be little doubt that it would pay to ban the low qualities. If one in a thousand bottles of milk was infected with cholera, the market would collapse. If standards of aviation construction and maintenance were of the level they were in the 1920s, when a pilot on the London to Paris run had a four-year life expectancy, there would be no mass market for air transport. As long as one supplier can produce a dangerous product, and this cannot be effectively distinguished from others, the market will remain tiny. It is in the interests of every producer to see that there are minimum standards which apply to everyone, so that one unscrupulous supplier cannot destroy the market for everyone. Some products harm people other than the producer or consumer. Society as a whole has to pay for treating the cancerous tobacco smoker, and the CFCs in my shaving cream help destroy the world's ozone layer. Some manufacturing processes produce harmless products at the expense of poisoned employees or a damaged environment. For this reason society as a whole may decide to control these products. The factors that make these examples so compelling are:

- The cost of failure is large, even though the probability of failure is small.
- Alternatively, there is a high probability of a less serious cost.
- Defective items cannot be distinguished by the buyer.
- Producers of defective items cannot be distinguished by the buyer.
- In the absence of any way of identifying or punishing the producer, it pays each producer to slacken standards, especially if he believes that his competitors will not slacken standards in response.
- Costs are borne by all consumers, not just those who buy the defective item. Risk and search cost are high.
- Costs are borne by all producers, even when only one or two are producing defective items. There is a very limited market.

Obviously, the case for minimum standards is weaker when these conditions do not apply.

It is possible to construct a model where the fact that the seller, but not the buyer, knows the hidden defect can cause market breakdown. This can happen even when for every quality there is a willing buyer and a willing seller, if the quality were known. Akerlof (1970) showed how this could happen in the second-hand car market; if someone sells a car six months after buying it new, the presumption is that he has found that it is a 'lemon' and is trying to get rid of it, so the price is low. He shows that this could conceivably bring all trade to a halt. The assumptions, implicit and explicit, of this model are rather restrictive, so one cannot generalize from them. Empirical tests of this model in the used-car market suggest that if there are slight adjustments to the basic assumptions to fit a real market, it does not work.[6]

Under the assumption of characteristics hidden from both buyer and seller, minimum standards cannot change consumer search.

Costly information

Cost of search

For many products the characteristic is not hidden, but it is costly to obtain. It takes time to examine every second-hand car: it takes time to test a consignment of cocoa beans before processing. A lengthy search is needed to find the information needed to arrive at the optimum purchase, finding the best single item at each price, then seeing which gives the best value for money. Since searching is expensive, buyers compromise with less search and an inferior but satisfactory purchase (Chapter 4). The search cost can be reduced by branding, labelling or sorting by the producer and by habitual purchasing strategies by the consumer.

Minimum standards may reduce the search cost if one grade is removed entirely. It will not have any effect if the standards are not related to consumer preference, as may be the case when the primary purpose of the standards is to reduce supply and give producers a monopoly profit. A review of the literature shows that the standards used in practice usually do not have much basis in consumer preference, and are almost never based on market surveys.[7]

Return from search

Obviously, customers will have little incentive to search if all items on the market offer much the same value for money: the search may produce little more value for money and perhaps none at all. If, however, a substandard item is dangerous, or if a lot of money is at stake – a purchaser losing three months' salary if his car turns out to be useless – or if a purchaser feels that there is a wide range of value for money on the market, he can be expected to search extensively. Because the returns from search are high, the optimum time spent on it is high, so it is expensive.

In cases like this, search may be a big cost even when the quality is easily examined or when each item is clearly labelled, if the cost of failure is sufficiently high. When someone poisoned half a dozen bottles of aspirin in Chicago, clearly labelling each 'Poison', it stopped all sales of that brand in the United States. There is always the danger that someone will not notice the label, or that the bottle was tampered with, and will be poisoned, as indeed did happen in Chicago.

When the cost of failure is this high, there can be a market failure. The consumer has to inspect every purchase carefully and the producer has low sales and low profit. If minimum standards can either reduce the probability of disaster or reduce the cost of the disaster, everyone benefits. Pressure from producers and, less important politically, consumers, has meant that most countries have adopted some minimum standards, on food hygiene, for instance.

Indeed, governments often overreact, imposing minimum standards at vast expense when the risk is small.[8] In many of these cases it is certain that most fully-informed buyers would be willing to buy the product and take the risk of a substandard item, but governments will not take the political risk of appearing to let people die by neglecting to take small precautions. For example, governments treat asbestos as a product as dangerous as plutonium, and spend vast sums to dispose of it safely, when most of those people born before the 1960s were constantly exposed to it, and used to play with it, with no ill effects: the few people who do die from it have millions of fibres in their lungs. People do seem able to make responsible and rational decisions when the data are available. For instance, when there was the scare about the possible side effects of measles vaccines, most people who were presented with the information asked for their children to be vaccinated in spite of the risk. There was the classic welfare argument here: all children are safer if all are vaccinated; my child is safest if she is not vaccinated but all other children are; therefore my duty to the public may not be the same as my duty to my child. I do not know if I would take the same decision with my daughter now as I did then, after quarter of a century of scandals about drug firms and about Ministry manipulation of scientists' results. The perceived reliability of the information has changed.

Both governments and individuals often have an unrealistic perception of danger. For example, there is constant pressure to improve already high standards of air safety, but very little to improve dangerous motor cars.

Full information

The situation where the consumer can readily assess the quality before purchase without cost will be discussed in the second half of this chapter, as the main example of a situation where it is difficult to provide justification for minimum standards. The same conclusions apply somewhat less directly where the quality cannot be assessed before purchase but there is repeat buying or habitual purchase of the product, where there is habitual use of one seller, or where there is branding.

Both manufacturers buying raw materials for processing and large retailing chains buying goods to sell apply quality control on their purchases, checking on a number of characteristics. It is often very little more difficult to check on the government-imposed minimum standard as well. Indeed, the firm will almost always demand a standard higher than the minimum standard, and so will check on the same characteristics at a higher level. Where this is the case, the marginal cost of checking to see that a product exceeds the minimum standards is zero.

Minimum standards to reduce risk

As a rule minimum standards make it an offence to sell a product that does not meet a certain minimum level of characteristic, though the standard could, of course, be defined in terms of standard deviation, tolerance, and so on. The penalties laid down are assumed to be sufficient to ensure that people do not in fact sell the banned qualities. This form of minimum standard is impossible to operate where the manufacturers cannot determine the level of the hidden characteristic and it is difficult to enforce when the cost of detecting and removing inferior items is high.

It does reduce the probability of buying an inferior item, particularly when it is a product that the consumer cannot or does not inspect (though the fact that the consumer does not inspect when it is possible to do so suggests that he may not think it worth the bother).

It can reduce search in two ways. First, the very lowest qualities are no longer available, so the incentive to search is lower. Second, there are fewer qualities on the market, so search is easier: there may be only two grades instead of three on offer.

It does certainly reduce choice and reduce supply. It puts up unit costs merely by the fact that a proportion of the output is not sold. It is likely to mean different production techniques and quality control.[9]

Minimum standards as guarantee

Instead of specifying that it is a criminal offence to sell any item that does not meet the minimum standards, the legislation may determine that the manufacturer has a statutory responsibility if the product does not meet the standards. This statutory responsibility might imply replacement, repair, money back, or it might imply responsibility for all damage caused by the failure. When government specifies that it is a criminal offence but takes no action to enforce the law, the effect may be similar.

The suppliers can then judge whether or not to change the quality of the output accordingly. At one extreme they may carry on producing the same mix of quality, and provide an instant, no-quibble, money-back guarantee. This might be the decision for a product like ball-point pens, where it is a simple matter to replace defective goods. It would not be acceptable to give a widow her money back for the poisonous mushrooms her husband ate. For some products the manufacturer would carry a terrific burden if he was responsible for all the damages caused by product failure, the destruction of a space shuttle because of the failure of a seal, the collapse of an accounting system because of the failure of a microchip costing 20p. It is normally recognized that no product is perfect, so electronics systems, for example, are designed to produce a perfect output in spite of imperfect components, and a lorry has two independent braking systems. It may be a lot cheaper to build in such fail-safe systems than to produce a product that is acceptably near perfect, given the contingent costs if it is not.

The compensation approach works even when there is a hidden characteristic and the manufacturer cannot identify and remove defective items. It also can work when the manufacturer works to tolerances: his quality control system is such that there is always some proportion defective, parts per million perhaps. This is usual, and indeed it is unavoidable when the product can only be classified by destructive testing.

In effect, this legislation means that the risk is switched from the buyer to the seller. It becomes a calculable, insurable risk. The buyer is no longer taking a gamble with unknown odds that his house will collapse, leaving him bankrupt: instead, the builder insures against any house he builds collapsing.

The removal or transfer of risk does not affect all customers equally. For example, the wealthy may be more willing to tolerate a risk of complete failure, but be more irritated by the inconvenience of claiming under guarantee.

Minimum labelling

An alternative to minimum standards and guarantees is to specify a minimum standard of labelling. This transforms a market from one where search is difficult to one where it is easy. It transforms a product with a hidden characteristic to one with an open characteristic. It enables people to avoid certain qualities if they wish, but it does not reduce the quantity on the market. This is, of course, impossible when there is a hidden defect which the manufacturer himself cannot identify.

A distinction must be drawn between labelling each item with a quality, and labelling the mixed product with its average quality, the implication being that some items may not meet the description. This is also a practical problem with minimum standards: with many products some items will not meet the standards, even when the consignment does, a problem that was discussed in the chapter on uniformity. Some caution is needed when referring to a low-grade product as defective: certainly it may be, but it may just be one with a slightly lower level of characteristic: 'defect' has value overtones which 'low level of characteristic X' does not.

While labelling may make search easier, it does not remove the incentive to search, as the range of qualities remains unchanged (in practice, if the product was individually labelled, pricing might change). The fact that search was easier might mean that more search was done: I can search for the kind of bread I want as long as it is properly labelled, but if it is not, then laboratory testing is needed to see if it is wholemeal rather than wheatmeal.

Beyond basic safety, labelling has a lot to offer. It does not sharply reduce the quantity on the market, though it does impose some costs and manufacturing inflexibilities. Instead, it identifies those qualities most suited to sub-markets and it permits market segmentation. For example, a minimum standard for food safe for all the population would have no sugar (diabetics), salt (hypertensives), cholesterol (heart disease sufferers), tartrazine (allergy sufferers) and so on. Instead of restricting supply to this extent, manufacturers can make a product which is perfectly safe for most people, and give the necessary information on the label to let the subgroups buy or avoid the product as they wish. This means less search for the subgroup than when there are no minimum standards or when they do not know the detailed specifications for the minimum standard, but much more search than if there was a very restrictive minimum standard. For the great majority of the population, labelling means more variety, a lower unit cost and less search.

A practical problem is that when there are minimum standards that are widely ignored as being unworkable, like the EEC grades, and there is compulsory labelling, the labels are often incorrect and the consumer gets the worst of both worlds. Labelling is inappropriate where quality is self-evident for reasons discussed in the previous chapter.

How high should a minimum standard be?

There is a declining marginal return to increased minimum standards. The first level, of removing the positively dangerous items, has a large impact and may be a necessary condition of having any trade at all. The next step, of removing totally useless items, also benefits the producer and consumer – very substantially in the case of expensive items like cars, but only trivially in the case of some very cheap items like ball-point pens. Increasing minimum standards beyond this only reduces the possibility of purchasing a somewhat substandard item, which may not be a serious cost or risk. Indeed, in some markets supply and demand have meant that the equilibrium price of each quality reflects the same value for money, and the lowest quality is also very cheap, so there is no obvious benefit to the consumer from banning its sale. As the standard rises, it helps fewer and fewer customers. Every time it rises it means that fewer people are allowed to buy their optimum quality, and they have to switch to other products or to Class I or Class II at a higher price. This effect is aggravated by the fact that the increase in price means that their optimum quality purchase falls – at the new price some of the buyers of Class II would have switched to Class III if it was still available. In many markets the only benefit from a further increase in minimum standards, banning Class II as well as Class III, would be to save those buying Class I the embarrassment of buying Class II by mistake, a Bentley instead of a Rolls.

How does the cost to the consumer rise as the minimum standard is increased? Often there is little or no added physical cost in removing Class III, because there is a sorting system already in place, but for some products like drugs, this elementary protection may be the most expensive. There may be a positive or a negative return from the outgrades, depending on whether they can be sold on another market or whether the producer has to pay to dispose of them.

There is no demand for the dangerous or useless items, so removing them from the market will not cause any scarcity. The increase in price will come from reduction in risk and search, not from a reduction in supply. However, once the standards start removing qualities for which there is a demand, there will be a price effect. (It has been assumed that the long-run supply curve is not perfectly elastic.) Those people who would have bought Class III now buy Classes I or II, putting up the price, or buy other goods. Assuming that quality is normally distributed about the mean, we can expect small price increases as the produce with a low level of characteristic is banned, and increasingly big price increases as the minimum standard approaches the mean level of characteristic.

It seems likely, therefore, that in many markets the first minimum standards, removing dangerous or defective goods, will greatly reduce search or risk, and will do so at little cost, but that progressive increases in minimum standard levels will result in decreasing benefits at increasing costs.

The producer gets two types of benefit from minimum standards. The first is very similar to the consumers' benefit. To the extent that consumers find it easier and safer to buy the product, producers and traders benefit from increased turnover. The other is a monopoly profit from restricting supply. This will be looked at later in this chapter under 'The case against compulsory minimum standards'.

Informing the consumer

So far it has been assumed, implicitly, that when minimum standards were introduced, all consumers knew what they were, understood them and believed that all producers had ceased to sell outgrades. This is, of course, a gross oversimplification.

In most countries there is a core of consumer protection laws offering some very basic assurances. There will normally be laws on food safety and hygiene,[10] laws like the Sale of Goods Act requiring goods in certain circumstances to be 'of merchandisable quality' and, in richer countries, laws like the Trades Description Act. In most countries the degree of enforcement is such that there is no real compulsion on the average seller to conform. However, there is a social expectation on the business community and by the business community to conform to some set of trading ethics – ethics that vary enormously in countries with the same Common Law and identical statute law.

The introduction of a minimum standard which merely repeats the social expectation is not likely to have any effect. One that merely duplicates existing hygiene rules or states that the good should be of merchandisable quality may be effective if the consumer can be convinced that, for some reason, the new standards will be enforced where the old ones were ignored. Sometimes meaningless standards may be set for a scheme when the real message is 'Made in Britain'.

It is quite common for a minimum standard to be set without the consumer having any real idea that there is any standard at all, much less knowing what it is. It is difficult to believe though that this can be an optimal strategy except in unusual situations, or when the standard is not aimed at the consumer at all, but at manufacturers and distributors. It may be an acceptable approach when the main objective is to reduce supply.

Sometimes the product is given a label indicating that it has met a minimum standard which is not defined. There may be a competitive advantage in stating that the product conforms to BS 1234 and using the kitemark, especially when it is obvious to the consumer that he would not understand the technicalities of the testing process. If nothing else, it may be seen as an implied smear on competitors who do not have it.

There has been a rash of 'quality assurance' schemes for food products in recent years, with a label, usually barely visible, suggesting that the product has met certain minimum standards.[11] There is no indication of what the standards mean, and when I wrote asking for clarification, I got nothing that could affect my purchase decision on most of the products. The cynical will suggest that the main reason for having such marks is to assure the producer that his levy is being well spent. In the absence of a lot of publicity on the meaning of the mark and the strictness of the enforcement, combined with a large and distinctive logo on each item, one may wonder what effect it has at retail. If they are intended to have an effect at wholesale, it is pointless to have a mark on the retail pack. Most of these schemes were introduced without any economic analysis.

BS 5750 (*ISO 9000*) assures buyers (in this case usually manufacturers or retailers) that the product has been produced by a firm using a quality control scheme which is acceptable to the British Standards Institute. It does not give any information whatsoever about the quality of the product or about whether we are talking of ships, shoes or sealing-wax. It is, perhaps, to be seen as an assurance of level of uniformity and of uniformity over time.

In Britain today grocery retailing is dominated by a handful of supermarket chains. Each has its own procurement system and a very strict quality control system. It is doubtful whether any government imposed system could be so carefully formulated or so rigorously imposed. It could be argued that the standards have to cover the other 25 per cent of the market perhaps, if the independent retailers are to be able to compete.

THE CASE AGAINST COMPULSORY MINIMUM STANDARDS

Assumptions

In this section I assume that the product consists of items which vary in one characteristic. They may be sorted into three grades, Class I, Class II and Class III. (The use of only three grades simplifies the analysis and does not change the conclusions.) Each item produced can only be sold in one grade: there are no tolerances or cumulative grades. The quality of the product is immediately obvious to a potential buyer, so there is no search cost and no possibility of buying an inferior product by accident. There are no costs in the form of pollution and so on. All producers produce some of all grades, as joint products. Different producers produce different proportions of each grade. The process may be altered in the medium to long period, at a cost, to produce a product with a higher mean or less variation about the mean. Minimum standards are then introduced, which ban the sale of Class III. These assumptions do assume away many of the complications discussed in previous chapters, such as cumulative categories, sale by package, tolerances, uniformity, multicharacteristic products, as well as many that arise when examining a real market. In spite of this, the scenario may be taken as a simplified model of the fruit and vegetable market.

While this model is built around a product for which the buyer can instantly assess the quality of the product, it applies, somewhat less directly, to the commoner types of search, like repeated purchase, habitual purchase of a grade or brand, habitual use of a retailer, and so on. Indeed, nearly every chapter in this book has shown new reasons for believing that sale purely on description is virtually unknown in the real world.

Market period

In the market period, the very short run, when supply cannot be changed, the effect of forbidding the sale of Class III is to reduce the total supply and to change the price of other grades by an amount which depends on the income elasticity of demand, the quantity of Class III, the elasticities of substitution between the classes and the rate of substitution between each class and all other products. If the grades are relevant to consumers, the effect of changing the supply of Class III is different from the effect of a change in quantity spread over all grades, so normal elasticities are irrelevant. The combined effect is to *change* all supply and demand functions, rather than just to cause movements along curves:

- the demand for Class I and Class II will rise, as Class III is no longer a possible substitute.
- the demand for goods which are substitutes will change (and the good which is a substitute for Class I is not necessarily the one which is a substitute for Class III – as a taxi is a substitute for a Rolls Royce, a bus for a Mini).
- The cross elasticity between Class I and Class II will change.
- The elasticities and cross-elasticities will change over time as consumers get used to the new product range and as their expectations change. It is widely recognized that cross-elasticities change during a product life cycle.[12]
- Production costs per unit sold will rise, and the rise will be greatest among those producers who produce the highest proportion of Class III in their output. It is assumed that Class III must be disposed of at a lower price than was possible before the minimum standards were introduced, being sold as a raw material for manufacture rather than being sold fresh at retail, for instance. It may be dumped, with the producer having to pay to get rid of it.
- The minimum standards may increase or decrease distribution costs, and the effect will be greatest on those distributors who previously specialized in Class III.
- The minimum standards reduce consumers' risk.
- The minimum standards increase the producers' and distributors' risk.
- Demand and supply curves can be expected to change shape as well as shifting, when, for instance, the demand of customers

who previously bought Class III becomes clustered at the bottom of Class II.

Each of these demand and supply curves will be further changed as a result of the change in search which is inevitable with any other assumptions but those made here. (The model becomes complex if it allows for situations where, for instance, consumers can select the best product out of a grade or where each item is priced separately according to level of characteristic.)

These changes in supply and demand functions impose serious restrictions on the economic analysis which is possible. For instance, it is not possible to do any meaningful analysis on the basis of historic elasticities, on the assumption that the supply and demand elasticities for grades or the product will remain the same, or on the assumption that the changes are calculable. It is questionable how far welfare economics is applicable under these circumstances.

In the market period all consumers are worse off because of the higher prices of Classes I and II. Those whose optimum purchase was Class III, generally people in the low income groups, suffer most, as they have both to buy a less desirable grade and to pay a higher price, so social costs may rise.

Where the sale of Class III is forbidden, retailers may get a higher or lower revenue, depending on the cross-grade effect and their policy on margins. Those retailers who sold mainly Class III probably lose a lot of trade; and social costs arise if they are mainly small family shops or neighbourhood shops, for instance. Fixed costs per item sold rise, and there is a drop, usually small, in variable costs. Procurement costs fall. Handling costs fall if retailers only have to handle two grades instead of three, but as a rule they handle only one or two grades, however many are available. Waste may fall, but it will not if stale or substandard Class I and II must be dumped rather than being marked Class III. Retailers incur increased supervision costs. The change in retailers' costs is not likely to be passed on to the consumer in the market period or the short run.

Wholesalers sell less at a higher price. If they sell on commission, their gross revenue may increase or decrease, depending on the cross-grade elasticity. If they buy or sell, their gross revenue depends on this and on their market power. The individual wholesalers who sold mainly Class III will be worse affected. Fixed costs per unit of throughput increase. The wholesaler dealing with a highly perishable product loses the flexibility gained from being able to sell over-mature Class I as Class III. It may take the wholesaler less time to sell the uniform Class I and Class II than to sell the mixture of classes that ends up in Class III and this may reduce his variable costs. In the market period, overcapacity may lead to higher wholesaling costs per unit sold. Administration costs also rise.

The total revenue of producers may or may not rise when Class III is banned, depending on whether the increase in average price is greater than the fall in quantity. Fixed and variable costs per unit sold increase. It is probable that those who produce Class III are worse off. Frequently it is small rural industries, small family farms and Third World countries that produce mainly Class III and are slow to change. If these are forced out of business by a minimum standard, the social and economic consequences are far reaching.

Some rather different conclusions arise if the assumptions are changed. Price (1967b, 1968) has shown that it can pay producers to restrict the supply of the lower quality even when the demand for the product is elastic. His model assumes that an increase in the culling rate improves the quality of all grades, by removing the smaller cherries from all grades alike, for instance, so that both the reduced supply and the improvement in quality of the existing classes increase the price. This might be an appropriate model where, for instance, one is introducing minimum standards of hygiene, pesticide residue and so on to a product which has already been sorted into grades on other characteristics. Nguyen and Vo (1985) implicitly assume in their model that *inter alia* the end product is a completely homogeneous bulk product, such that removing the lowest quality increases the quality of all the rest. Carley (1983) discusses a practical example, milk, where the quality of all produce is increased (by adding solids rather than discarding low quality milk) and he is guarded about the net benefits. A somewhat different example occurred in Britain where a milk factory receiving a tanker full of milk with a higher lead content than permitted, mixed the contents with another tanker load to produce an end product which did meet the minimum standards. In my model, where one grade is banned and the specification of other grades are unchanged, these effects do not arise. Waugh (1971) shows that it is not necessarily the most profitable option to withdraw the lowest grade; in some cases the industry could gain more from withdrawing Class I or some of each class.

Government must negotiate the minimum standards, legislate, inform the users of the new regulations, provide inspectors at producer, wholesale and retail levels, warn offenders and prosecute persistent offenders. These costs are negligible in relation to the costs incurred by the other sectors.

Longer-run implications

In the short run, it may be expected that supplies will increase and prices will fall below the market period level, so consumers will not be as badly off as in the market period. Those consumers who previously bought Class III will be worse off. In the long run consumers' tastes may change and they will no longer accept Class III.

In the short run retailers and wholesalers, particularly those who formerly sold mainly Class III, sell less and may go out of business, so a smaller quantity is sold by fewer firms, which may lead to a rise or fall in the turnover per firm. Those retailers who built up a reputation for quality may get a lower premium for this when Class III are removed. Consumers frequently judge quality by price, assuming that the more expensive items are better, but this implies that some cheap items, Class III, are available for comparison.

The total supply is affected in several ways in the short run. Some of those firms which produced large proportions of Class III switch to other products or go out of business, so the Class I and II they produced is no longer on the market. Other producers, especially those producing mainly Class I, use their capital at a greater intensity and produce more. Producers also have a greater incentive to change their techniques, producing more Class II and less Class III, as the return from improving an item from unsaleable to saleable is greater than that from improving it from a saleable Class III to Class II.

In the longer period producers may adjust their production systems to produce an intermediate product that has a higher proportion of Class I and II, so that less need be discarded in the sorting and quality control processes. This may require a large scale of operations or a high level of capital, so that small producers are forced out, or a consolidation of the marketing system is forced.

Minimum standards are sometimes used to protect home producers from competition: for instance, the EEC tomato grading regulations could at one time be used to protect the northern European glasshouse industry from southern European outdoor tomatoes. Maximum standards are sometimes used in the same way, as when it is forbidden to add yellow dye to margarine so that it will be a less close substitute for locally-produced yellow butter.

It is sometimes argued that the chief reason for poor quality is bad management, and that the firms will improve their quality if they are told that they cannot sell Class III (the 'pull yourself together, man' argument). There is an implicit assumption that this has little or no extra cost. This is not necessarily unreasonable: in agriculture better quality is often associated with high yields, and in industry better quality can result in a sharp drop in post-sale maintenance and repair under guarantee. If the policy did work and all Class III were upgraded to Class II at no extra cost, there would be a reduction in the price of Class I and Class II below the previous levels, and Class I, Class II and some Class III customers would be better off, though some Class III customers would still be worse off. However, the fact that entrepreneurs produce Class III when there are no minimum standards and there are very high premiums for producing Class I, suggests that they do not think that it is financially sensible to change to producing these qualities. It also suggests that, when minimum standards increase the supply of Class I and Class II and push their prices down, it will be a still less attractive proposition financially.

Unfortunately, the decision to produce Class III is often treated as a sign of moral turpitude by people pushing for minimum standards, rather than as a production decision which may be fully justified economically. It is worth considering the political and social implications of forcing a man to work harder for a return which is unlikely to be bigger in the long run, when the economic benefits to society are doubtful. Even if quality could be improved at no extra cost, one could not assume that this would be done just because minimum standards are introduced. Some producers go out of business or switch to other products rather than submit to what they consider to be mindless bureaucracy – a reaction particularly common among farmers. Others find that the increased price and the reduced quantity gives them the same income, so there is no incentive for them to change their production methods. The more efficient producers, often those who produce a high percentage of Class I anyway, are likely to respond to the increased price by increasing production to the point where marginal cost equals marginal revenue, and so increasing production cost.

Poor quality need not be due to bad management. It may well suit the producer to produce large quantities of Class III and to dispense with sorting. The decision faced by the producer is extremely complex, and it is seldom possible for the producer to calculate his optimum sorting plan, though sometimes he may find a position that is clearly not far wrong. No outside observer could have any grounds for saying that the producer is not adopting an economically optimal plan. Still less could anyone say that all producers are mistaken in producing Class III.

In imposing a minimum standard the state must also allow for the market effects described above, which will alter market prices for each grade, particularly Grade III, and so will change the marginal return from sorting. It is sometimes argued that producers adjust their production according to the demand curve facing the firm rather than the market demand curve, and if a market supply reduction can be managed by means of a minimum standard, they will obtain monopoly profits. While this is true in the market period, its effectiveness in the short run, or for long-run periods, depends on there being some form of supply restriction, like quotas.

It is generally uneconomic to export low-quality products, because transport is a relatively high proportion of their final value, so exporting countries usually consume Class II and Class III at home and export Class I. If the importing country sells Class III and has a low price for Class I and II, imports will not be high, as prices may not cover transport and production costs. If Class III is forbidden in the importing country, supply on the market falls and Class I prices rise, so it becomes more profitable to import. For this reason restriction of home production may not increase home producers' Class I price much even in the market period, and may reduce profits substantially. Even if the exporting country does not have the advantages of favourable climate, cheap labour and cheap raw materials, it does have the advantages of lower unit costs, as it sells all grades at home, not just Class I and Class II; it can build up a highly-organized distribution system; and it can use discriminating monopoly, with a high home price subsidizing exports: these advantages often compensate for the higher transport costs. The importing country with minimum standards is choosing to compete in the grade where transport costs give it least advantage.

It may be felt by government that each producer on the home market is sufficiently identified by his brand or reputation to make industry-wide minimum standards unnecessary, but that on the export market all producers are lumped together as 'British' or 'Japanese'. In these circumstances one unscrupulous or inefficient exporter can destroy a country's reputation for that product and possibly for related products. For this reason, minimum standards for export may be set so that nobody can harm the reputation of, say, Danish bacon, by selling inferior bacon, or of Israeli celery by selling inferior Israeli melons. In effect, the national name becomes one of many competing brands on the market. Interestingly, New Zealand has abandoned these compulsory minimum standards, apparently on the grounds that they are costly and time consuming to enforce, and anyone who flies substandard raspberries to Europe will lose so much money that he will not do it twice.

However, it has been shown that the strict standards on Canadian wheat exports have meant that farmers could not switch to higher-yielding varieties with different or lower quality even when they were clearly more profitable. In order to maintain Canada's reputation for top quality, hard wheats, government made it illegal to produce very-high-yielding soft wheats. These would have got a lower price and a higher yield, resulting in a much higher profit.[13]

Practical problems

The practical problems of forecasting the effects of legislation to impose minimum standards or of evaluating the effects of standards already imposed are insurmountable. One cannot forecast the effect of removing a substantial quantity of a product, all from one grade, particularly if, as with horticulture in the EEC, similar minimum standards are applied simultaneously to all close substitutes. *All* elasticities and cross-elasticities in the market change. Long-run supply responses for Class I cannot be estimated from experience of producers' response to short-run price changes. Lack of statistical data, mislabelling (which is common) and insufficient identification makes econometric analysis impossible in most markets.

What minimum standards?

The impact of the minimum standards depends largely on their specifications. It is most unlikely that the category specifications which are optimal when three grades are marketed will also be optimal when one grade is thrown away: the boundary between Class I and Class II should shift. The minimum standard may specify minimum or average levels of perhaps twenty characteristics, and it may set down tolerances. If the specifications for any one of these characteristics changes, then the supply, demand and cross-elasticities for all classes will change. If the specifications for several characteristics are changed at the same time, the result is impossible to forecast.

If any one of the characteristics is not relevant to any group of customers, then any increase in the level of the specification increases the price without increasing their satisfaction. The more characteristics that are specified in a minimum standard, the more likely it is that several will be irrelevant to a large proportion of customers. When the customers have different tastes, particularly in the EEC where the same regulations apply to very diverse countries, one can expect that many of the characteristics in the minimum standard are irrelevant at the margin in most countries, and that the English working class pays high prices because the standards list characteristics of interest only to the German or French professional classes.

The model

The model presented here would have to be adapted and expanded to apply to the circumstances of any industry, though it is similar enough to some real industries, like the fruit and vegetable industry, to influence decisions. It is obvious that the theoretical and practical problems of justifying any minimum standard are enormous. It is also obvious that the immediate costs to producer and consumer are likely to be high when any substantial amount of the product is Class III. The long term costs may not be so high, but in practice they cannot be forecast. Except for a few goods when there are public health and safety benefits, any benefits are vague and insubstantial.

One cannot say from an outline of the theory and no data whether minimum standards are justified in any case. One can say, though, that many of the costs are large, certain and immediate, while all the benefits are uncertain, distant and may be small, so the onus is on the legislator to justify his action with facts, theory and hard analysis. This conclusion of mine is by no means extreme: other economists have argued that minimum standards necessarily reduce social welfare (though the assumptions are very restrictive).[14] I know of no case where there has been a serious attempt to analyse the impact of minimum standards before introducing them, and I know of one major European country which introduced minimum standards on a wide range of products without consulting an economist.

CONCLUSION

In this chapter it has been shown that compulsory minimum standards are introduced for a range of reasons, and for reasons which are often not clearly identified. Most important are consumer protection, helping producers by preventing market failure through inferior products, and helping producers get monopoly profits.

The first two objectives can be tackled by reducing the possibility of buying an inferior product, by removing it from the market, reducing the cost of avoiding it, or reducing the damage if it is bought inadvertently. Minimum standards which prevent it being sold are a possible solution in some circumstances. Elsewhere it may be possible to achieve the objective by making the seller liable if the product does not reach certain standards, giving a guarantee rather than removing the product from the market. A minimum standard of labelling may also be effective. If the objectives are seen as valid, these alternative approaches should be considered.

The second part of the chapter showed the sort of price response that could be expected from minimum standards. This reinforced the conclusion that minimum standards might not help producers or consumers. It also called into question whether the minimum standards were an effective means of obtaining monopoly profits for producers, though a full policy analysis of a specific industry would be necessary before conclusions could be drawn.

Attention is drawn repeatedly to the complexity of the market, and to the fact that elasticities and cross-elasticities, short run and long run, change as a result of these changes in marketing.

Chapter 10

Price as an indicator of quality

It is commonly observed that buyers sometimes use price as an indicator of quality, assuming that if a product is more expensive, it must be better. In this chapter a research programme which examined this phenomenon is examined critically, and its weaknesses exposed.[1] The lessons are of wide application in the economics of quality.

Academic research on a subject may consist entirely of well-designed experiments competently carried out, and may still fail to produce any useful results or any advance in our knowledge. One line of research on the price/perceived-quality relationship over the past half century has followed this pattern, combining poor scientific method with good experimental technique to produce little of value.

In 1944 Scitovsky commented on the commonly observed phenomenon that people frequently judge the quality of a product by its price, assuming that the more expensive item is better, and he discussed the reasons for this and its implications. Since then there have been over 100 academic articles and PhD theses, implying perhaps 150 years of research, testing the hypothesis that some people sometimes judge quality by price,[2] but we know no more than we did in 1944.

In the typical experiment, university students were given a set of cards, each card bearing a description of a product and its price, and were asked to choose which product they thought they would buy if they had the choice. Statistical analysis showed whether, other things being equal, they were more likely to buy the more expensive product. The result of this enormous research effort was to show that American university students and a few other populations sometimes do appear to judge quality by price in such situations. (None of these experiments can match the elegance of that devised by a French politician who cut a cheese in half, charged 50 per cent more for one half, and watched the expensive half sell many times faster than the other.)

What is the value of this result? There can be few businessmen who do not believe that sometimes, but not always, some people think that the more expensive good is better. The research confirmed this belief. However, once one experiment had confirmed their belief, the other experiments were superfluous, at best providing a little extra corroboration for a self-evident hypothesis. Even if all the subsequent experiments had failed to show the relationship, it would have meant nothing: nobody expects that the relationship would apply *always* and in all markets. The tests were incapable of showing that nobody ever judged quality by price: all they could do was to show that nobody appeared to do so in the experimental situation.

The series of experiments did not show how frequently people judge quality by price, or how strong the effect is. A statistical estimate of the frequency and strength of the relationship might perhaps be made if a probability sample of a carefully-defined range of market situations was taken and an experiment was carried out in each of them. Samples would be drawn from different populations depending on whether one was interested in the average product, the average consumer, the average transaction or the average market. No attempt was made to sample in this way.

The research programme made no attempt to sample situations typical of the real world. In most of the studies reported, the experimental design demanded atypical products like carpets or curtain material which the consumers would not be able to judge objectively or be able to recognize by brand or other characteristics. It was necessary that the students should not be able to judge from experience, or from any other quality cues, if the price effect was to be isolated. In some studies the consumers did not see the product: they sat in a classroom and made their choices from written descriptions.[3] The consumers were nearly always students, and were not typical of the population as a whole. Researchers usually put a ritual caveat in their reports, saying that someone should see if the experimental results on any product have any application to the corresponding market in the real world.

Until experiments or observational studies have been carried out to compare the results of these laboratory experiments with purchasing patterns in the real world, we have no reason to believe that they give any indication of actual purchase behaviour even in the markets they do examine.

Many of the weaknesses are recognized by the writers themselves: it is a classic case of the view that

> If you are appraising an entire research programme, a very effective approach is to make a collection of the literature and read it through. In their introductions or discussions many of the authors comment on the difficulties that they have encountered. Often the weaknesses an author admits to are enough to invalidate his paper. One wonders why he submitted it: there seems to be a superstition that if you confess to the weaknesses, they will go away. The authors are even more forthcoming in discussing the mistakes of previous writers in the field. These include errors of method, of theory, of technique, and of data. Add up all the admitted weaknesses of all the papers in the research programme, and you will often end up with an overwhelming attack on the whole research programme.[4]

Nevertheless, nearly all authors state, implicitly or explicitly, that an examination of the results of the various experiments will produce a kind of general law on the strength and frequency of this price/perceived-quality relationship. Indeed, if this was not their aim, there would have been no point in carrying out experiments based on artificial or imaginary products. The scientific method here is clearly wrong: one cannot generalize from experiences with a few, atypical, products to all products. One would not expect a scientist observing trace element deficiencies in tomatoes growing in peat in a controlled environment to forecast from this the frequency of trace element deficiencies for all plants in all soils throughout the country. Still less would one expect a businessman to forecast the behaviour of a New England housewife buying a refrigerator from his experience of the Congolese salt market.

Even if it were possible to produce a general law, that in 75 per cent of cases people think that the more expensive product is better, it would not be much help. The businessman wants to know how consumers react to *his* product, after taking into account all cues and the reputation of his competitors. Commercial research aimed at answering these questions is valuable and by its nature is unlikely to suffer from the weaknesses of the academic research. Some firms do carry out this commercial research, but only a handful of the academic experiments reported in the literature could possibly have had any commercial relevance.[5]

OTHER HYPOTHESES

These criticisms also apply to the minor hypotheses tested in the studies. They are very nearly as trivial, they have been tested with the same poor scientific method and the results of the tests are no more likely to be general laws. The hypotheses are:

1 Customers are more likely to buy the expensive product when price is the only information available. As they get more information on brand, store image and other quality attributes, price becomes relatively less important. The weighting given to the different cues depends on how useful the consumer thinks each is for prediction, how much experience he has of the product, when he last bought it and how much confidence he has in his ability to use the cues to judge quality.

2 They are more likely to buy the expensive brand when they think that there are large differences in quality between brands, and, by implication, when there are large differences in the price of brands.

3 They are more likely to buy the expensive brand when an inferior quality causes a big drop in satisfaction, when the risk of poor quality is high, and when expenditure is high in relation to income.

4 A product is often evaluated with reference to a standard, perhaps the price or quality of the last purchase.

5 The consumer's evaluation of a product frequently depends on the price structure in a market, the order of presentation of the alternatives, the 'preferred prices' for those products and whether prices were rising or falling.

6 There is generally a range of acceptable prices: if the product is too cheap, the consumer is suspicious of it: if it is too expensive, he thinks he is being overcharged.

If these hypotheses are correct, there are clearly so many market situations that each marketing situation is unique, and it is impossible to generalize.

No criticism is made here of the techniques used by researchers. They use a sophistication of experimental design and statistical analysis that must excite the envy and admiration of those of us who deal with real markets. It might be argued, though, that it is this obsession with technique that has led to the neglect of relevance, scientific method and economic theory, which caused the failure of the research programme.

ALTERNATIVE RESEARCH STRATEGIES

The alternative to poor testing of a trivial hypothesis should not be the rigorous testing of a trivial hypothesis, but the rigorous testing of an important hypothesis. For this reason, there is no point in discussing better ways in which the hypothesis could have been tested or in giving examples of suitable research strategies. There are plenty of real problems in the world, and attention should be concentrated on them.

Even where the price/perceived-quality relationship is of commercial interest, it is not necessary to inflate its importance by treating it as a distinct major research programme. At the level of the firm it is no more than a special case of work done on consumers' perceptions of quality in relation to quality cues, where price is treated as another quality cue. Similarly, in the wider economics of quality, it may be handled by adding a price axis to those of money, quantity and characteristics.

DISCUSSION

In spite of half a century of research on the subject, no more is known than in 1944. This must be blamed on poor scientific method, trivial hypotheses and a lack of interest in the needs of industry and the relationship of the results to the real world.

It is significant that of all the people working on this line of research since Scitovsky, few seem to have asked why it was of any general importance (though those doing commercial research have dealt with specific problems). Generally researchers seem to have no deeper or more-clearly-defined aim than to try and find out more about the price/perceived-quality relationship. Surprisingly, of the many hundreds of references quoted in this research programme, there are only one or two to the literature of the economics of information, which has analysed in depth the causes and effects of treating price as an indicator of quality.[6] Less surprisingly, the economics literature ignores this research programme.

Knowledge advances by testing and trying to disprove hypotheses rather than by trying to support them.[7] With the price/perceived-quality relationship, researchers have been intent on gathering evidence to confirm their hypothesis 'that some people do in some circumstances sometimes appear to judge quality by price'. The tests were incapable of testing the hypothesis or disproving it: if no evidence was shown by the experiment that people judged quality by price, the hypothesis never said that they *always* would, for *all* products in *all* circumstances. Indeed, it is difficult to formulate it in such a way that it can be tested (except as a product-specific, market-specific, commercial test). Each experiment after the first one adds a little further corroboration to the hypothesis, though it is so well established by now that a further experiment can do nothing to increase our belief in it. If, instead, researchers had attempted to formulate the hypothesis in a form in which it could be tested, its weakness and lack of explanatory power would have been shown. A hypothesis that cannot be tested and that is consistent with all possible outcomes has no explanatory power – to say that some consumers sometimes do something and sometimes do not, explains nothing to the businessman.

It is sometimes believed that an experiment 'confirming' a hypothesis, however trivial, is more likely to be published in an academic journal than the rejection of a hypothesis or an inconclusive result, and some academic researchers, whose careers depend on the number of their publications, have become expert in developing hypotheses that are not too obviously true, but that will still give the required result.

It is interesting that there still exists the belief that there are broad generalizations about people's economic behaviour that apply everywhere at all times. The laws beloved of the Victorians, Malthus's Law, Say's Law, Engel's Law, the Law of Labour, have been discredited, and economists have been concerned in recent years to find systems of analysis that can be used to find the truth in any particular case, instead of universal truths.

One may speculate that one reason why so many workers have examined the price/perceived-quality relationship is the band wagon effect. Because so many people have worked on it, it was accepted as a respectable area for research, and it was thought that all one had to do was to develop a slightly different experiment and a rather more complex analysis to get one's paper published or one's thesis accepted.

This research programme is exceptional in providing so few useful results, but in most programmes a substantial number of papers exhibit the same lack of relevance, lack of economic theory and poor scientific method. Research like this provides ammunition for those who condemn all academic research, and it leads to a reduction in research budgets and to demands for political control of research programmes.

Chapter 11

Market effects

Throughout this book the point has been made that grades and brands operate in a market, and that the effect of grading or branding a product cannot be analysed independently of the market. In this chapter the message is emphasized by giving examples of situations where the impact of a grading scheme appears perfectly obvious, but because of the market structure, the actual effect is exactly the opposite to that expected.

THE IMPACT OF A COST-SAVING INNOVATION

In this section it is shown that producers who introduce a cost-saving innovation, an improvement in retailers' quality, can end up worse off as a result.[1]

The assumptions

Retailers tend to have customary levels of margin. For example, they may decide that 33 per cent is the correct mark-up for vegetables, 15 per cent for hard groceries and 10 per cent for cigarettes, and then continue to charge the same mark-up whatever the level of waste or turnover. The mark-ups on all lines within a product group tend to be the same: retailers commonly charge the same 33 per cent mark-up for all fruits and vegetables; the expensive ones, the ones with high waste and the ones that require a lot of handling, as well as those that are pre-priced and pre-packed. There seems to be little doubt that nearly all retailers have a traditional margin for all products (except those pre-priced by the manufacturer) in the short run, and my experience is that they maintain these margins in the long run in spite of major changes in the level of waste. A profit maximizer would charge a different margin on each line, allowing for variable costs, waste, elasticity of demand and so on, but, because of the time involved, the lack of information and the fact that supermarkets handle over 5,000 product lines, this profit maximization is impractical. Instead, supermarkets may concentrate on optimizing allocation of shelf space with given margins.

The difference between the margin that the retailers charge, the theoretical margin, and the margin that they achieve, or actual margin, may be shown as follows. If a retailer buys 100 items at 12p and sells them at 16p, he is charging a mark-up of 33.33 per cent and a theoretical margin of (16–12) ÷ 16, or 25 per cent. Normally, though, there is some waste because of poor packing, rough handling, natural decay, short deliveries or theft, so the calculation then becomes:

100 items bought at 12p	1,200p
10 items discarded	0p
90 items sold at 16p	1,440p
Actual margin = (1,440 – 1,200) ÷ 1,440 = 16.7 per cent	

Often retailers set the theoretical margin for the department or for the whole shop as their goal and they try, by reducing waste and other leakages, to bring the actual margin as near to the theoretical margin as possible.

We now consider the impact of a costless improvement in quality which has no effect except to reduce the level of waste at retail. The consumer cannot tell the difference between the new product and the old. Examples might include the use of Charolais bulls to produce carcasses with a higher proportion of saleable beef, and a lower proportion of bone and fat, the purchase of yoghurt with a longer shelf life, or the purchase of sweets packed so there is less pilfering. The quality being improved is retailers' quality, not consumers' quality.

The improvement in quality

For illustration we take a situation where the total theoretical distributive margin is 25 per cent, a mark-up of 33 per cent. It is assumed that this percentage mark-up is charged whatever the level of waste. Initially, 10 per cent of the product is wasted so the actual margin is $(0.9 \times 133.33 - 100) \div (0.9 \times 133.33) = 16.67$ per cent, as in the example above. With the improved product there is no waste, and the mark-up remains the same, so the actual margin becomes 25 per cent. This means that the retailer does not have to make any complex calculations: he just adds one-third to the purchase price. He does not have to work out the implications in terms of perceived supply curves: if he has too much in stock at the end of the day, he reduces his order next day. It is assumed that retailers buy in a perfect market, but because of locational monopolies and so on, they can sell at different prices.

Effect on supply and demand

The effect on the market supply and demand curves is shown in Figure 11.1, in which all quantities have been measured in terms of quantity sold at retail, in order to avoid the confusion that arises when some figures include the rotten apples, while others do not. W_1 is the original supply curve at wholesale, the number of saleable apples that the farmer is willing to provide at that price per unit saleable. (Table 11.1 shows how these curves are derived, using figures for a hypothetical market.) R_1 is the original supply curve at retail. For any quantity, the supply price at wholesale, per unit saleable, is 11 per cent higher than the supply price for all units, including 10 per cent rotten; for any quantity the retail price is, by assumption, 33.33 per cent higher than the supply price for all units: R_1 is, therefore, $(133.33 \div 111.11) = 1.2$ times W_1.

With the change in the product there is no waste, so the quantity on offer at wholesale is higher and the wholesale supply curve becomes W_2. The amount offered at W_2 is not just 11.1 per cent greater than that at W_1 because the price per unit falls at the same time as the amount of waste falls. However, R_2, the retail supply curve with no waste, is 11.1 per cent further over than R_1.

DR_1 is the demand at retail in both periods: by assumption, the customer is not affected by the change in quality. DW_1 is the derived demand curve per unit saleable at wholesale in the first period. Because 10 per cent of the purchases are being wasted the actual margin is 16.7 per cent, and DW_1 is 16.7 per cent below DR_1. When there is no waste, the wholesale demand curve DW_2 is 25 per cent lower, because there is a 25 per cent actual margin.

Figure 11.1 shows that the result of the improvement in quality is to increase the margin of the retailers and their total gross profit. The retail price per unit falls by an amount depending on the

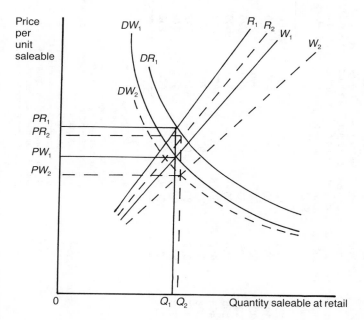

Figure 11.1 Supply and demand curves per unit saleable at retail
Key: W = wholesale
R = retail

elasticities as the quantity sold increases. Since all prices are shown per unit saleable and all quantities are in saleable units, the effect on the producer is not clearly shown here, so it is shown in Figure 11.2.

In Figure 11.2, the actual quantities, including waste, are given, and the unit price is for all units including rotten. W_3 is the supply curve in both periods (the number of packets of sweets remains unchanged, even though the number of packets pilfered falls). DW_3 is the demand at wholesale in the first period, and DW_4 is the demand at wholesale in the second period. Because of the increased margin, the derived demand is 10 per cent lower in the second period. As long as demand curves are negatively sloped and supply curves positively sloped, producers sell a smaller quantity at a lower price. If the retail demand (DR_1) is perfectly elastic, producers sell the same quantity.

The assumption that retailers have traditional margins and identical demand functions implies that the excess profit of

Table 11.1 Derivation of supply and demand curves shown with hypothetical data

(1) Original wholesale price	(2) Original retail price per unit saleable	(3) Original wholesale price per unit saleable	(4) Original amount supplied (incl. waste)	(5) Original amount supplied (saleable)	(6) Original amount demanded (incl. waste)	(7) Original amount demanded (saleable)	(8) New wholesale price per unit (saleable)	(9) New retail price per unit (saleable)	(10) New amount supplied (saleable)	(11) Amount demanded at retail (saleable)
10	13.3	11.1	100	90	2,700	2,500	10	13.3	100	2,500
20	26.6	22.2	200	180	1,389	1,250	20	26.6	200	1,250
30	40.0	33.3	300	270	925	833	30	40.0	300	833
40	53.3	44.4	400	360	694	625	40	53.3	400	625
50	66.6	55.6	500	450	555	500	50	66.6	500	500
60	80.0	66.7	600	540	463	417	60	80.0	600	417
70	93.3	77.8	700	630	396	357	70	93.3	700	357
80	106.6	88.9	800	720	347	312	80	106.6	800	312
90	120.0	100.0	900	810	308	278	90	120.0	900	278
100	133.3	111.1	1,000	900	278	250	100	133.3	1,000	250

Notes
(a) Columns 1, 4 & 6 are arbitrarily chosen figures.
(b) Column 2 is column 1 plus a mark-up of 33⅓ %.
(c) Column 3 is column 1 X 1.11, to allow for 10 % waste.
(d) Column 5 is column 4 less 10% waste.
(e) Column 7 is column 6 less 10% waste.
(f) As a result of the improvement, there is no waste, so the new wholesale price per unit saleable (Column 7) equals the old wholesale price for all items including waste (Column 1). That is to say the reported wholesale price remains unchanged.
(g) Column 9 is column 8 plus a mark-up of 33%.
(h) Column 10 is the same as column 4 because there is no waste.
(i) Column 11 is the same as column 7 because there has been no change in consumers' taste.

Derivation of curves
To get R_1 plot column 2 against column 5.
         W_1 plot column 3 against column 5.
         R_2 plot column 10 against column 9.
         W_2 plot column 8 against column 10.
         DR_1 plot column 2 against column 7, or column 9 against column 11.
         DW_1 plot column 3 against column 7.
         DW_2 plot column 8 against column 11.
         W_3 plot column 1 against column 4.
         DW_3 plot column 1 against column 6.
         DW_4 plot column 8 against column 11.

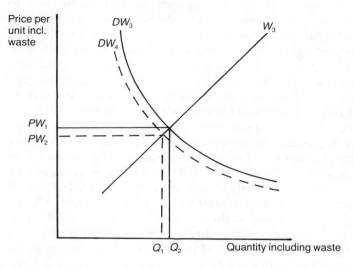

Figure 11.2 Wholesale supply and demand curves per unit including waste
Key: W = wholesale
R = retail

retailers arising from the improved retailers' quality will not be competed away by price cutting. Instead, in the long run new retailers will enter the market and take a share of the trade. All firms still charge the same margin, but sales per shop are lower, so only a normal profit is obtained from each shop. This chronic over-capacity, with a large number of retailers operating at a low turnover per shop is typical of greengrocers, butchers and small grocers, who all charge traditional margins.

Discussion

The limitations of market margin analysis and the dangers of generalization from a model like this are too well known to need repeating.[2] This scenario is based on a very specific model and the results are dependent on the assumptions, especially those on the level of waste, margins and competition. A realistic model of the beef market, for instance, would have to allow for many other factors such as the different cuts of meat sold and differences in butchers' cost curves. The assumptions are sufficiently close to those in some industries to cause alarm, especially where the predictions are in line with experience: there is chronic over-capacity in retailing, producers do not inevitably get richer as they produce a better product, and the increased price obtained for a better product often does not cover the increased production cost.

Whenever a product is improved in such a way that retailers' waste is reduced, the possibility should be considered that it will result in a fall in producer price and amount sold, and a large increase in margin. The innovators among producers are likely to benefit at the expense of others. The improvement may be necessary to improve the long-term viability of the industry though: if a product is consistently difficult and expensive to handle, retailers will be reluctant to stock it, and will immediately switch when a competing product without these problems is introduced. There is a strong message to producers here: if they do improve quality in the way mentioned, they should try and persuade retailers to cut their margins accordingly.

A PERVERSE QUALITY-PRICE RELATIONSHIP

This example shows how the dominance of the market by super-market chains can lead to a situation where the highest qualities get lower prices than the mediocre qualities.[3] The market described is one that is widely believed to be one of the closest approximations to perfect competition in the real world, horti-culture, but the problems apply *mutatis mutandis* to other markets. In this market empirical observation has found that:

1 Retailers and consumers complain that they find it difficult to obtain produce of the quality they want, even if they are willing to pay extra for it.
2 Producers complain that they receive little or no premium for top-quality produce, a complaint that is confirmed by an examination of their sales records.
3 Producers find that they get a higher average price if they split consignments between several wholesalers, though costs to producers, wholesalers and retailers are increased by this, and bulk buyers are not interested in such small consignments.
4 There is no apparent relationship between retail price and quality if a random sample of shops is taken, but there is if

shops with a similar purchasing power are compared, all large supermarket chains or all corner grocers for instance.[4]

Discounts

One explanation is as follows: if a retailer buys two or three packages in a wholesale market, he will be charged the full wholesale price. When a retailer buys 500 packages, he will get a discount of as much as 30 per cent on occasion (the examples of very high discounts for which I have evidence were in glut periods). In general, the bulk buyers (supermarkets, variety stores and greengrocery chains) want Class I produce and will use their market power to obtain it. The small greengrocers and corner grocers must take what is left, and many of them do not buy Class I, as their customers do not want it. As a result, the full discount is given on large orders of Class I, while no discount is given on small orders of Class II, so the prices for Class I are below those in a perfect market, while those for Class II are unchanged.

As the difference in price falls, it will pay fewer producers to sort their product, and there will be a shortage of Class I. The equilibrium position depends on the elasticity of demand for Classes I and II, their cross-elasticity, the marginal cost of sorting and losses in sorting.

Naturally, this is a simplification. Large buyers buy a range of qualities, usually at the top of the scale, while many greengrocers buy only the best. For some products caterers buy large amounts of 'low' quality (In this context, low quality implies a low score in attractiveness when displayed on a supermarket shelf). Instead of a reduction in price, the large buyer may get better quality at the same price, but this is effectively a discount. Discounts are sometimes given when costs are reduced, when, for instance, produce is delivered direct to the shop instead of going through the usual market channels, but these discounts do not come within the scope of this argument.

The explanation is economical, being based on the observation that discounts are given mainly to firms buying Class I, but it explains a wide range of other observations, such as those set out above.

Other factors

While it is convenient to examine one factor at a time, most economic phenomena must be explained by several factors working together. In this case we should consider the possibilities that the grading system used by the producers may not bear much relation to that used by the consumers, that the quality of the product changes between the producer and the consumer, or that the phenomena are due to temporary disequilibria in the marketing system with the oversupply of Class I reducing the grading premium below the costs of grading (in their widest sense).

Implications

The explanation given here suggests that the practice of giving discounts for bulk sales reduces marketing efficiency in many ways. The producers who produce the most desirable quality in the right amounts get a lower price. Consumer preferences are not communicated to producers. Producers are encouraged to split consignments among a number of wholesalers, so that they cannot offer a bulk discount. Small retailers are forced out of business though they are no less efficient than the bulk buyers. The wholesaling sector does not benefit from discounts as the total quantity sold is not increased, as average price and commission may be reduced and, indeed, as lower prices may reduce total supply, though there may be an increase in the proportion of bulk sales, which cost little more to administer than small sales. Individual wholesalers benefit only if they attract more business or a greater proportion of bulk sales. Market discrimination pays the individual wholesaler when discounts are given to the buyer with the most elastic demand – the bulk buyer. If bulk buyers have the most elastic demand at market level too, total revenue to the industry may be increased by the discounts, though the other inefficiencies remain.

Chapter 12

The costs of producing quality[1]

INTRODUCTION

In the literature on quality control, quality assurance, total quality management and so on there is often a discussion of what is called 'the costs of quality', or even 'the economics of quality assurance'.[2] The 'cost of quality' approach is essentially one carried out by quality assurance engineers using cost accounting data, rather than one that would be used by economists. There has been a certain amount of criticism of the approach within the paradigm (for example, Plunkett and Dale 1988, and Fox 1989), partly a criticism of the method itself, and partly an assertion that the results quoted were not realistic. In this chapter, however, a much more fundamental criticism will be presented, from the point of view of an economist. The main thrust of the argument will be that the writers on the subject have used a wide variety of variables as axes to their graphs, more or less interchangeably. They have failed to define what exactly is the variable they are using for their axes, or how they measure the variables. In Figures 12.3 to 12.18, some 48 curves will be plotted, all showing the same cost to an imaginary firm (Table 12.1), but defined according to the different variables used in the literature (the numbers attached to the curves refer to the corresponding row in Table 12.1). The curves are completely different in shape.[3] It follows that the arguments in the literature about typical shapes for the curves are pointless: everybody is plotting different variables, so of course different curves can be expected. It will be argued that this confusion implies a lack of a theoretical basis for the costs of quality. This chapter will also show that there is often a major misinterpretation of the graphs, attempting to draw conclusions that the graphs do not permit. Finally, it will be asked whether the 'costs of quality' approach is asking the right questions.

THE 'COSTS OF QUALITY'

The 'costs of quality' is an approach which asks a question that economists seldom ask, but someone employing a quality assurance engineer may: 'How much should I spend on quality assurance and control?' The specifications of the product are taken as given. It will be shown at the end of this chapter that the questions that would be asked by an economist, under 'the economics of producing quality', are very different.

The analysis used for the 'costs of quality' is generally one like that in Figure 12.1 or Figure 12.2. The Y axis is generally total cost or unit cost, and the X axis ranges 'from measures of quality dimensioned at their extremes to undimensional process capability, arbitrary quality management stages or time' (Plunkett and Dale 1988). Time axes will be discussed later.

It is argued, in BS 4891: 18, for example, that in Figure 12.1 'to the right of the optimum, the costs are uneconomic due to "perfectionism" and in this region the cure is perhaps worse than the disease, so that "better" quality assurance costs more'. Figure 12.2 is based on similar concepts without the same startling increase in prevention and appraisal costs, because 'the author has not yet found one organization in which the total costs have risen following investment in prevention' (Oakland 1989).[4] The difference in the two is essentially one of belief in the magnitudes of the different costs rather than the analysis. I do not want to get distracted here by considerations of what are or are not realistic costs, when the objective is to see what is a valid way of measuring and analysing them.

What is quality?

In these diagrams a great deal of confusion arises from the fact that it is not made clear what the X axis is meant to measure. It certainly does not measure, as some of the graphs in the literature would indicate 'increasing ability to meet customers' requirements' (Oakland 1989), nor 'quality level' (Robertson 1971) nor 'quality' (Urwick Group 1981). In no way can it be seen as a quality continuum, like the one from a Ford Escort Popular to a Ford Escort

XR3i Cabriolet at twice the price or from page 3 of the Sun to Botticelli's Venus.

An examination of what the figures are used for suggests that the following are more realistic descriptions of what the authors think they are measuring: 'product defect level' (Besterfield 1979), 'quality of our production (= quality of conformance)' (Caplan 1972), 'increasing quality of conformance' (Kirkpatrick 1970), 'product defect level' (Harrington 1976).

Even here the meaning of the X axis is far from clear. It appears to mean something like 'percentage defectives', but it is not clear whether this is as a percentage of

- number of items entering the production line;
- number of items leaving the production line;
- number of items sold to the distributors and leaving the company's premises;
- number of items sold to the distributors less waste in distribution and returns by distributors and customers.

It will be shown below that each of these definitions used for the X axis results in different curves for cost and so on. It is also not clear whether the defectives are the ones found on inspection, or those passing inspection 'including not only lots accepted by the sampling plan, but also lots rejected by the plan, that have been given 100 per cent inspection in which all defective items have been replaced by non-defective items' (BS 4778: 13). It is not clear whether defects per hundred items are considered, or the very different number of defective items per hundred.

However, there are a lot more complications that have not been sorted out. It is not clear how rework and waste early in a process is taken into account: are defects early in the process taken into account when counting defects in pre-despatch delivery, for example? If a product is despatched with zero defects after repeated inspections and heavy waste and rework costs, is this zero defects? Clearly there can be an enormous difference in cost between replacing a faulty oil seal in an engine immediately it is put in and disassembling the engine to do so when the fault is noticed on final assembly, or, worse, when the customer's car breaks down. One would also like to know whether critical, major and minor defects are treated the same: a faulty light bulb is not of the same importance as a seized big end. Are these defects treated as identical? The time dimension of reliability is also ignored in the models.

The distributor is concerned with consignment quality – risk, percentage waste, probable cost of repairs under warranty, complaints by consumers, and so on – factors which are *not* the same as quality as the consumer sees it. There is an important practical difference between percentage of total sales defective, and percentage of consignments defective. The question of uniformity must be settled: uniformity within package, uniformity between packages, and uniformity over time.

There is a big difference in the concept when we are talking of bulk goods like milk, petrol or flour, where the whole consignment or batch either is, or is not, out of specification, and a product like radios where each set either does, or does not, meet specifications.

Production capacity

The capacity of a production line frequently varies with the level of defects. If, say, 20 per cent of the items reaching the end of the production line are defective and need extensive reworking, the line may be producing at only half capacity, with only half as many items leaving the line as when there are no defectives. Here, 20 per cent defectives is the same *number* of defects as 10 per cent of theoretical capacity. As the percentage defectives falls, so does the total output increase. This means that there will be very substantial differences in the shape of curves, depending on whether they are plotted against number of defects or percentage of defects. Accordingly, great caution is needed in distinguishing between costs of rework and costs of low capacity.

To further confuse the issue, economists will point out that doubling the capacity does not mean doubling the output: it may be necessary to reduce prices to sell any increased production, and it may not be possible to sell twice as much at any price. This, again, changes the definition of the X axis. The change in capacity alters the cost curve at all levels of output, so it may pay to increase output, even bringing in another shift or increasing overtime.

THE Y AXIS

There are many different labels to be found on the Y axis in the literature. The following are sometimes used when the X axis is 'Defects':

'Cost' (Caplan 1972; Robertson 1971; Kirkpatrick 1970; Harrington 1976; Urwick Group 1981; Thoday 1976; BS 4891, 1972)

'Operating quality costs' (Besterfield 1979)

'Quality costs (direct)' (Oakland 1989)

'Cost per good unit of product' (Juran and Gryna 1980)

The following are sometimes used where the Y axis is time or the degree of implementation of a quality management programme.[5]

'Percent of cost input' (Campanella and Corcoran 1983)

'Quality as percent of cost of turnover' (Veen 1974; Hagan 1986)

'Quality as percent of sales' (Kohl 1976 and two companies cited by Plunkett and Dale 1988)

'Percent of manufacturing cost' (Huckett 1985)

'Quality assurance cost for quality acceptable to consumer' (Lockyer 1983)

'Quality related costs' (BS 6143)

Plunkett and Dale (1988) say that all these are 'absolute cost or a simple variant of it'. However, it can be seen from Table 12.1 that these are very different concepts, and from Figures 12.3 to 12.18 that they result in very different shapes of curve.

The costs

It is usual to plot costs, unit costs, and so on. against something like level of defects or conformity. The 'quality related cost' is taken to be the 'cost in ensuring and assuring quality as well as loss incurred when quality is not achieved' (BS 6143). These quality related costs are subdivided into prevention costs, appraisal costs, internal failure costs (for example, waste and rework costs) and external failure costs, and a figure looking something like Figure 12.1 or Figure 12.2 is produced. This seems to be generally interpreted in the literature as implying that as one increases prevention costs, for example, so internal failure costs are reduced, and there is some discussion in the literature on how realistic the different curves are in indicating the pay-off from prevention and appraisal expenditures (see Fox 1989; Oakland 1989; Plunkett and Dale 1988). However, there are several problems that arise:

- It is not possible to present four interdependent variables on a two-dimensional graph. Both internal and external failure costs are changed by prevention costs, so it is not possible to read off one level of prevention costs on the graph, and derive from it the level of external failure costs that can be expected from it.

– It cannot be assumed that one level of appraisal costs will result in a single level of internal and external failure costs. Checking of incoming raw materials has a totally different impact to checking the finished product leaving the firm. A different range of pay-offs can be expected from changing the effectiveness of each quality assurance or control process. Lumping together totally different processes, with totally different costs, totally different effects on the product leaving the factory, and totally different pay-offs causes more confusion than it cures.

– It is far from clear why the appraisal and prevention costs should be separated, except to emphasize that the quality assurance professional using the figures belongs to one or another school of quality assurance. The economic importance is not obvious. The economic costs of internal and external failure are by no means simple to calculate.

– An economist would want to take into account the effect on sales and prices of a change in quality, allowing for changes made by competitors: I know of no attempt to allow for this in the paradigm. BS 6143 talks only of 'loss of profit due to cessation of existing markets as a consequence of poor quality' – a far cry from the economist's reckoning. In the economics of grading it is normal to ignore the physical costs, as being tiny in relation to the price effects and waste (Chapter 6).

– One normally talks of increased revenues arising from increased costs. While it is possible to redefine increased revenues as reduced lost potential revenue, or the cost of imperfect operations, or quality cost, it is not in line with the way economists or management usually think, and it does lead to confusion, as the literature shows. The BS 6143 definition includes only some of the lost potential revenue, so it is difficult to see how confusion could be avoided.

The only way that one can make any sense out of diagrams like Figure 12.1 and Figure 12.2, is to take it that the grandaddy of these diagrams did not refer to 'total costs', but to 'minimum total costs', and that it includes lost revenue as a cost. The proportion

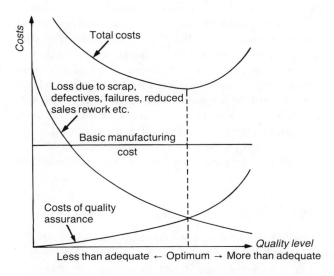

Figure 12.1 BSI quality costs model 'economics of quality assurance'

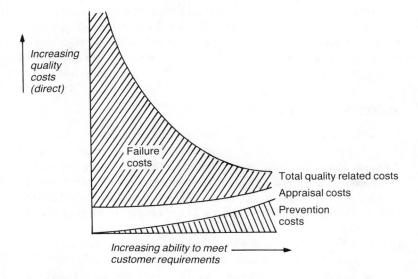

Figure 12.2 Relationship between direct costs of quality and organizational capability (Oakland, 1989)

of the different costs shown then means the proportion that exists at the least cost level of producing an output with a given defect rate. It does not in any way imply that changing the level of one cost will have any given effect on another cost. However, while it is easy to conceive of such a curve, it is extremely difficult to draw one in practice. It would be necessary to calculate at each process level a quality cost curve, and to do sequential costings through different possible processes, comparing high input inspection, with high output inspection, high prevention with high appraisal, early stage appraisal and inspection with later stage appraisal and inspection. I have not come across any such economic analysis in the literature.

THE TIME AXIS

One would normally be critical of any economic model which did not take into account time, and at least distinguish between short run, medium run and long run, if not analysing the dynamic effects. The 'costs of quality' approach, however, has handled time, not by adding an extra time axis to a static economic analysis, but by removing the static economic analysis entirely, and replacing it with a time axis. What is left is a description of how the quality assurance expert would like to see costs moving over a period of time (with complications like inflation, changed input costs, changed market conditions, changed specifications and changed technologies tacitly ignored). It is of no analytical value.

PLOTTING THE CURVES

In Table 12.1 I have set out some quality costs for an imaginary firm. In Figures 12.3 to 12.18, the costs have been plotted against different axes. The numbers attached to the curves correspond to the rows in Table 12.1, with each row being a different way of looking at the same cost. It is not suggested that they are typical for two reasons. First, in the absence of an economic theory on the production of quality there is no incentive to collect the data required for economic analysis. Second, there are so many firms using so many processes that it is unlikely that figures for one firm will have any general application. However, the figures are not presented because they are typical, but because they can be used to show that, using the different concepts of quality and cost used

Table 12.1 Relationship between quality costs, total costs, total revenue, unit costs and percentage

1 No. of items entering factory	200	200	200	200	200	200	200	200	200	200	200
2 No. of items defective during process	80	69	58	45	31	21	15	18	7	0	0
3 % of items not defective during process	60%	66%	71%	78%	85%	90%	93%	91%	97%	100%	100%
4 No. of items leaving line	120	131	142	155	169	179	185	182	193	200	200
5 No. defective at end of line	10	10	10	12	15	15	12	0	2	0	0
6 % of items not defective at end of line	92%	91%	93%	92%	91%	92%	94%	100%	99%	100%	100%
7 No. into store	110	121	132	143	154	164	173	182	191	200	200
8 No. defective on final inspection	10	11	12	13	14	14	13	12	11	10	0
9 % not defective on final inspection	91%	91%	91%	91%	91%	91%	92%	93%	94%	95%	100%
10 No. leaving company	100	110	120	130	140	150	160	170	180	190	200
11 No. wasted in distribution	20	20	20	20	20	18	16	14	12	10	10
12 No. of returns	10	10	10	10	10	10	10	10	10	10	10
13 Number consumed	70	80	90	100	110	122	134	146	158	170	180
14 % of sales believed consumed	70%	73%	75%	77%	79%	81%	84%	86%	88%	89%	90%
15 Total Quality Cost $	$100	$110	$120	$130	$140	$150	$160	$170	$180	$190	$200
16 Total cost of production	$2,430	$2,375	$2,320	$2,261	$2,200	$2,150	$2,111	$2,090	$2,041	$2,000	$2,000
17 Value of sales	$2,000	$2,200	$2,400	$2,600	$2,800	$3,000	$3,200	$3,400	$3,600	$3,800	$4,000
18 Value of sales less returns, waste	$1,150	$1,350	$1,550	$1,750	$1,950	$2,210	$2,470	$2,730	$2,990	$3,250	$3,450
19 Quality cost as % of prodn cost	4%	5%	5%	6%	6%	7%	8%	8%	9%	10%	10%
20 Quality cost as % of sales	5%	5%	5%	5%	5%	5%	5%	5%	5%	5%	5%
21 Quality cost as % of consumption	9%	8%	8%	7%	7%	7%	6%	6%	6%	6%	6%
22 Quality cost per unit leaving company	$1.00	$1.00	$1.00	$1.00	$1.00	$1.00	$1.00	$1.00	$1.00	$1.00	$1.00
23 Quality cost per unit leaving line	$0.83	$0.84	$0.85	$0.84	$0.83	$0.84	$0.86	$0.93	$0.93	$0.95	$1.00
24 Quality cost per unit entering line	$0.50	$0.55	$0.60	$0.65	$0.70	$0.75	$0.80	$0.85	$0.90	$0.95	$1.00
25 Quality cost per unit consumed	$1.43	$1.38	$1.33	$1.30	$1.27	$1.23	$1.19	$1.16	$1.14	$1.12	$1.11

Note: the 'quality cost' is here limited to prevention and appraisal costs. The figures have been selected purely to demonstrate that what is a straight horizontal line with one set of axes, may be upward or downward sloping, or have a reverse slope, with another. It is not possible to know how realistic these figures are as, in the absence of a suitable theory, these variables do not appear to have been measured empirically.

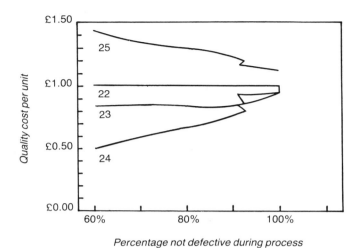

Figure 12.3 Quality cost per unit and percentage not defective during process

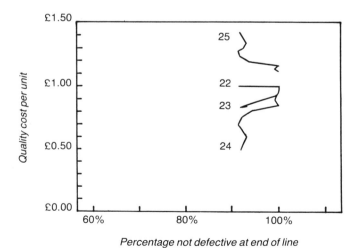

Figure 12.4 Quality cost per unit and percentage not defective at end of line

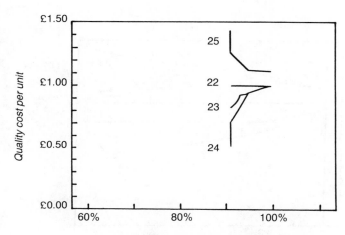

Percentage not defective on final inspection

Figure 12.5 Quality cost per unit and percentage not defective on final inspection

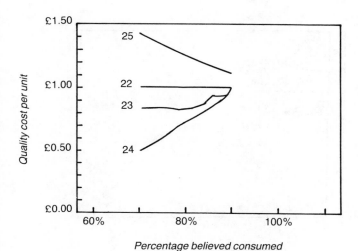

Percentage believed consumed

Figure 12.6 Quality cost per unit and percentage believed consumed

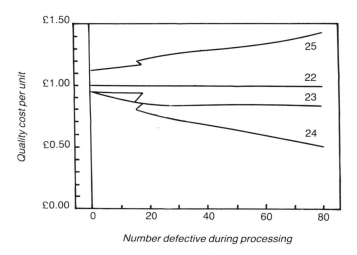

Figure 12.7 Quality cost per unit and number defective during processing

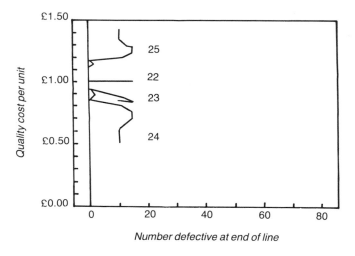

Figure 12.8 Quality cost per unit and number defective at end of line

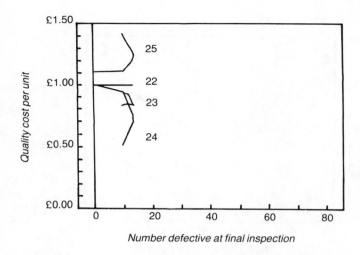

Figure 12.9 Quality cost per unit and number defective at final inspection

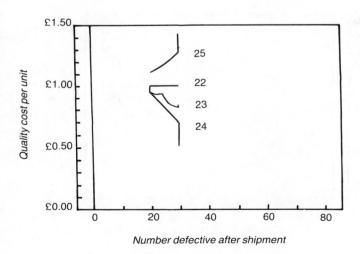

Figure 12.10 Quality cost per unit and number defective after shipment

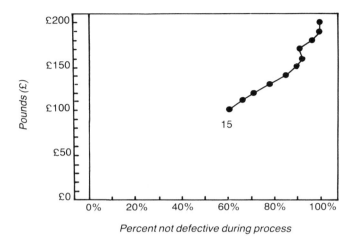

Figure 12.11 Total quality cost and percentage not defective during process

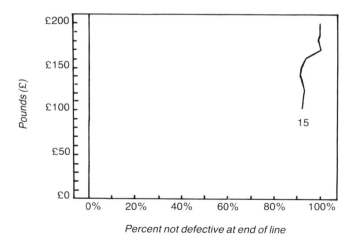

Figure 12.12 Total quality cost and percentage not defective at end of line

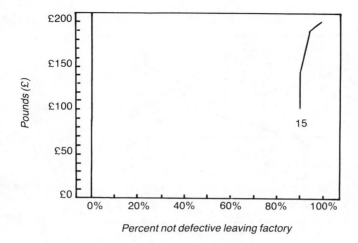

Figure 12.13 Total quality cost and percentage not defective leaving factory

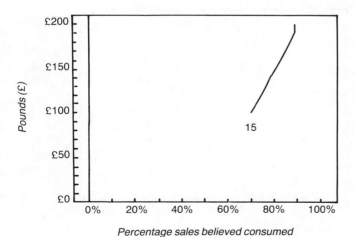

Figure 12.14 Total quality cost and percentage sales believed consumed

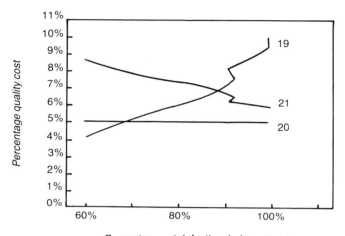

Figure 12.15 Percentage quality cost and percentage not defective during process

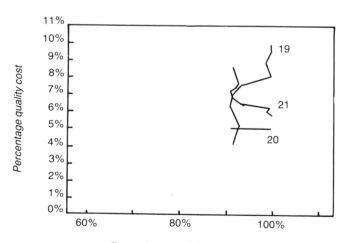

Figure 12.16 Percentage quality cost and percentage not defective at end of line

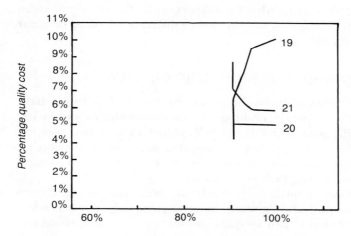

Percentage not defective on final inspection

Figure 12.17 Percentage quality cost and percentage not defective on final inspection

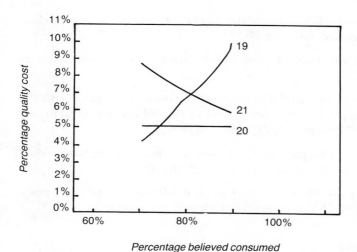

Percentage believed consumed

Figure 12.18 Percentage quality cost and percentage believed consumed

in the literature and set out above, there can be a vast difference in the graphs drawn. What the authors evidently considered to be virtually the same graphs with slightly different labelling turn out to be totally different.

THE ECONOMICS OF PRODUCING QUALITY

In twenty years of researching the economics of quality, I have come across virtually nothing on the economics of producing quality. Plunkett and Dale (1986) report that in two comprehensive literature searches 'it was noted that there is virtually no information available on the costs or economics of common quality-related engineering practices'.

The 'costs of quality' approach asks only 'How much is deviation from perfection costing the firm, [ignoring certain marketing costs]?': it does not ask questions that an economist would ask, such as:

Changing the product

- How much will it cost to increase the level of a single characteristic?

- How much will it cost to increase the level of several characteristics at one time?

- How much would it cost to produce a different characteristics mix?

- What is the trade-off in production cost between producing the same product with lower tolerances, and producing to higher specifications with the same tolerances?

- Would it be possible to produce an entirely different product that met the same needs more cheaply?

- What are the cost curves for the different production possibilities? How do costs vary with quantity produced?

The market

- How far are the present specifications optimal? Would consumers prefer a different characteristics mix?

- Would they pay more for a different characteristics mix? Would they buy more?

- Would they pay more for the same product supplied to closer tolerances?

- To the consumers what is the trade-off between the same product with tighter tolerances and a product with higher specifications and the same tolerances?

- How does consumer demand differ from distributor demand, for example, waste in the distribution system, repair under guarantee and so on are costs to the distributor, not the consumer.

- What is the cost of changing consumer perceptions by advertising?

- What is the cost of changing consumer search?

- What is the price effect of changes?

- What is the demand curve facing the manufacturer for the different qualities that might be produced?

Production

- What is the optimum production level, given the cost curves for the different quality options, and their demand curves?

- Would it be possible to use different processes to produce the same product?

- Would it be possible to redesign the product to make production cheaper and less defect prone?

CONCLUSION

It has been shown that there are major conceptual errors in the cost of quality approach as practised, and that there are a large number of unresolved questions. There has been very little work done on the economics of producing quality, a much larger research programme. It is concluded that a major economic input into the production end of the economics of quality is urgently needed.

Chapter 13

The time dimension

In this chapter the time dimension is introduced into the analysis. While this is usually ignored in the economic analysis of quality, it is important in the marketing literature.[1] This book has already emphasized the importance of the time element in search, notably in Chapters 4, 5, 8 and 9. This chapter will cover delays between buying and consuming, demand for a varying product, changes in demand and demand for durable goods.

DELAYS BETWEEN BUYING AND CONSUMING

It is convenient for analysis to assume that a product is consumed immediately it is bought, but of course it is far more common for there to be some delay and perhaps a storage period. The home-maker may go shopping on Saturday and consume the perishables over the next three days, the tinned and frozen food over the next fortnight, and the spices and sauces over the next six months.

Two examples will show what problems can arise from the assumption that products are consumed as they are bought – a fundamental, though implicit, assumption of hedonic/characteristics theory. The logic of Lancaster's (1966, 1971, 1979) model falls away if one accepts that drinking a bottle of whisky bit by bit over a week is not the same as drinking a whole bottle on Saturday night,[2] or that buying 14lb of potatoes does not imply eating them at one sitting. The indifference curves he constructed, on the basis that consumption and purchases were identical, would no longer apply. If one tries to avoid this problem by constructing a model of the household as a market, taking into account multiple users and uses of the product, storage space, amount in stock at time of purchase, frequency of shopping, location and so on, one moves far beyond the theory of revealed preference, and one cannot use the indifference curves as he does. Rosen's (1974) model, where consumers choose between different product lines rather than cooking up a product line in the kitchen after purchase, is marginally less seriously affected.

A second, explicit, assumption of hedonic/characteristics theory is that there is constant demand. Each individual is assumed to buy exactly the same goods in the same proportions each day, as long as the price relationship remains the same. Again, the theory falls away if this is not true.

The decision on whether to purchase is strongly influenced by how much is in stock at the time of buying. As long as there is some in stock at home, the buyer will not feel pressed to buy if the quality or the value for money is not very good. This means that price elasticity of demand and quality elasticity of demand are influenced by the amount in stock. This is why one group of market researchers ask whether buyers have deep freezers, refrigerators and pantries, while another group is interested in world stocks of rubber, chrome, and so on.

At consumer level it is not common for buyers to buy more than one product line or level of quality at a time. Some economists have cited this phenomenon as evidence of the predictive accuracy of quality appraisal models that led to corner solutions, with consumers always buying the same quality or product line, but this is not correct, for two reasons. First, it is certainly not true of manufacturing, where several qualities may be bought at one time and blended or used for different components or end products. Industries like tobacco, coffee and steel fabrication are examples, and they use products that closely resemble the ones used in theoretical models. Second, the fact that consumers do not normally buy two or more competing product lines at a time does not indicate that their decision process has led them to buy one and only one quality, and to avoid any diversity. On the contrary, it indicates that in the short run they want the maximum diversity, different products rather than different product lines of one product. Over time they can get a different type of diversity, buying different lines and qualities of one product. When buyers do buy several qualities of the same product at one time it may be that they are buying for a range of consumers, breakfast cereals for the family, or a range of alcohols for a party: this would be compatible with each consumer wanting a different product each time. On the other hand, it is normal for goods to be bought in relatively large quantities and to be consumed bit by bit over time, so the fact that a buyer buys only one product at a time does not necessarily mean that only one quality is consumed at a time: food from different shopping expeditions may be consumed at one meal.

DEMAND FOR DURABLE GOODS

Much of the economic theory on the quality of durables has been carried out in abstract models of consumer choice, which defined the quality of a product as the life of the product. The assumption that a product that lasts twice as long is twice as good, is a way of getting round the problems of comparing the quality of consumer goods with different levels of characteristic in a consumer model. The approach implies that a consumer gets exactly the same characteristics in the same quantities and proportions in each period. It also implies that the satisfaction produced by the product, be it a car or a vacuum cleaner, is constant over the period. It does not permit comparison of products with different characteristics, or the utilities obtained from consuming different quantities of the product at one time.

Buying durables involves many more considerations in the real world. Quality is not consistent. The cost of replacing the durable changes over its lifetime, its second-hand or scrap value changes, and its operating cost and reliability changes. In an era of technological change the replacement is seldom a perfect substitute: it is likely to be cheaper, to do the job better and to have more features. The possibility of new, better, and cheaper variants being introduced in the short to medium term strongly influences short-run replacement decisions. The changing quality over time, plus the fact that a manufacturer may have several items of different ages may change the use to which a good is put: for example, a haulage firm may use old trucks, with their higher risk of breakdown and low resale value, to fill the gap at peak periods and to do various odd jobs. Buying a durable is an act of faith: buying a television may require the belief that there will still be an electricity supply in five years, the belief that the programmes will still be worth watching, and the belief that the promised new satellite channel will be operating.

Often consumers get utility from a product long after they have forgotten what they paid for it, and businessmen may get utility from a product long after it has been written off. This gap between purchase and consumption, and the ignorance of the price paid, or the belief that one is getting something for nothing, may influence what brand to buy when the time comes to replace it.

VARIATION IN PURCHASE OVER TIME

In this section the variation in purchase behaviour over time is discussed, and the reason why people purchase a variety of goods over time, switching brands and buying new products, is discussed.

Variety seeking

People like change, and it can be argued that the search for novelty and variety is a basic survival trait for humanity, when other species have died out from over-specialization. Van Trijp (1989), in his review of the literature, covers the psychological and market research literature on the reasons why people like change. The main conclusions are:

- People like to try new products and 'New' is the commonest advertising flash. Novelty, itself, is desirable.
- People like short-term variety. The most wonderful food in the world loses its savour after a week. This appears to be partly boredom with this product setting in as the novelty wears off, while at the same time the desire for novelty, and a new product, increases. This is reflected by people buying a wide range of foods every week, not just different qualities. Interestingly, staple foods are usually bland, like bread, rice, maize and potatoes, so that one does not get tired of them as quickly, and they can be given a different taste with a relatively small addition of another product.
- People like long-term variety. When I was a student we had the same menu each Monday for three years, the same each Tuesday and so on. Certainly, there was short-term variety, with a different meal each day, but there was long term boredom from the certainty that if it was Monday it was beef stew. This may explain why people acquire a brand loyalty and then after a period get dissatisfied and change their loyalty. Again there seems to be an increasing positive desire for change, which may get stronger with time, combined with increased dissatisfaction with the old.

– In the medium to long term there are significant changes in taste. This may be constant fluctuation as in fashions for clothes or a deeper and more fundamental change like the one we have seen in British eating habits over the last twenty years.

Other reasons for varied purchases

There are several other reasons for variable purchases apart from just a liking for variety and novelty.

They may arise because the buyer is buying for several consumers who may have different tastes and who may even have different uses for the product. The reason may be 'It's your turn to choose the breakfast cereal, dear', or 'This time we need lawn fertilizer, not rose fertilizer'.

Demand may change because of changing situations – the house needs painting – or changes in the buyers' circumstances, like a change in income. It is not always easy to distinguish conceptually between a change in circumstances and a change in purchases arising out of a desire for change, especially a long-run change, and empirically it may be more difficult.[3]

Purchases may change while demand remains constant, even though quality and price are also unchanged. This could happen because of a change in the prices or availability of competing lines or because of the introduction of new product lines.

Perceptions of a product may change over time, even though it is physically unchanged. It is easy for a product to acquire an 'old-fashioned' image for instance.

Demand may also change as a result of previous purchases. Consumers who once buy a CD player or a microwave can be expected to change their demand for LPs and frozen food as a result. One's tastes change as one consumes a product, and people develop a taste for classical music, or for fine wines. More seriously, one can become physically addicted to a drug.[4]

CHARACTERISTICS OR PRODUCTS

Variety seeking can be looking for new characteristics and features on a single product, or the switching from product to product for variety, and both may be combined. In empirical work it is not always easy to distinguish between a consumer being an occasional buyer of apples and a consumer being a regular buyer of fruit who sometimes buys apples. Here fruit is an easily identified product group from the retailer's point of view, but an individual's product group might include apples, crisps and sweets as close substitutes, with oranges and bananas being another group entirely.

ELASTICITIES VARYING WITH TIME

With most products one expects the price elasticity of demand to depend on whether it is calculated on a daily, weekly or yearly basis. A homemaker may choose the cheapest vegetables on display on any one shopping expedition, but over a week the aim will be to serve the family a variety of produce, so the demand may be less elastic. Demand may be less elastic on Saturday when buying for weekend meals than on Monday and Tuesday, when the family are taking some or all their meals away from home and when purchases can be more easily postponed. It is certainly true, in western countries, that most vegetable sales are on Friday and Saturday and that Monday and Tuesday are slack days. Analysis of the demand for hogs in Chicago showed that the elasticity of demand was –5.8 on Saturdays, –2.8 on Wednesdays, –2.5 for weekly data and –1.0 on yearly data.[5] As these are wholesale prices, the very elastic demand on Saturday is largely because the hogs bought then will be sold retail on Monday and Tuesday, and the less elastic demand on Wednesday is for hogs that will be sold retail to weekend shoppers.

Supply elasticity can vary in much the same way: the farmer with no storage may be compelled to sell immediately: wholesalers can store for months or even years; bakers must sell bread within 24 hours of baking. The market period of the wholesaler may be the short-run period of the farmer or the long-run period of the baker.

If the elasticities of supply and demand in relation to quantity purchased can vary in this way over time, one can expect some change in elasticities relating to quality. Indeed, in so far as quality may be a substitute for quantity, this is inevitable.

CONFUSION

Van Trijp and Steenkamp (1990) point out the many possible reasons for variation in buying behaviour and argue that the terminology used in the literature encourages confusion, particularly between seeking variety and buying different qualities for other reasons. As a result, much of the empirical work on the subject is of doubtful value: it is not clear what has been measured or what the results can be used for.

IMPLICATIONS

The fact that people vary their purchases over time has a wide range of implications in marketing. For example, if buyers of a product do vary their purchases, it will be relatively easy to introduce a new product on to the market: the major problem of getting people to try the new product solves itself in time. On the other hand, if people switch brands frequently, it is more difficult to build up a large market share with a single brand: if one in three purchases is a 'new' brand, the maximum possible share is 66 per cent, and the probable share is much lower. For this reason, in a market where variable buying behaviour is common, manufacturers often introduce parallel brands or sub-brands.

Variable buying behaviour is a function of the individual, so it is normally investigated from panel data or market research aimed at the individual. It is possible to quantify this data and to cross-tabulate it against the usual marketing variables like age, income, social class, shopping patterns and so on. It is, however, extremely difficult to separate out the reasons for the variable behaviour, and I am sceptical about it being done at all.

One approach to quantifying the variety seeking as opposed to other reasons for variable buying behaviour is to design laboratory experiments in which the 'other' motives are held constant. As with all laboratory experiments, this requires one to believe that the consumer behaviour in this situation is realistic, and that the results of an artificial laboratory experiment can be generalized to the real world.

Some attempts have been made to generalize from the fact that buyers exhibit stronger variation in purchases with certain types of product or in certain markets. Again, it is questionable whether such generalizations are valid. Even if they were, it is difficult to imagine a firm acting on such a generalization, rather than finding out what are the facts in relation to its own product.

CONCLUSION

This chapter has argued that buyers have an innate demand for novelty as well as a capacity for boredom, or satiation over time, which means that they normally switch purchases from one product to another and from one product line to another even in the short term. This has long been recognized by marketing, and the implications on product launching, brand loyalty, and market share have been explored fully in the literature. In economics it has normally been ignored, with the result that many of the models built up cannot cope with this touch of realism.

Chapter 14

Subjective attributes and objective characteristics

Manufacturers like to think that they perceive a product in terms of objective characteristics, of a product specification that is measurable and controllable. Consumers have a purely subjective appreciation of the satisfactions that a product can give, an appreciation that may be strongly influenced by the objective characteristics, but that may not. Marketing professionals and economists may be concerned, not with the quality of an individual item, but with qualities of the product line as a whole: elasticity of demand, market size, market segments, wastage rates and so on.

A great deal of the business of the firm, and of the marketing and product development departments in particular, is to bring these very different concepts together, to relate a consumer's satisfactions to the nuts and bolts of a product specification, to relate one consumer's enjoyment of an item to product sales to AB consumers in the Central television area.

It is easy to do quantitative research based on manufacturing specifications, but it is of limited value if it cannot be related to consumer perceptions and consumer satisfactions. It is far more difficult than is generally appreciated to do accurate quantitative research on consumer satisfactions, and more difficult still to relate consumer satisfactions to manufacturing specifications. Often the different approaches are confused, with unfortunate results.

A product has objective characteristics like redness, weight, or sugar content. Attributes are the subjective perception of the consumer. He may attribute redness, weight or sugar content to the product, more or less accurately, but he may also attribute ecological soundness or social status – attributes that have no corresponding physical characteristic. An objectively measurable

physical characteristic like lead in paint may have no corresponding attribute if the buyer has never thought of the possibility that
there might be lead in the paint, but may have an important
corresponding attribute if the buyer is afraid of lead poisoning.

This chapter will distinguish between subjective attributes and
objective characteristics, between beliefs of different kinds and
between different types and levels of characteristic. These distinctions are of great practical importance: if researchers do not
realize exactly what it is that they are researching, they will make
major conceptual errors, some of which will be examined in later
chapters. If they are doing quantitative work, the specification
errors can easily invalidate the results.

The chapter identifies many of the confusions that run through
the different traditions of the economics of quality, and dissects
them. These confusions have invalidated many of the analyses in
the past, particularly those which used two completely different
concepts of characteristic as though they were the same one, and
those which used overlapping concepts of characteristic, and so
double counted one aspect of quality. The only way to avoid such
errors in empirical work is to be aware of the possible confusions
between characteristics and attributes, between the characteristics
of an item and of a product line, between the different types of
characteristic, and between the different types of characteristic at
different levels of the marketing chain.

SUBJECTIVE ATTRIBUTES

Quality can be thought of as being purely subjective. Any change
in a product's design, manufacture, specifications or objective
characteristics is only an improvement to an individual consumer
if he likes it better – or, as argued in Chapter 1, if he thinks it is
better for someone else. What one consumer thinks is better,
another may consider worse: you may like a Rolls Royce, I think it
is too big to park. Wants are not unchangeable: you can be edu-
cated to enjoy music, or revel in fast cars and so on. This is
particularly noticeable from the enormous range of cuisines
around the world, and their spread.

Purchase decisions are influenced, not just by this personal
subjective perception of quality, but by a whole range of subjective
beliefs, which may or may not approximate to the truth. These
include an individual's

- beliefs about what he really wants;
- beliefs about what product characteristics might satisfy these wants;
- beliefs about what products in the market might have these characteristics.

A change in the objective characteristics of a product cannot be expected to change sales unless these beliefs change.

The consumer's beliefs about his own desires are often inaccurate – attics are full of gadgets bought eagerly but only used once. Subconscious desires may not be recognized, and this may mean that people do not buy what they think they want or what they think they ought to want rather than what they 'really' want. Marketing may approach this by persuading people that they do have wants that they never suspected, for spa baths for instance, or that some wants that they recognize are more important than they thought. Inevitably, much of quality theory must be based on the assumption that wants are static, if the analysis is to be kept manageable, but there are times, particularly when discussing brands and advertising, when it must be accepted that wants can be influenced.

Similarly, the buyer's beliefs about the consumer's desires are often inaccurate. When someone buys a product that will be consumed by others, the buyer's beliefs about the desires of the consumers and how best to weight them are necessarily imperfect. Advertising aims to change the home-maker's beliefs about what kind of foods children like, or to persuade him to give more weight to what is good for them than to what they like. At the same time it works on making the buyer feel satisfied that he is getting a bargain or is doing the best for his family.

The buyer's beliefs about what product characteristics are needed to meet the perceived desires are also imperfect. One may know that a house is damp, but not know all the possible ways of treating it. Demand for certain qualities (in the sense of characteristics mixes), or certain products, may be limited as a result. For this reason a marketing campaign may have to tell consumers that a different type of product can meet their needs before trying to sell a specific product line.

Again, consumers may not be aware of the need for vitamins or trace elements to ensure health. The objective fact that certain characteristics will help achieve the perceived aim, health, is not matched by a subjective belief, either in the existence of these characteristics or in their desirability, so there is no demand for them. On the other hand, they may believe in a purely subjective attribute that has no objective parallel: dietary fibre in meat, yin or yang in potatoes. The market exists nevertheless. Consumers may attribute their feeling of well-being to having a cup of tea, when it really arises from taking a break from work and sitting down. The placebo effect is also important.

Even if the buyer is perfectly informed about his wants and the product characteristics needed to satisfy his wants, he will have an imperfect perception of the product characteristics on offer. For most products one could argue that the consumer's perceptions are limited to perhaps half a dozen product lines out of dozens or hundreds on the market and even for this half dozen lines perceptions are generally imperfect – what do I really know about my car? How is it made? How reliable is it? How safe is it? How does the engine work? What fuel consumption does it have, today?

The consumer will try to match his requirement for a particular mix of characteristics to a particular product type.

He may believe quite strongly that vitamins are a Good Thing, or that pesticides are a Bad Thing, but if he has no information about the relative levels of the different lines within a product group, he cannot apply his beliefs to his choice between product lines. He can, however, switch to another product group, fresh organic vegetables rather than canned vegetables, where he may perceive that there is less risk of a low level of vitamins or a high level of pesticide residues. Having no beliefs about the level of pesticide is not the same as believing that there is no pesticide.

The buyer will also have beliefs about the probability of any given purchase within a product line having certain characteristics. He will have beliefs about risk, about quality variations within the product specification and so on. The seller will, of course, have his own beliefs about the characteristics of his product, which may not be very closely linked to reality.

It is argued therefore that buyers' quality can be thought of as being subjective, as long as quality is thought of as what gives satisfaction: the identical product will give different satisfactions to different consumers. People's perceptions of their own wants, of what product characteristics will meet their wants, and of what product lines and specific purchases have those characteristics, are subjective. A seller can change the quality of the product without altering its physical specifications by changing consumers' beliefs. An advertising and marketing programme can change people's wants in some real sense: it can change what they think they need, it can change their perception of what product characteristics best fill that need, it can change their perception of what characteristics a given product line has and it can change the perception of the probability of getting those characteristics in a given purchase from that product line. A cynic might even argue that a quality product is one that has been lied about convincingly.

Changing the physical characteristics of the product will not necessarily change quality. It will not change demand or change consumers' satisfaction if consumers' beliefs and perceptions do not change. Some changed products will, of course, produce changed consumers' satisfaction at the time of consumption, a product with a new flavour for instance – but it may be necessary to change consumers' perceptions before they are willing to buy it. Some product changes, in design and presentation, for instance, may change consumers' perceptions without necessarily changing satisfaction at the point of consumption. There is, of course, a feedback effect: you can persuade a customer that your product is wonderful, but if it proves not to meet these expectations, you may lose a customer.

What then do we mean by improving the product? Certainly improved production methods and quality control can reduce actual (as opposed to perceived) risk of product quality deviating from the mean, and advertising and experience may then change consumers' perceptions towards the new reality. Changed product design and product specifications can produce a product line nearer what the consumer thinks he wants – again requiring advertising or experience to change the consumers' perception of that product line. New product development can produce a different way of meeting well-recognized needs. These are examples of the characteristics changing, while the product line is continuous in a sense. Finally, a totally new product, a spa bath, a Walkman, a space shuttle, can unlock new wants that were dormant, if indeed they ever existed.

I have been talking as though all consumers were the same. A product can be improved, meeting consumers' needs more exactly, if it is advertised differently to different market segments, so that each has its own perceptions. It can be improved by redesigning it so that each market segment has a purpose-built product, again with advertising and experiences bringing the product and perceptions closer over time.

Sometimes, of course, the consumer will have wrong perceptions about what wants he has, what product characteristics he requires, what products have those characteristics and what product lines have those characteristics in what proportions. Occasionally, these will all average out in the end, so that he chooses a 'wrong' product that does meet his 'real' wants and this experience confirms his wrong perceptions.

In one very practical sense a product does not have attributes at all: individual buyers have the attributes, the beliefs about the product. One cannot analyse quality in terms of a product's attributes, but in terms of what individuals, market segments and markets think and do.

For analytical purposes it is convenient to think of these different levels of perception separately. In practice a buyer may squeeze these different levels, thinking that he wants a Coke, rather than going through wants, characteristics needed to satisfy these wants and, what characteristics each product has. This does imply though, that at some stage he has gone through the processes, and that a search and learn process has enabled him to short-circuit the process.

The main points to bear in mind are that:

- Many, indeed most, characteristics do not have a corresponding attribute.
- Not every attribute has a corresponding characteristic.
- The attribute is a function of the individual buyer or consumer, not the product.
- Individuals can be expected to differ in their attributes for a given product. This is particularly noticeable for individuals in different market segments (indeed market segments could be defined in terms of common attributes), and at different levels of the marketing chain.
- Attributes can be changed while characteristics remain the same by

  * changing the end use
  * changing the information available
  * changing search costs
  * changing advertising
  * changing availability and location

* changing uniformity, tolerances and so on
* changing guarantees
* selling in shops with a different reputation

CHARACTERISTICS

Why use characteristics?

When one is selling a product to a customer, there are obvious advantages in describing it in terms as close as possible to the consumer's own perceptions of his wants, in terms of subjective satisfactions given. This may mean advertising a cigar as restoring the smoker's calm and contentment when he lands up in a particularly embarrassing situation. This is not always possible: it may be that the satisfactions offered are so crass that the advertiser cannot afford to make them explicit or delicacy may prevent him from stating any purpose for lavatory paper except being a puppy's plaything. The range of possible satisfactions from a product like a car is so wide that they cannot all be mentioned.

When it is not possible to describe the satisfactions directly, the product can then be described in more concrete terms, aiming not at the consumer's perceptions of his wants but at his perceptions of what product will meet these wants.

Describing a product in terms of its subjective attributes is not very helpful to the production division. They need production specifications giving the raw materials and the production process. These must be set out objectively and they seldom bear much relationship to the satisfactions the product produces. When the product moves from the manufacturing department to the marketing department, the perceptions change.

Quality control can take the form of ensuring that manufacturing specifications are carried out, of checking raw materials and procedures (for example, 'Right First Time') or of checking the characteristics of the output defined more in terms of the marketing department's criteria (for example, 'Does it work?').

The retailer and the marketing department will probably find manufacturing specifications rather irrelevant and will have a different way of describing the product, perhaps in terms of its performance, its appearance and its warranty, in characteristics which bear more relation to what the consumer perceives. Later in the chapter I will discuss a range of other factors apart from physical characteristics which come into the picture here.

A complete, unambiguous definition of a product's physical characteristics is not necessarily helpful. With music, for example, we have the score, as the manufacturing specification, and the sound engineer can give the most detailed, unambiguous, description of the sounds it produces, but neither of these definitions indicate whether it would appeal to someone who loves Mozart.

Economists will often carry out an analysis of the objective characteristics of a product to determine what a producer ought to want. This is very useful with products like pig food, and similar manufacturing inputs, where the relation between the inputs and the satisfaction gained is a technical one, and the satisfaction can be defined in such unambiguous terms as weight gain or profit. This analysis will produce a bad fit where there is a significant subjective input – brand image, information gap, imperfect perception and inaccurate beliefs – and pig food buyers are subject to these biases as much as anyone else. It is also important to bear in mind the different concept of manufacturer's quality for an intermediate product, discussed in Chapter 1. There is a danger that economists dealing with these products will not see the bad fit as a sign of specification error, but treat it as a positive result, a quantitative measure of the difference between the subjective and objective elements, of the value of the brand.

Throughout this section I have emphasized that the choice of objective characteristics to describe a product is itself subjective: which characteristics one should use depends on one's purpose.

THE PRODUCT OR ITS CHARACTERISTICS?

We may make a broad distinction between a product which is consumed as a product, and a product which is consumed as a bundle of characteristics (or attributes).

A glass of wine, a radio, a stew are, basically, consumed as a unit, and changing some of the more important characteristics (or attributes) changes the nature of the product, though changing others like the level of alcohol just modifies the effect.

There are other products which are valued more for their constituent characteristics (or attributes), as ore is valued for its gold content or the oilcake going into a cow's diet is valued for its protein, calories and so on. Much of the analysis in the literature has been devoted to products like this.[1]

Level of characteristic

A product may be described in terms of objective characteristics at several levels:

- What the product does (cures athlete's foot).
- What the product is capable of doing (150 mph).
- What the product's components can do (32 megabyte hard disk).
- What the product is made of (5 per cent alcohol).
- What processes it has undergone (hand-made).
- What its end use is.
- What it produces: a radio produces music, a machine produces shoes, and the product is valued for the music or the shoes.
- What it is: a Rolls Royce may be valued for being a Rolls Royce, independently of being a means of transport, a mix of components, and so on.

It is not unusual for a product to be described in terms of several levels of characteristics: Daimler Sovereign, 6 cylinder, 4235cc, OHC, 11.23 miles per gallon, air-conditioned. This gives precision and it describes characteristics of interest to different market segments. However, great care is needed in dealing with this information in economic analysis or market research to avoid double counting. Since engine capacity affects fuel consumption, the two cannot be taken as independent variables. Morris (1975) points out that most studies give a negative valuation to miles per gallon and guesses that this is because the characteristic is negatively related to other characteristics buyers value: size, speed and so on. Technical constraints mean that some products are necessarily produced with good and bad as joint products.[2] Another point to note is that a manufacturer with a limited range may produce only an expensive, fast, car with a host of extra features, and a cheap, slow, car with no extras, so the variables are not independent. As there is a great temptation for an economist to do an analysis with different levels of characteristic, it seems likely that many consumers do the same, and that there is a certain amount of double counting when they evaluate before purchase. This must be taken into account when interpreting the results of quantitative research.

What wants it satisfies

Describing a product in terms of what wants it satisfies often makes sense: two antibiotics which are quite different chemically may attack the same range of bacteria. It is seldom possible, though, to give the degree to which it meets these wants (unless, of course they are defined in terms of increased profit to a firm, and so on). Defining a product in terms of one of the wants it satisfies may mean accidentally excluding some wants that are important in the market. Describing it in terms of several of the wants gets the message to different market segments, but it introduces serious specification biases to any econometric analysis.

It may be easy enough to specify an attribute of a product, status, for instance, but it may not be easy to find a characteristic which bears a close relationship to that attribute, and which can be used for description, especially when the status may be changed by advertising it or selling it in a high-status shop. There is also a risk that describing a product in terms of one attribute, or of a characteristic closely linked to that attribute, can mean that buyers who value it for other attributes do not realize that it is a suitable product.

What the product is capable of doing

Describing the product in terms of what it is capable of doing is still quite close to what the consumer buys it for, but some problems remain. First, the consumer may not expect to use it to the limit of its capacity. He may never exceed the 70 mph speed limit even though the car is capable of doing twice that speed. He may use his AT computer as a word processor when a very much less powerful computer would give the identical performance in this role (and one of my clients had fitted a maths co-processor to the AT he was using purely as a word processor). The buyer may think that the car which can do 140 mph will have better acceleration from the red light, and may use top speed as a cue for acceleration (probably wrongly in this case, as sports cars are normally geared for fast cruising rather than fast take-off).

Some products are named for what they do rather than for their components or characteristics: vacuum cleaner, delivery van, destroyer, word processor. No two word processor software packages will operate in the same way, for copyright reasons, but they do virtually the same job, and may share many of the same features, like spelling checks, so components or characteristics are not a useful way of describing them.

What the product components can do

Personal computers are usually described in terms of what their components are capable of doing, rather than by what they themselves do. Again, the fact that, when an appropriate programme is run, they have 36 megabytes of storage, or that they can operate extremely rapidly does not mean that the buyer uses these characteristics when a routine word-processing programme is run. To some extent this may be over-engineering, like building a bridge to take twice the load it is ever expected to take.

One reason that they are described in this way is because they have far more possible uses than any user could want, so listing everything they could do would be impracticable, and listing only a few would miss possible markets. It also reflects the fact that even though the vast majority of computers are used for rather similar word-processing and spreadsheet applications, one user is irritated by a cramped keyboard, another by inadequate ROM, another by slow storage, another by inadequate RAM, another by a monochrome monitor. Partly because of this range of demands, the product has developed so that it is easy to expand or modify it by plugging in different components. With the computer, too, it is possible to work out pretty accurately what jobs it can tackle by describing what its components can do.

What the product is

Some products are normally described by what they are. Sulphuric acid, for example, has so many potential uses in industry that it cannot be usefully described in terms of what wants it meets or what it does (except in the trivial sense of reacting in certain ways to standard chemical tests). It is assumed that the purchaser has a pretty good idea of how it will react in his process. Similarly, the different qualities of sulphuric acid, the different purities or concentrations are expressed in terms of what they are, rather than what they do.

While this is understandable, and is closer to the manufacturer's specification, it is increasingly far from what the consumer wants. We can get precise quantifiable relationships, but at the expense of ignoring what a product is used for and what the purchasers believe.

In a very different sense, a Burberry, a Rolls Royce or a Holland and Holland is what it is: it gives a satisfaction in addition to the level of characteristics, the components, or what it can do.

What the components are

A product can be described in terms of what its components are. Fertilizer is described in terms of its component nutrients 12N:12P:6K. A house is described as a pebble-dash, 3-bedroom semi. These are rather different examples, the fertilizer being valued for its component nutrients rather than as a product, the house being valued as a product, with the bedrooms being a core characteristic, the finish being a feature.

For many products, describing by the components would be counter-productive. It is not very helpful to describe a motor car in terms of percentage steel and rubber. It is not very helpful to most users to describe a radio in terms of its production specifications.

What process it has undergone

Products are often marketed as having been subjected to a process – Kosher, halal, organic, BS 5750 (ISO 9000), *methode champegnoise,* – hand-made, Made in Japan. It is objectively verifiable that a factory is operating under these conditions, though it may not be possible to prove objectively that a product in a supermarket has undergone this process. For this reason some warranty process may be needed to reassure the customer, though it is surprising how often they believe the label when they have no reason to do so.

For most products the satisfaction comes from a possibly unfounded belief that the product has undergone the process rather than from any change in satisfaction when the product is consumed. It is not possible for the customer to tell halal from ordinary meat; it is not possible for the customer to tell organic vegetables from outgrade standard vegetables; few people can tell whether the bubbles were added to the wine during or after fermentation.

With processes like 'Hand Made', 'Made in Japan', 'BS 5750', there is no suggestion that the average purchase will be of a different quality: the suggestion is rather that there is a lower risk of getting a purchase that does not conform to specifications.

THE CONSUMER'S PERCEPTION OF A PRODUCT

The consumer's perception of a product and of a product line may differ in important respects from his perception of a single purchase within that product or product line.

The product

A product may be thought of as what a consumer thinks of as being those product lines which are a close substitute for a single purpose.[3] The product cannot be objectively identified: it is the subjective opinion of the buyer (and the seller) whether two items are in the same product group.[4] To one person 'vegetables, fresh or processed' may be a product group, while other buyers may not see processed vegetables as being alternatives to fresh at all, just being an emergency supply. One buyer may see 'cabbage' as a product, while another may classify white cabbage with salad ingredients, red cabbage with pickling ingredients, and see brussels sprouts and savoy cabbages as two virtually non-competing products, though the biologist would classify them as being slightly different cultivars of the identical plant species.

Cognac may be seen by one person as something to get drunk on, a close substitute for cider, by another as a fine flavour, a substitute for a single malt whisky, and possibly even a substitute for a Stilton. For some purposes a typewriter and a computer may be close substitutes, for others not at all.

When one item can be used by the individual for different purposes, it may in fact be two products, with a different set of substitutes. Flour has one set of substitutes if it is being used for wallpaper paste, another if it is being used for cooking. A one-pound can and a half-pound can of marmalade may be thought of as the same product, while a 14lb catering pack may be thought of as quite a different product.

The consumer's perception of what is a product line is also subjective. Unless the consumer believes that the brands of baked beans on a supermarket shelf are in fact different – and this requires more than just brand recognition – they may be treated as one product line. Two cleaning fluids of quite different composition may be considered to be the identical product line.

Uniformity

The buyer has perceptions of the uniformity of the product, of the risk of buying an inferior purchase within a product or within a product line, which are not the same as his perceptions of buying from a given supermarket display.

Once he has purchased an item, the risk changes: either it meets specifications, or it does not. His perceptions of the item he has bought need not square with his perceptions of the average for the product line, in which case he may be indignant and ask for his money back. Someone who has bought a bad car may be seriously out of pocket, while the fleet owner, who buys a lot of cars, may see the probability of a bad car as a statistical risk, a hidden addition to the cost of purchase. An individual who buys small quantities of a cheap product regularly may be in a position to treat product failure as a statistical risk in the same way that a fleet owner might.

Uniformity is covered in some detail in Chapter 7. Here uniformity is considered (a) as a characteristic (or attribute) of the purchase, (b) as a characteristic of the product on offer, in a given display or shop, (c) as a characteristic of the product line, and (d) as a characteristic of the product lines within the product group (are they all much the same or is it worth searching?). The distinction between a product meeting its specifications, but being variable because there are wide specifications, and a product having tight specifications, but often not meeting them, is important in practice.

Warranties

Warranties are given to a product line or a brand as a whole, and they enable the consumer to change his view of the product line. They need not change his appreciation of the product once he has bought it, though they may lessen his annoyance if the appreciation is less than expected. On the other hand, there may be a significant pleasure from the fact that there is a warranty, and that you are covered if your new car breaks down, or even from the belief that if there is a warranty, it must be good quality. Chapter 9 considers warranties and guarantees in more detail.

Availability and location

Availability and location of the product, which do, of course, affect purchases, are also functions of the product rather than the item purchased. There is a big difference in search costs and in perception of quality between having the one item I buy as the only one in stock in one shop in town and having it as part of a big display in every grocery and supermarket.

Information and search

Information and search are also functions of the product line rather than the item purchased. Again, they have a very different impact on the consumer before and after search. Brand loyalty, desire for variety and habitual purchase strategies apply to the product line.

Brand image

Brand image is a function of the brand and the product line. It will certainly affect search and buying behaviour. It may also affect perception of quality after purchase, and it may be a quality attribute in its own right, as with designer clothes or own-brand groceries.

SELLER'S PERCEPTION OF PRODUCT

The product

The seller, unlike the buyer, gives little consideration to a single purchase, but is extremely interested in the product group and the product line. His perception of the product group is likely to be rather different. It may, for example, take into account all products produced by one process, whatever they are used for. A product line is often very closely defined, meaning the can with the '3p off' flash, but not the ordinary can. Any presentation with different marketing characteristics may be treated as a separate line, so that the seller can evaluate the success of his marketing strategy. On the other hand, a product group may be 'organic' or 'health foods' rather than 'frozen foods' or 'meat'.

Waste

The level of waste in a product line is very important in
determining its profitability (see Chapter 7). Waste in store never
reaches the consumer, so it is not a characteristic of the purchase.
Customer complaints, repairs under guarantee and arguments
with the supplier are also, in the retailer's eyes, problems with the
product line rather than individual items. All these may vary from
item to item and from consignment to consignment, so the
retailer, the multiple anyway, has a perception of the statistical
probability of these effects. From my experience of working with
retailers and manufacturers, though, this perception is usually far
from correct. For example one manufacturer was losing 17 per
cent of his turnover in loss of product, and loss of quality between
purchase and sale, without realizing it. Most retailers had only a
hazy idea of their losses on a product group like greengrocery, and
none at all of their losses on particular lines, when a little thought
and observation showed that more was wasted than was sold of
several lines.

Sells well

The knowledge that a product sells well or sells slowly, that its sales
are price responsive or not, is knowledge about the product as a
whole, not single items. This is perceived as a function of the
product, though it might be more accurately described as a statistical regularity in the behaviour of buyers *en masse*. It is not, however,
a perception of buyers.

Similarly the knowledge that most people like their apples red,
or small, or in plastic bags, is a perceived statistical regularity in the
behaviour of customers. It is not a characteristic of an apple.

Brand image

The retailer will have a completely different brand image to the
consumer. At one level he is concerned with his own problems:
delivery reliability, wastage and customer complaints with that
brand. At another he is concerned with what consumers *en masse*
think of it: does it have the image of reliability, status and so on
which is appropriate to his operation? To the consumer, of course,
all this is invisible: he does not see what is wasted, he does not

handle the complaints, and he does not have the same perceptions of status, and so on as other customers.

MEASURING THE PRODUCT

Most models of quality assume implicitly that the characteristics can be readily identified and measured at the time of manufacture and at the time of consumption, though there is usually some confusion as to whether they can be readily measured at the time of purchase. However, there are practical problems here which would have to be taken into account in a study of a real product in a real market: it is clearly wrong to build a model based on the assumption that consumers can measure the component characteristics of a product at purchase if they do not do so in fact; there is also a temptation to base a model on what can be measured easily, rather than what is important. Chapter 9 has looked at some of the changes in market structure that occur when the product quality is known only to the seller or when quality is hidden at the point of sale: in some cases this asymmetrical information can lead to the collapse of a market.

In studying a real market it is useful to have an idea of how producers, distributors and buyers measure characteristics, especially as they are likely to have different methods available to them. They are also likely to have different concepts of quality (see Chapter 1) which may mean that they measure different characteristics, that they measure them by different criteria, and they process the results differently. Consumers are likely to assess quality differently at purchase, at consumption, and in recollection – and consumers gain utility at each stage, and each stage influences future purchases.

One may distinguish between 'easy to measure', 'hard to measure', and 'hard to measure objectively, but easy to assess by eye' (like the quality of vegetables). The product may be measured by machine during manufacture, by machine in the final sorting and quality control process, or by eye. If it is measured by eye, the consumers' perception and the sorters' may not coincide. Sometimes measurement is expensive, and it may not be possible to measure the product except by actually consuming it – meaning that a quality assurance programme, controlling the manufacturing process rather than the product, is needed, or that there is destructive testing of a sample.

MEASURING ATTRIBUTES

We have set out areas where the consumer's perception of the item bought may differ from his perception of the product. In some of these areas the perception is purely subjective with little or no objective parallels.

Techniques for measurement of consumer attitudes and retailer attitudes have been developed by market researchers, and will not be covered in this book. I stress here that they must only be used where appropriate. Some constraints on analysis that may arise are as follows:

> Individuals' perceptions of a given purchase and perceptions of the product as a whole are different phenomena, and must be measured and interpreted differently.

> Individual consumers, buyers, retailers, marketers and manufacturers have different subjective perceptions of product quality, which are incommensurable.

> Linking attributes to objective quality is seldom easy. Since consumers, buyers, retailers, marketers, and manufacturers have different attributes, different objective characteristics will be appropriate.

> There may be big differences in the perceptions of buyers.

> There are big differences between perceptions of an item that has been purchased, an item on the shelf (a possible purchase), a product line and a product group. The importance of these for marketing are important. I must stress, therefore, the need to keep these concepts entirely different in empirical market research.

SOME TYPES OF CHARACTERISTIC

Throughout the literature it is usual to think of characteristics as ingredients. This is convenient, it is easy to understand and it is easy to analyse. Earlier in this chapter some types of product which did not conform to this model were described, products which were better described by what they did, what they produced, what satisfactions they produced, what their components were or what their components did, for instance. For these products characteristics have to be thought of as something quite other than ingredients.

The approach of using ingredients as characteristics is particularly attractive when the characteristics are defined so that they can be manipulated easily mathematically. It is convenient, for example, to assume that all characteristics vary continuously, and that everybody values a product more if it has more of any characteristic. In this section, some of the characteristics that do not vary in this way are considered.

Vertical and horizontal quality

The distinction between vertical and horizontal quality is often made in the literature, and most theoretical models assume vertical quality. Colour, for example, is usually a horizontal characteristic, as not everyone would agree that one colour is better than another, while the gold content of an ingot is a vertical characteristic, with more being seen as better by most consumers. The distinction causes more confusion than it avoids. It means that an objective characteristic of a product is classified as vertical or horizontal by the subjective perceptions of consumers and of those potential consumers who choose to buy something else. It is not practical to measure this perception. It is difficult to imagine a product for which one can say that all consumers value the product more the more there is of each characteristic. In practice, as one characteristic is increased, its marginal utility can be expected to fall and then become negative if it is an ingredient characteristic, so it is not vertical over the whole range of possible levels (while this may not be so obvious for a performance characteristic, most models assume ingredient characteristics). Similarly, in practice most characteristics are horizontal over some possible levels: not everybody has the same optimum level of characteristic. This is particularly clear when the product has several uses or gives several satisfactions: with the gold ingot, for example, a jeweller may prefer a harder 9 carat gold to 24 carat gold. In quality theory it is best to take it that all characteristics can be valued positively or negatively, horizontally or vertically, until this is proved not to be the case.

Critics of the hedonic/characteristics approach to quality sometimes point out that there are products which do not fit the assumption of vertical quality which is basic to the approach. The theory would suggest that two size 6 shoes were of the same utility as one size 12 shoe. The problem arises, again, because the distinction is not preserved between an individual's appraisal, and the objective physical characteristic. In the next chapter it will be shown how this example could be handled using indifference theory.

Continuous or discrete characteristics?

It is also convenient in abstract modelling to assume a continuous characteristic, where the level of characteristic can vary continuously from zero to the maximum possible. Again, this assumption is unrealistic: there are many characteristics where the variable is discrete, like the number of wheels on a motor car. Others may be continuous in principle, but discrete in practice, because of manufacturing considerations or the traditions of the industry. At the extreme there are dichotomous products where either the characteristic is there or it is not.

Filler characteristics

There are some characteristics which do not add to the enjoyment of the product. These may be fillers and makeweights, like water, which add to the volume of the product. In most theory these are ignored, and it is assumed that one can simply increase the level of some characteristics without cutting the level of others. This may be a reasonable assumption for some products, like ointments with an active ingredient of 0.5 per cent of the whole, but for many products there is a cost incurred in extracting the filler and disposing of it. It is not usually reasonable to assume that one can remove or add filler without changing the taste and the utility to the consumer, as is implied in most theory, but for some products it is, as when a more or less concentrated chemical can be added to a process. Another type of filler, or disposal, characteristic is the peel of an orange or the tin the sardines came in. The characteristic comes with the product; it does not add to utility in consumption (though it may contribute to how the product survives the distribution process); and a certain cost is incurred in disposing of the characteristic. It is not always possible to dispose of a characteristic though. One cannot remove the acid and sugar of a cooking apple to make a dessert apple. On the other hand, if one cooks dessert apples with sugar and malic acid, one gets an acceptable apple purée. This means that the product has a very different marginal utility if it is being added or removed.

Availability of product

The product may be available in continuous quantities, as petrol is readily available in fractions of a gallon, but on the other hand it may only be available in discrete amounts, one car or two. Some products like milk could conceivably be available in continuous quantities, but are in fact available in pint bottles. Some goods, too, are conceivably available as discrete items or as bulk goods but are normally marketed in packages.

This non-continuous availability is a constraint to some types of analysis. For example, it makes it very difficult to use those approaches where consuming more of a product is seen as a close substitute for eating a better product, or where two bland oranges are seen as a close substitute for one sweet one. The most important of these systems of analysis, the hedonic/characteristics approaches of Lancaster and Rosen, are discussed in the next two chapters.

Availability of information

Availability of information could be thought of as a characteristic. The fact that a product has a printed label listing its contents changes the consumers' purchase behaviour, and often does so without changing the perception of the product when it is consumed. To this extent it is a characteristic of the product line as a whole, rather than of the item purchased. However, the fact that the product is properly, or reassuringly, labelled can also change perceptions of the item, at the time of purchase, when it is consumed, or when it is remembered.

Proxy characteristics

Consumers often use proxy characteristics as an indication of quality, when the characteristics they really value are invisible. They may buy 'Scotch Beef', brown eggs, or organically-grown vegetables because they believe that the product with these characteristics will taste better: they do not value the Scotchness, the brownness or the 'organic' process at all. The proxy may be considered instead of the characteristic, or it may be used to reinforce the buyer's perception of the level of the characteristics he can observe, giving him more confidence. This may well be a rational search strategy (Chapters 4, 5, and 8). Proxy characteristics may also affect consumers' perception of the product when they consume it. In effect, the existence of a proxy characteristic implies a subjective belief that one attribute is linked to another characteristic. For many purposes, economists and marketing professionals may be justified in analysing quality as though these proxy characteristics were the ones really valued, but the analysis can be seriously misleading when, for instance, the underlying characteristics are changed, so that the taste of Scotch beef changes over time, and consumers adjust their search accordingly. A mechanical approach to quantifying consumer response, finding the statistical response to real and proxy characteristics, might find a strong market demand for these proxy characteristics, and get a very poor fit for the underlying characteristics. The risk here is that the mechanical approach double counts, taking into account *both* the real characteristics which the consumer values when the product is consumed, *and* the proxy characteristics which the consumer takes into account at the time of purchase.

Most economic theory, the hedonic/characteristics approach, for instance, ignores the possibility of proxy characteristics, and as a result, does not draw attention to the possibility of these errors arising.

The brand as a characteristic

The brand is a proxy characteristic for other characteristics, in that consumers may buy a certain brand because they believe that it is more reliable, that it tastes better, or that it has a better resale value, for instance. Chapters 4 and 5 have shown how brands can be used as a proxy characteristic to make search more efficient.

The brand can also be a proxy for a subjective attribute that does not have any corresponding physical characteristic. For example, it gives reassurance that the product is socially acceptable; it gives reassurance that you will not be considered a Philistine for liking it; it gives reassurance that the product is fashionable.

The brand label can also be an objective characteristic valued in its own right: some consumers get satisfaction from displaying the label on the designer jeans, or the GT label on a car otherwise externally indistinguishable from all other cars in the line.

For these reasons, consumers may be willing to pay more for a branded good, and may be more likely to buy it regularly.

However, since brands are almost always proxy characteristics, it follows that nearly all analyses taking into account both brand and characteristics will involve double counting, and will introduce biases. For example, any product with the brand Weight Watchers can be expected to be low in calories, so a regression with both the brand and the calories will produce odd results. Products with the brand names Rolls Royce, St Michael and Boots are expected to have certain levels of characteristic, so any analysis with level of characteristic and brand will double count. It will also be extremely difficult to separate the value of the brand as a brand from the value of the brand as a proxy characteristic.

Price as a characteristic

Price is also a proxy characteristic in some circumstances, where consumers judge quality by price (see Chapter 10). Here, since both price and characteristics will both be included in any analysis, some double counting is inevitable.

Price as an objective characteristic is usually valued negatively, as a cost. It is sometimes valued positively, when, for instance, a consumer gets satisfaction from 'being able to afford a high price' or 'being able to afford the best' in which case it is a proxy for an attribute which has no objective characteristic. It may also be used as an indicator of the quality of the product, or the level of a characteristic, to save on search, in which case it is a proxy for other characteristics, in the same way that 'Scotch beef' is.

'Value for money' also appears to have a meaning a bit beyond that of making the optimum purchase. There is a certain temptation to buy a product that is obviously a great bargain, even if it is not the quality you want to buy, and even if you would be embarrassed if someone gave it to you as a gift.

THE PRICE OF A CHARACTERISTIC AND ITS SUPPLY

Much of the literature on quality makes use of a 'hedonic' price (the price of a characteristic), or even of a supply function for a characteristic. If one is to talk of a price for a characteristic, one must first conceive of a market in which that characteristic can be traded. There is, for example, a big difference between saying that the world supply of phosphates affects the price of a fertilizer mix with phosphates as an ingredient, and saying that, on average, a

4-bedroom house in my suburb costs £5,000 more than a 3-bedroom house. Chapter 16 looks at the theory of hedonic prices and shows its limitations.

Similarly, talking of a supply function for a characteristic requires a concept of how the supply of a single characteristic can be increased and at what cost. There is a difference between the supply of carrots of different grades, which can only be changed by adopting new production methods in the long run, the supply of curry powder with different levels of chilli powder, which is a matter of increasing one ingredient, and the supply of cars with a different engine capacity. Some sorting models, for example, assume that there are equal supplies of all qualities before the sorting process, others that the supply is normally distributed: in both cases, the supply of a blended or packaged product is changed by the sorting process. Some models, especially the ingredient models, assume that the supply of a characteristic is perfectly elastic. The difficulties of deriving supply functions for characteristics are discussed in Chapter 16.

BUNDLES AND GROUPINGS

In basic economic theory two dimensions are taken into account, price and quality. Bringing in one quality aspect, such as the size of the apple, brings in a third dimension, and three-dimensional graphs are required. Colour, variety, bruising, shape and so on are all quality aspects, and each introduces another dimension to the analysis. It would be impossible for the consumer to take into account all the possible characteristics in making a decision on such a multi-characteristic surface, for reasons which will be elaborated on in Chapter 15. Here it will be suggested that consumers bundle together characteristics into broader groupings to make the data manageable.

For example, the food scientist looking at onions is concerned with how the propenecysteine sulphoxide in the onion reacts with the enzyme alliinase to produce the propenesulphenic acid content, which breaks down to form either propanethyl oxide, which makes the eyes water, or thiosulphinate, which gives the raw onion smell, and which turns in the frying process to the sweeter smell of bispropenyl disulphide.[5] At this stage some product-based quality analysis may be appropriate. One step later in the chain, all these characteristics and reactions are bundled into two, pungency and flavour, as the plant breeder and agronomist try to develop onions for different markets, while at the same time developing characteristics in other characteristic groupings like 'keeping quality' (such as thin necks and many skins) or appearance. The consumer may rank flavour as good or bad, or even take it for granted, and buy mild, attractive, Spanish onions for salads, and the more pungent, brown-skinned varieties for cooking.

What appears to be happening is that there is a combination of characteristics into another characteristic, which may later be combined into yet another characteristic. Eventually the consumer values a single characteristic, taste, rather than a multitude of organic sulphur compounds. This alone is enough to invalidate the idea that market transparency, with information systems using the same characteristics through the marketing chain, is a Good Thing.

However, at this level there are still some broad characteristic groupings which are extremely important to anyone planning a marketing or production strategy. It seems likely, for example, that there are several characteristic bundles like taste, texture and appearance, which are closely related in the consumer's mind, and which may be substitutes for a particular decision. Similarly, there may be matters of environmental concern which influence the consumer's purchase decision – CFCs, the greenhouse effect, pollution. Again they are closely related to each other, but only distantly related to characteristic in other groupings, such as taste.[6]

The characteristic bundles cannot be expected to be the same for different products. For a consumer durable like a motor car, for instance, several new bundles come into play. There are a lot of characteristics that relate to the durability of a car, such as resistance to rust, engineering design, manufacturing care, springing, and so on and it is convenient to lump them together under the heading of durability. They could, of course, be classified differently; there will be overlaps between durability and reliability or performance, for instance. At the same time, characteristics affecting one characteristic grouping frequently affect others, positively or negatively. The paint job that reduces rust affects aesthetic quality and the springing that improves durability gives a rough ride.

Why is it necessary to talk in terms of characteristic groupings at all, rather than just deal with the characteristics themselves? It has been found that when consumers are concerned about safety, for instance, there are several characteristics of a product that can be marketed as safety. Equally it has been found that when a product is excellent in some characteristics groupings, it is possible to establish a competitor which outperforms it on another dimension, which may be of more concern to one segment of the market. The Japanese entered the photocopy market with machines that did not try to perform as many fancy functions as the market leaders, but which scored higher on another grouping, reliability. Foods may compete on nutritional value, on flavour or on such factors as '3p off' flashes. A great deal of competitive advantage can be obtained by rethinking the nature of the market and the nature of the groupings in which there is quality competition.

For this discussion I have taken the following characteristics groupings, safety, performance, aesthetics, features, environment, price, value for money, durability and confidence. The groupings are arbitrary, they will not be equally applicable to all products, and there will be some overlaps.

SAFETY

Safety is the fundamental grouping with food. If the consumers do not believe that a product has a certain minimum level of safety they will not buy it, and legal minimum safety levels may be necessary to ensure that a market exists at all (see Chapter 9). There may be a sharp divergence between actual and perceived safety, with, for example, people forced to eat unhygienic food deluding themselves that it is safe (cognitive dissonance) or, at the other extreme, people being far more worried about the danger of salmonella in eggs than the danger of cholesterol.

The distributor does not want to handle unsafe products, not so much because of the damages payable to a consumer who falls sick, but because of the damage to reputation and sales if he sells corned beef that spreads typhoid, for example. There is also a direct personal satisfaction to the seller in knowing that consumers get safe products and that the people manufacturing or handling the product are not at risk. This may seem quaint in modern Britain, but it was the influence of the Victorian Quakers and nonconformists that created today's retail industry, because they refused to bargain as this involves telling lies, and instead quoted what they thought was a fair price, and because they refused to sell adulterated goods. This cannot be put down to enlightened self-interest: the Quaker chocolate manufacturers stopped buying cocoa from Fernando Po, which produced nearly all the world's supplies, when the atrocities on the plantations there were exposed at the turn of the century, and they went through a very rough time trying to find alternative supplies until they managed to establish the Ghanaian industry.

It appears that once a certain minimum level of safety is achieved, the consumer is prepared to pay relatively little for more safety, and starts to look for quality on other groupings. With aeroplane travel, for instance, most people would assume that all the major western airlines operate to the same standards. Selling an airline on safety is apparently less productive than selling it on comfort, and indeed it may raise unpleasant thoughts and be counterproductive.

This is not to say that safety standards remain constant. From time to time there may be a sudden burst of consumer awareness followed by a sudden improvement in safety and, one might guess, a determination by manufacturers not to have the worst safety record. This happened with motor cars in the 1960s.

The increasing preoccupation with E numbers, wholefood and fibre could be taken as being a progression in the same safety grouping, with minor issues taking over as major issues seem to be under control. There are other groupings they might come into, ecological, features, and so on, and I have no doubt that marketing professionals are analysing these in some detail right now.

Performance

Another basic quality grouping is performance: how well does the product do its job? Does a stereo give good sound? Does a vacuum cleaner pick up dirt? Does a breakfast cereal give energy? Do fish and chips give healthy nutrition? These performance concepts are not analogous when comparing a stereo with fish and chips, but then who wants to? Good sound is an excellent measure of performance when comparing different stereos, and that is what matters.

With food one might require that it performs by providing a tasty, satisfying meal. Energy is very important to the poor, but the rich are looking for the maximum of other characteristics and the minimum of calories. Performance is not an absolute; it is related to the job in hand. The use of salmon for fish cakes or new potatoes for mash does not mean that quality is very high in the performance grouping, just because expensive 'high quality' (in the product-based concept) ingredients are used. This means that a ranking of quality in terms of one characteristic may not be related to performance quality: a 60-watt bulb is too small for a reading lamp, while a 200-watt bulb is too big. A pair of size 9 shoes is too small, size 12 too big.

The distributor's concept of quality is based very much on performance, though the definitions of performance are in terms of speed of turnover, waste, handling problems, pilferage, and so on.

Again, there is a sense in which performance is of key importance up to a certain level, but after this other groupings come into play, with improved performance adding relatively little to perceived quality, and other aspects coming into prominence.

Aesthetics

Some goods like pictures and flowers are valued mainly on the aesthetics grouping, so much so that aesthetics is the performance grouping. For most food products, aesthetics, including factors like taste, smell, texture and even sound (Snap! Crackle! Pop!), are a very basic quality grouping. Most foods are bought because they produce some purely aesthetic satisfaction, and mushrooms, for instance, produce no other.[7]

When one is dealing with consumer durables it may be worth separating out the aesthetic benefits of the good sound quality produced by a stereo (performance) and its appearance (aesthetics).

Here again, the producer and distributor may be expected to get a direct personal benefit from producing and handling beautiful things, and perhaps a spin-off effect with a beautiful shop attracting customers.

Features

Features are the less important measures of quality which do not determine a product's safety or its ability to do its job, but which do influence sales, the free drink on the aeroplane, for instance. It is not always clear what is a feature and what is a safety, performance or aesthetic factor.

It appears likely that once a product has met basic safety and performance criteria, features may be an easier and cheaper way to compete than improved quality, and indeed it may be the only way to distinguish products. Consumers may use features as tie-breakers for otherwise identical products.

It is also argued that features are used to indicate that a product is aimed at one market segment rather than another. A basic product like a motor car can be given one set of features for the family car market, another for the speed crazy, another for those wanting luxury and so on. The features may not be much used, and may not even give much utility, but they indicate to the buyer that the product is aimed at him.

Environment

Ecological aspects may be considered as a different characteristic grouping, partly because they have recently become so important that it would be unwise to ignore them. They are, however, dif-ferent in a clearer way than most: they have very limited effect on the buyer or user directly. Whether or not I use shaving cream with a CFC propellant will have no measurable effect on the total amount of CFCs in circulation, and I will be dead long before the gap in the ozone layer means any more than my having to wear a hat on a sunny day. I, as a buyer, am taking a product which may give less satisfaction in use (it doesn't) to confer a benefit on others (and, of course, to acquire some of the satisfactions of good citizenship including self-righteousness).

The ecologically-minded are concerned with damage to the environment from the manufacture, use and disposal of the pro-duct. Similarly, damage to the health of workers is taken into consideration. Political concerns, consumerism and animal rights concerns would be in the same grouping.

Manufacturers and distributors are careful not to be branded as polluters in case they lose sales, but no doubt they too get a direct personal satisfaction from the protection of the environment.

Price

Price, together with variants like discounts, special offers and so on, can be thought of as a characteristic grouping. Chapters 4, 5, 8 and 9 examined how far search cost, location and so on can be taken to be in the same group.

Value for money

Value for money is another characteristic, or rather attribute, grouping on which quality can be measured. At the simplest we may take the situation where a buyer has a family of indifference surfaces between price and quality and compares them with the price curve.[8] The good and bad value for money lines are the ones for which the indifference curve and the price curve are furthest apart. If, for example, the buyer is indifferent between 1lb Grade 1 tomatoes and 2lbs Grade 3, then Grade 1 are good value, as long as they cost less than three times as much per pound.[9] This means that value for money is a composite of other groupings such as price and performance.

There is an implicit assumption here that a consumer has already decided to buy tomatoes and not a camera or oranges. While one lot of tomatoes may be better than another, tomatoes in general may not be. It may well be true that once he has decided to buy a camera nothing else comes into his calculations.

How exactly does one define value for money? In one sense one can talk of determining the best buy for each of the 'products' of standard economics, and then deciding the best buy of the different qualities within that market. In another sense, though, I may recognize that tomatoes in one shop are good value for money, even though I have no intention of buying them. Here, perhaps, there is a more dispassionate feeling that if I were to search I would not find that quality at that price very easily. Similarly, tomatoes may be particularly good value in August, in the sense that they would be three times as expensive in December, but still be less attractive than lettuce.

There are three separate strains in this. First, good value for money implies the best combination of quality and price on the market, economic man at his simplest. Second, the man who wants to minimize regret, or who does not like the feeling that he has been taken for a sucker, wants to know that he did not pay much more for it than everyone else. Third, most people want something that is both good value for money and of at least a certain quality level.

Durability

When one talks of consumer durables instead of a product like food which is used once only, other factors come into play. The characteristic grouping durability probably includes such factors as reliability in operation, and quality of after-sales service and availability of spares. The better all these are, the longer the durable product will give service. To some considerable extent, durability may be seen as performance: the longer the product lasts, the more service it gives.[10]

Confidence

Those characteristics which give a buyer confidence in his purchase might be thought of as a characteristic grouping. It is important to buyers that they do not face an unacceptable risk of getting poor quality by mistake, because of hidden defects. It is important that they can buy an unfamiliar product, and know that it is good value for money, even though they are unable to assess this themselves. It is important to many that they do not feel that someone has taken them for a sucker, making them pay far more than most people did. It is important to minimize regret. The marketing package that scores heavily on this characteristic grouping is likely to be extremely complex, taking into account factors like labelling, guarantees, reputation of store and so on.

Marks and Spencer, for example, have cashed in on this by providing assurances of value for money in several senses. There is an assurance that the price for a line is reasonable, though one could probably find better goods cheaper, after searching. There is an assurance that because of both quality control and guarantees no one item in a line is of particularly low value for money. At the same time there is the knowledge that the shop is targeted fairly heavily at the middle classes, and that if you are wearing Marks and Spencer clothes you are acceptably dressed when you are moving among such people, and there is the assurance that in some sense the tomatoes, oranges, shirts and pot plants on sale all offer the same value for money and the same acceptability. Interestingly, the same acceptability seems to vary from cheap and durable underwear, through less cheap clothes to rather expensive food.

CONCLUSION

This chapter has set out some basic concepts that are needed to analyse the quality required by consumers and buyers, and to analyse the quality that a given product offers. If a realistic market analysis is to be carried out, the researcher must be aware of the different types of quality characteristic, different ways in which they may be combined, and the difference between subjective attribute and objective characteristic, as well as the pitfalls that arise from double counting and overlaps. The analysis is not simple or straightforward, and requires careful attention to detail, but then quality is not simple or straightforward, and the very poor success rate of new product launches shows how easy it is to get things wrong.

The many types of characteristics, the overlaps and double counting, and the difference between objective and subjective perceptions of quality, mean that mechanistic models of quality will certainly get the wrong answer. Any useful model must be built up for the product being examined, and must take into account the characteristics and attributes relevant to that product at that level in the marketing chain.

Chapter 15

Errors in characteristics theory[1]

INTRODUCTION

This chapter covers the tradition of economics sometimes referred to as the 'characteristics approach' and sometimes included in 'hedonic theory'. This is a tradition that draws on the seminal work of Rosen (1974) and Lancaster (1966, 1971, 1979). As virtually all traditions of quality economics make use of characteristics, it is confusing to refer to one tradition alone by this name, and I shall refer instead to the hedonic approach.[2] There is a substantial literature on this approach to quality – some 566 mainstream citations in the last five years for the basic papers by Lancaster and Rosen. The approach is by now so well established that it is diffused through marketing and marketing economics, to the extent that the basic papers are often not cited, and that authors appear to rest their papers on the concepts without realizing that they are doing so.

In this chapter some of the basic concepts underlying the programme, the fundamental assumptions on indifference curves and utility which underlie the whole theoretical structure, will be challenged. In the next chapter another set of fundamental assumptions, on hedonic prices, will be challenged. As the discussion proceeds, it will become increasingly clear that the concepts that have already been presented in this book effectively limit the hedonic approach so much that even if the fundamental logic had been correct, the theory would have had virtually no practical application.

The chapter is not going to review the work done on the subject over the years, or examine in detail the successes and failures of various workers in the field. Instead, it is going to examine the basic assumptions on which *all* these papers are based, assumptions which are *fundamental* to all their analysis and conclusions. The first question to be asked is whether the assumptions are correct. The second is whether the simplifying assumptions are too restrictive. Obviously, every economic theory has to make some simplifying assumptions, or it would be too complicated to use. However, by definition, each simplifying assumption means that there are fewer real situations that the analysis can apply to. By definition, too, each explicit assumption introduces a host of implicit assumptions: in previous chapters, for instance, it has been shown that the assumption of full information implies a lot about the amount of labelling, method of purchase, market structure, and so on, and raises questions like 'Does the buyer have full information about each item, each consignment or the product line as a whole?', 'Can he select out the best item in a grade or does he get a random selection?' A good economic theory is one which uses simplifying assumptions which make analysis easier, but which do not restrict the possible application too much. A bad economic theory can make one or two simplifying assumptions which do little to make the analysis easier, but which make the theory have no practical application at all. It is like assuming that the moon is made of green cheese: it certainly makes the astronomy easier, but at what cost in applicability? There are other approaches to quality apart from the hedonic one, so there is no reason why we should stick with one which can be shown to be wrong.

THE SHAPE OF INDIFFERENCE CURVES

The hedonic approach analyses the individual's choice of product quality. Product quality is defined purely in terms of the objective characteristics that the product has. The fundamental principle is that the optimal quality for an individual is one where the individual's outlay curve is at a tangent to the indifference curve between two characteristics of a product. This is very close to the argument that with the traditional indifference curves between two goods (rather than two characteristics of a single good), the buyer's optimum choice was one where the outlay curve was a tangent to the indifference curve between the two goods: the argument closely follows that used in traditional, two-good, indifference theory.

An indifference curve for two goods is drawn on a graph with quantity of one good on one axis and quantity of the other on the other axis and is a curve joining combinations of two goods that a buyer is indifferent between. In hedonic theory, the figures have level of characteristic instead of level of good as the axes. The indifference curves are assumed to be the same shape as two-good indifference curves, and the same assumptions are made that the indifference curves are strictly convex to the origin, with the usual assumptions of transitivity, completeness, continuity, non-saturation and all characteristics being positively desired.[3] The resulting set of indifference curves, Figure 15.1, looks just like those for a two-good product in a microeconomics textbook.

In traditional, two-good, indifference analysis, one is dealing with two quite different goods consumed separately, postage stamps and butter perhaps, so this means that the amount of butter consumed does not change the utility produced by the stamps. In quality analysis we are concerned with the utility when the characteristics are consumed together.

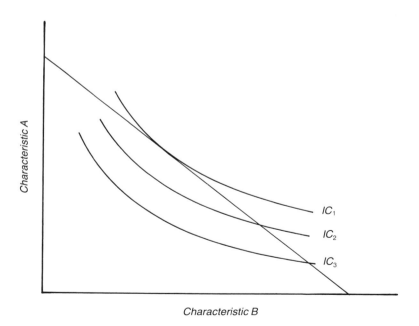

Characteristic B

Figure 15.1

One way is for the product to be consumed as a complete whole: one cannot consume an orange without consuming its sweetness characteristic and its acidity characteristic. If the level of its acid changes, this changes the utility that the sweetness produces.[4] A consumer does not get the same satisfaction from two bland, low acid, oranges as from one acid orange (unless one juices them, in which case the product is different).

A second way of consuming the product is to buy the characteristics separately and join them together to make a product. More realistically, one can buy a product which is a mix of characteristics and combine it with another mix of characteristics to produce a combined product which has a third mix of characteristics. This is common enough with intermediate goods, with manufacturers blending coffee, fertilizer or the ingredients of soap, to make an end product with the desired mix of characteristics. Consumers purchase food as products with different characteristics, and combine them by cooking or preparation to make a different product. A salad, for example, is a mix of ingredients, which has a greater value than its constituents taken separately (why else would anyone make a salad?).[5] If one takes into account the complexities of consumption discussed in earlier chapters, the analysis becomes impossibly complicated, so hedonic theory assumes (usually implicitly) that

1 The buyer is the consumer. There is no discrepancy between the buyer's and the consumer's preferences (see Chapter 1 and Chapter 4 for the opposite view).
2 The cooking or preparation process is purely mixing, so a good and a bad cook produce identical end products.
3 The ingredients for a meal are consumed at the same moment they are bought. There is no possibility of storage or of a bag of potatoes bought today being eaten in several meals over the next month (see Chapter 13 for the opposite view).
4 The indifference curve at the time of purchase is identical to that at the time of consumption and the time of recollection. This assumes away changing perceptions, and, at the extreme, the possibility that a homemaker buying vegetables in a supermarket may not have decided what meal she is going to serve them in.
5 There is only a single end use possible for the product or characteristic.

6 Characteristics are the same as attributes: every consumer is perfectly informed.

There are not a lot of products for which these simplifying assumptions are realistic.

The question now asked is 'Given the fact that the different characteristics of a product are necessarily consumed together, while the two products of traditional, two-good, indifference theory are normally consumed separately, what is the effect on the shape of the indifference curves?' This question is not tackled in the literature.

The bull's eye

One example of a quality indifference curve is given in Figure 15.2.* This is a bull's eye, a target. The centre is the combination of the two characteristics that produces the greatest satisfaction. If one moves away from the centre point, increasing or reducing the level of Characteristic A, the product gives less utility. This set of indifference curves is a good approximation to the indifference surface between many pairs of characteristics in a great many products. For example, it would apply with sweetness and acidity in oranges, salt and vinegar in crisps, length and width in shoe sizes (so size 12 is not twice as good as size 6). This shape of indifference curve is assumed away in hedonic theory.

It is argued here that some such relationship is normal when we are dealing with aesthetics – taste, touch, beauty, scent and music. In all these it is the balance between the elements that counts, not the level of characteristic. It cannot be argued, as the hedonic models based on the indifference curves in Figure 15.1 *must* imply, that Mozart's clarinet quintet would have been perhaps 20 per cent better if it was a sextet, or that increasing the level of violets in a scent must improve that scent.

It is clear from Figure 15.2 that the normal indifference curve analysis cannot apply here: the assumptions necessary for calculation of substitution effects and maxima do not hold. In particular, the indifference curves are not convex to the origin and there is saturation. As the analysis proceeds it will become increasingly

---

* This is for unit quantity. The indifference curves are contours of a third dimension, utility, so in effect a three-dimensional surface is being presented in two dimensions. The area of peak utility is shaded, for emphasis, and because buyers may be indifferent between points near the peak.

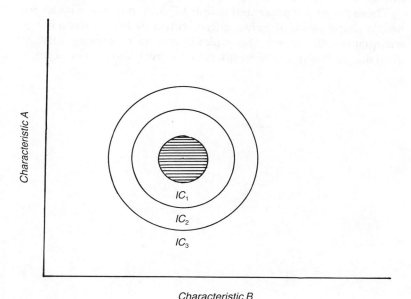

Figure 15.2

clear that the shape of indifference curves does not meet any of the assumptions made by hedonic theory. In the next chapter it will be shown that the price and cost assumptions are also questionable.

Quantity

Figure 15.2 deals with unit quantity of a product. To put in a quantity variable (number of units rather than size of units in this case) another dimension has to be introduced and this is done in Figure 15.3. The bull's eye has been shown at 1, 2 and 3 units. If we were talking instead of an infinitely divisible product like petrol, any quantity would be consumed, and there would be a continuous surface joining the bulls' eyes (and here the distinction between number of units and size of units falls away). Figure 15.4 shows one such surface, where the consumer is indifferent between one unit of the best quality, two of the next best and three of the third quality. Sometimes, of course, no quantity of third rate quality can substitute for one unit of top quality.

These curves are presented mainly to show that even with a very simple shape of indifference curve, with only two characteristics and quantity, the degree of complexity very soon becomes difficult to manage. If the other indifference curves shown below were

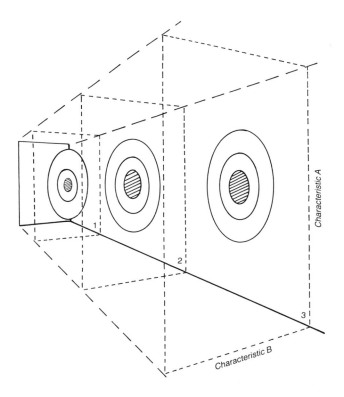

Figure 15.3

used, or if there were more than two characteristics, it must be asked whether the analysis would be manageable at all.

Satiation

The assumption of non-satiation is important in hedonic theory, so its implications will be examined here. It will be shown that

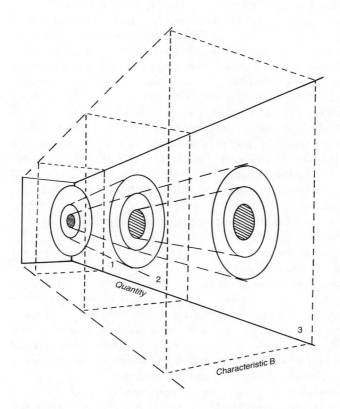

Figure 15.4

there are five distinct ways of getting more of a characteristic, and that each of these can lead to a different type of satiation – these are hopelessly confused in the literature with the result that the practical implications are not understood.[6] The ways of increasing the level of characteristic A consumed are:

1 Consuming more of the identical product. The satiation that follows is that of eating a third helping of turkey at the same sitting: there is eventually a negative utility from further intake. Figure 15.5 shows this situation, with the consumer being somewhat more likely to have a third helping if the quality is excellent.

2 Consuming the same number of units of a product which is more concentrated – having more of each of the products in the same proportion. The satiation is similar. However, the increased concentration usually implies that one has removed a bulk, or filler, characteristic like water, which is not itself valued by the consumer. The reduced bulk may mean that it is physically easier to increase consumption, eating vitamin pills instead of food, for instance. The increased concentration may also alter the palatability of the product.

3 Consuming the same number of units but switching to a product which is identical except that it has more of characteristic A. The satiation here comes from increasing the amount of chilli powder in the curry, while keeping all other characteristics constant. Doubling the quantity of chilli in a very mild curry may improve the curry, while doubling the quantity of curry will cause satiation, but if a curry is already hot, doubling the amount of chilli powder, may cause more satiation than doubling the quantity of curry.

   Generally, one may expect a different response curve when increasing the quantity of a single characteristic and when increasing the quantity of several characteristics at the same time, adding a balanced curry powder instead of chili powder for instance. For many products it is only possible to add one characteristic, like the potatoes in a stew, by reducing the quantity of other characteristics, so it is implied here that the proportion of other characteristics remains constant. Figure 15.2 is appropriate for this type of satiation.

4 Consuming a different mix of products, so that the total amount of characteristic A consumed is increased, while the total level of other characteristics is increased. This means

consuming more of products with a high level of characteristic A and less of those with a low level. This is seldom done except for intermediate products like pig food or coffee. This example is very demanding in its assumptions: for example, if it is used to calculate a least cost diet, it assumes that consumers are indifferent between the protein in beef and the protein in potatoes. Conceivably, if the switch in diet did not change flavour, texture, aroma and appearance (and pigs have preferences as do the humans who buy pig food) the satiation effects would be like that in the previous paragraph.

5 Consuming more of the product over time leads to a different sort of satiation, which has been discussed in Chapter 13. The hedonic approach assumes away the time dimension.

Each of these different ways of increasing the consumption of characteristic A can be expected to change utility in different ways, so they will each produce their own set of indifference curves and will each produce their own type and level of satiation. None, of course, correspond to Figure 15.1, the template of hedonic theory.

One quality at a time?

It is convenient to assume that consumers buy only one quality at a time, possibly buying Class 1 if a single unit is bought, Class 2 if two units are bought, and Class 3 if several units are bought, and Figures 15.3, 15.4, and 15.5 are drawn up on these assumptions. In the real world this assumption cannot always be made. For example, someone may buy a large family car if he is buying a single car for family use. If he then decides to buy a second car, he may decide on a small, traffic-friendly car for going to work. If, on the other hand, he buys two cars at the same time, rather than buying one as a supplement to another, he may buy a sports car, and a smallish family car. Similarly, someone shopping for clothes is unlikely to buy several identical dresses. Indeed the fact that consumers often buy only one quality at a time does not imply that they dislike diversity, as sometimes argued,[7] but rather that consumers like diversity so much that they will buy two products, apples and pears, on one occasion, rather than two qualities of one product. Over time they may buy different qualities of one product. The importance of this time dimension was shown in Chapter 13.

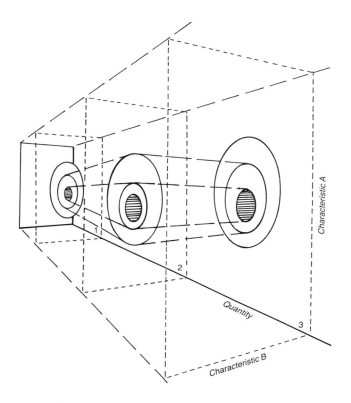

Figure 15.5

These possibilities are important for practical marketing, but a very large number of complex diagrams would be needed to analyse the indifference surfaces for someone buying a variable product like clothes or shoes, for instance.

Milk and kerosene

Traditional, two-good, indifference curve analysis assumes that two goods, say milk and kerosene, will be consumed separately. In quality theory, the assumption *must* be that milk and kerosene are two characteristics of a single product, so they are consumed together. The two products each have their utility when consumed separately, the milk being drunk, the kerosene used for a lamp for instance, so traditional indifference curve analysis is appropriate. When the two are combined to produce a single product, that product is useless. This is shown in Figure 15.6. Here the buyer is indifferent between one unit which is 100 per cent milk and one unit which is 100 per cent kerosene, so the indifference curve is two points, one on each axis. At all other points the mixture is equally revolting to drink, or equally clogging for the lamp, so all fall on the same indifference surface. This surface has nothing in common with that of Figure 15.1.

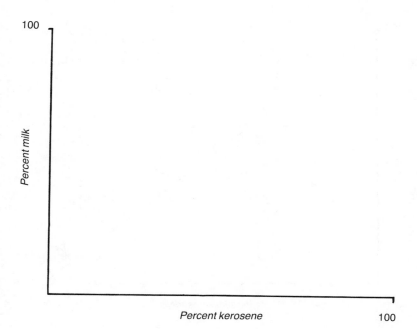

Percent kerosene   100

Figure 15.6

In Figure 15.7 the assumptions are relaxed slightly. The consumer will accept a very little milk in the kerosene, and some kerosene in the milk. The line between the 100 per cent points shows all possible combinations of the two that can exist: 70:30, 50:50, 33:67, and so on so it is the product possibility curve for a product consisting of these two characteristics alone. If other characteristics were taken into account, other dimensions would be needed.

It can be argued that indifference curves like this exist for virtually every product. There is always a characteristic like dioxin content, level of cholera bacteria, water in the brake fluid, and so on, where the product is only acceptable where the level is within strict limits, and where the consumer is indifferent between all other (unacceptable) mixes.

With yes/no characteristics, there are only two possible levels to go on the curve. In one sense, perhaps, an indifference surface consisting of just four points exists between left foot/right foot and lace-up/slip-on for shoes.

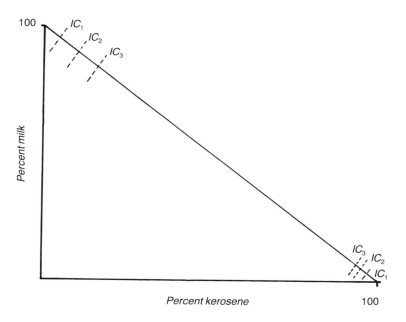

Figure 15.7

Multiple peaks

In two-good indifference analysis there is a single point which gives maximum utility, and by assumption it is not possible to have two or more such peaks scattered round the graph. In hedonic theory it has been assumed that the same applies, and the theory depends on consumers choosing combinations of characteristic which give this one single maximum utility for a given outlay. However, these assumptions are totally unreal. I like Laxton Superb apples, which are moderate in sugar and acid content, but I also like Bramley cooking apples which are very high in both acid and sugar, but I do not like the intermediate apples which are no good as either cookers or eaters. This is shown in Figure 15.8.

These multiple peaks are not just a matter of personal peculiarity. For example, the laws of physics determine that if one plots the superconductivity contours as indifference curves (a product

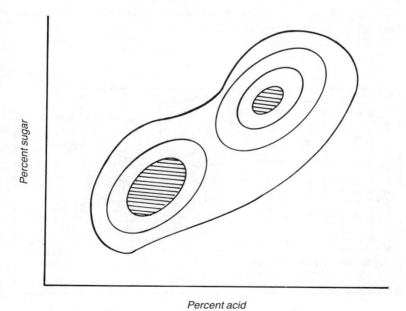

Percent acid

Figure 15.8

with a high superconductivity temperature is more valuable)
against the yttrium content and lead content of a superconductor,
one gets two peaks (Figure 15.9). One would be indifferent
between points on the 78K contour on the main mountain and the
separate 78K peak – so one could choose on such factors as price
and reliability, and here it seems that a slight error in
manufacturing would cause a sharper fall from the 78K peak than
from the ridge. Similarly, the combinations of two notes which
produce a chord or a discord, produce multiple peaks of
satisfaction (chords) for reasons determined by the laws of physics
rather than just personal preference.

Convex curves

Two-good analysis and hedonic theory both assume that all curves
are strictly convex to the origin, but it has been shown above that
while they may be convex for some parts of the curve, they are
unlikely to be for the whole of the curve. Figure 15.10 shows a
common situation with industrial raw materials where the value
falls off sharply with the level of impurity.

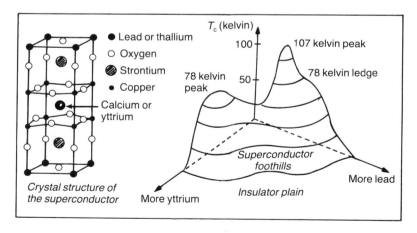

Figure 15.9 Topography of a superconductor
Source: Emsley (1990)

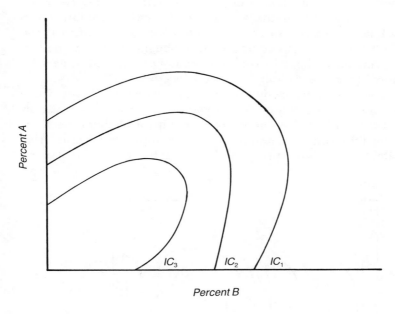

Figure 15.10

Other shapes

There is an enormous range of possible shapes of indifference curves for common products. Figure 15.11, for example, was derived from a market research study examining the optimum level of tea and sugar in iced tea.[8] This is only very roughly equivalent to an indifference curve under perfect knowledge: market research studies do not, of course, attempt to meet utility theory's definitional requirements for an indifference curve. The study asked respondents to compare tea with different levels of sugar and tea: water, lemon and colouring were held constant. They made preference judgements on sixteen alternatives, pair by pair, judging (a) similarity, (b) preference, (c) strength of preference, (d) whether they would prefer more or less sugar, and (e) whether they would prefer more or less tea. It took three to four hours to examine each respondent (and it is assumed that their tastes remained constant over this period). A SYMAP contour mapping

routine analysed the data, estimating the height (preference) of
each point as a function of the level and trend of the surrounding
points.[9] If the requirements of revealed preference utility theory
had been adhered to and the only information obtained was
whether or not the product had been bought, instead of the rich
information of these five complex questions on sixteen choices, far
more observations would have been necessary.

The curves here are quite unlike those of hedonic theory. There
is almost no convexity of curves to be seen. Increasing the quantity
of tea from 0 to 6 has no effect on utility for medium sweet tea:
indeed this consumer seems to be quite happy with anything from
water to moderately strong tea as long as it has five spoons of sugar.

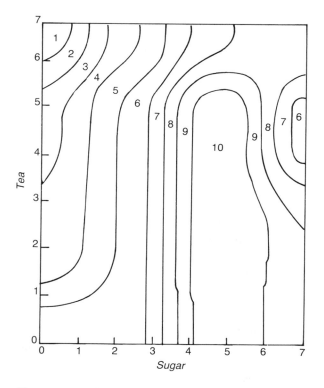

Figure 15.11 Symap approximation to preference surface for subject
number 1

Source: Huber (1975)

In Figure 15.12, the situation is shown where one unit of characteristic A (negatively valued) exactly counteracts one unit of characteristic B. The neutral indifference curve passes through the origin at 45°.

Three characteristics models

So far it has been assumed that a product has only two characteristics, and with indifference curves being the contours of a utility surface, it has been possible to present it in two dimensions, or in three if quantity purchased is taken into account. For a third characteristic to be considered, another dimension must be introduced. Figure 15.13 shows such an indifference curve, for a three characteristic item with a single item being bought. The indifference surface between any two characteristics is the bull's eye of Figure 15.2. Accordingly the three characteristic indifference surface is likely to be like an onion, a ball with layer upon layer of indifference surfaces one upon the other. Where the axes cut the

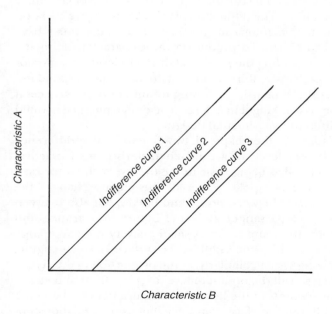

Figure 15.12

onion, it shows the bull's eye. This indifference surface has the preferred quality being one where the consumer gets a moderate level of all three characteristics.

The shape becomes extremely complex when an indifference curve between one pair of characteristics is like Figure 15.9 and that between another pair is like Figure 15.11. If a quantity dimension is added the shape becomes even harder to conceive.

How can such a surface be mapped? One would have to take several levels of one characteristic and map the indifference surfaces of the other two characteristics at this level to get cross-sections. It cannot be assumed that, because an indifference curve between characteristics A and B is of one shape at one particular level of C, that it will be of anything like the same shape at another level of C. For every level of C there will be a different indifference curve between A and B. Similarly, when four characteristics exist, each level of D will produce another indifference surface between A, B and C. The estimates of two-dimensional indifference surfaces between A and B at each level of C could then be used to estimate the surface as a whole. Indifference theory requires that the indifference surface should be calculated for a single individual, rather than at market level. The difficulties of calculating Figure 15.11 on the basis of taste tests comparing possible tea and sugar mixes have been described above. To produce a three-characteristic model would require repeating the process at different levels of lemon or of colour – perhaps a thirty-hour test for a single respondent. Adding a quantity dimension, allowing for different preferences if the consumer is drinking it in a demi-tasse or in a pint glass, would require a different experimental design.

This variation in the shape of two-dimensional indifference curves at different levels of a third characteristic is of practical importance, as well as being basic to the theory. With motor cars, for instance, increasing the power of the engine changes the indifference surface between power and brakes, but also between roadholding and passenger capacity, luxury appearance and sporting appearance, and so on. A small delivery van and a large truck do not have the same indifference surface between engine, tyres and braking system. Similarly, as the proportion of dried fruit in a cake rises, so will the optimum level of spice, flour and eggs.

There are attempts in the hedonic literature to describe multi-attribute indifference surfaces, but since they assume relationships like that in Figure 15.1 for all pairs of characteristics, it is difficult

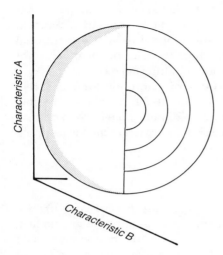

Figure 15.13a 'Onion' indifference surface, segmented to show higher indifference surfaces

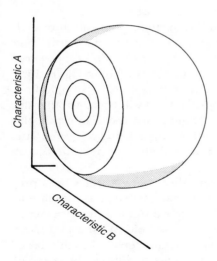

Figure 15.13b 'Onion' indifference surface, showing 'bull's eye' where axis cuts indifference surface

to see what application they can have to any real good. There is a safety element in nearly all goods, for instance, so a curve like that in Figure 15.6 or 15.7 would be expected for some characteristics. It is difficult to take a mathematical model of an n-dimensional indifference surface seriously, when the author clearly cannot construct a realistic two-dimensional indifference curve.

Given the practical difficulties of mapping even a three-characteristic indifference curve, and the lack of any credible mathematical models for a realistic n-dimensional curve, one may ask whether this hedonic characteristic approach to quality mapping can have any practical application.

Applicability

Hedonic theory depends on a small number of very precise assumptions on indifference curves. These assumptions are explicit, and if the assumptions do not hold, the theory collapses. The theory assumes that *all* indifference curves are like those in Figure 15.1, strictly convex to the origin, with assumptions of transitivity, completeness, continuity, non-saturation and all characteristics positively desired. The assumption must apply to *all* indifference curves between *any* two characteristics (a) at any level of quantity, and (b) at any level of any other characteristic.

If this is not so, then all the utility maximization conditions fall away. One cannot talk of the optimal purchase being at the one point where an outlay curve is tangential to an indifference curve in Figures 15.2 to 15.13 in the same way as one can in Figure 15.1. This is clear even when the constant outlay curve is a straight line, as in Figure 15.1, but in the next chapter it will be shown that the constant outlay curves, too, are nothing like those shown in the hedonic theory, with bull's eyes, for example, being common. This makes the simplistic mathematical modelling of hedonic theory totally inapplicable to real life.

Since there might be, say, twenty-five characteristics for a product, there are 25^2 or 625 pairs of characteristics, and each and every one of these pairs would have to exhibit indifference curves like those in Figure 15.1 for the theory to hold. What is more, this would have to apply for every level of characteristic – as the size of a motor car engine increased from 500 cc to 8 litres, the shape of the indifference curve between brakes and comfort would have to remain the same. Even assuming only ten different engine sizes, this implies 6,500 cross-sections where the indifference curves of Figure 15.1 would have to apply. If there are ten cross-sections for each characteristic, there are billions of two-dimensional indifference curves.

There are additional complications if indifference surfaces between the product and its substitutes at different levels of characteristic are taken into account.

If a single one of these billions of indifference surfaces does not conform to the Figure 15.1 convex indifference curve, then hedonic theory does not apply to that product. The indifference curves of Figures 15.2 to 15.13 definitely apply to some important characteristics of most, if not all, everyday products, so hedonic theory does not apply to this set of products. The question arises 'Is there any product in the world for which the assumptions of hedonic theory apply for all the billions of possible cross-sections'.

It is sometimes suggested, explicitly by Lancaster and implicitly by others, that when one is analysing two qualities of the same product, one can ignore any characteristics that are identical in both product lines, and concentrate on the characteristics that vary. If this were so, the number of planes on which the indifference curves would have to be convex would be smaller, though still substantial. However, this is clearly incorrect: if one takes a Robin Reliant, which is a small, lightweight, economical, three-wheeler car appropriate to its market niche, and replaces its engine with a Jaguar engine, the new car is wrong in all respects. Instead of being a car which achieves its performance specifications well, it would be highly dangerous in terms of speed, roadholding, braking, and so on. The optimum relationship between shock absorbers, tyre size and suspension would change. The optimum relationship between comfort and trim would change. Similarly, putting chilli powder into a stew upsets all the balances of flavour. A blend of spices is needed to restore the balance and produce a curry. Ratios, proportions and balance are important. This means that we cannot just ignore characteristics because they themselves are unchanged.

THE LANCASTER MODEL

The most used models in hedonic theories are based on Lancaster (1966, 1971, 1979). His objective was to produce something very similar to the two-good indifference curve model:

to express consumers' preferences in terms of the utility function of the neo-classical kind with all its first-order-partial derivatives positive

(Lancaster 1971: 21)

His writings are largely an attempt to define a product which could be analysed in this way, and in order to do this he had to make very restrictive assumptions on how the product was constructed and how it was consumed.

Types of product

In the Lancaster model the following assumptions are made:

- 'goods are considered not as entities in a gestalt sense but as bundles of properties or characteristics. These characteristics are objective, and the relationship between a good and the characteristics it possesses is a technical one. . . ' This assumption appears to rule out consideration of any products which are consumed as a single entity, a car, a house, a meal in a restaurant, or a film.
- The satisfaction one gets is directly defined by its objective characteristics. The weaknesses of this assumption are shown throughout this book and especially in Chapter 14.
- There is perfect information about the characteristics of a product and the level of characteristics in a product. Again, much of this book has argued that information is necessarily imperfect so search costs are a key ingredient of any meaningful economics of quality.
- 'The characteristics which appear in the analysis are assumed to be objectively quantifiable, as well as objectively identifiable, even though there are important characteristics (color for example) that do not fit this specification. Although color can be objectively *defined* by primary color composition and degree of saturation, color differences cannot be put on a simple scale like size or horsepower or vitamin C content so that everyone agrees that good A has twice as much per pound as good B.'[10]

This is an extremely restrictive assumption. It appears to rule out beauty, taste, smell and sound as well as many characteristics. A Mozart quintet is excluded, as is a car's

appearance, style, handling, or the taste and texture of a Mars Bar.
- Characteristics are thought of as ingredients, though the definition is a little broader. They are defined to exclude 'satisfactions as characteristics', and 'what the product does'.[11] This rules out many of the types of characteristic discussed in earlier chapters, particularly Chapter 14.

Consumption technology

Lancaster then defines the way in which a consumer must consume the product if it is to fit in his model, a consumption technology. This covers the way in which the different products purchased are combined to make the product consumed, and the way in which it is consumed.

A major constraint in defining this appears to have been the desire to present four dimensions on a two-dimensional diagram (utility, quantity purchased, level of characteristic A and level of characteristic B). Utility is presented as contours or indifference curves, which removes one dimension of the diagram. Another is removed by defining the product so that quantity of product and quantity of characteristic are the same thing: so that it is assumed that the same utility can be obtained from consuming a little of the product with a high level of characteristic, or consuming a lot of a product with a little of that characteristic. Lancaster's assumptions include:

- 'preferences over characteristics are taken to have the proper-
ties usually assumed for preferences over goods in traditional theory: that is if a diagram is drawn with quantities of different characteristics along the axes, instead of quantities of different goods, the indifference curves will have the properties of being convex towards the origin, of being non-intersecting and of representing the more preferred collections when further from the origin, assuming all characteristics to be desirable ones.'[12]

This assumption has been dissected at length above and has been shown to be virtually impossible to meet in real life.
- 'Individuals are interested in goods not for their own sake but because of the characteristics they possess'.[13] This assumes away much of what was discussed in Chapter 14.

- 'the relationship between goods and characteristics was *linear* in the sense that quantity x of a good contained exactly x times as much of every characteristic as a unit quantity of the same good.'[14]
- 'It was also assumed that characteristics were *additive* in the sense that the characteristics obtained from joint consumption of specified quantities of two or more goods could be determined by adding up the quantities of each characteristic contained in the specified quantities of the two goods.'[15]

These assumptions imply that the consumer gets the same satisfaction from two cups of tea, one with no milk and one with 50 per cent milk, as from two with 25 per cent milk, and indeed from two cups with 25 per cent milk and one with 50 per cent milk. The assumptions also appear to confine the application of the theory to products like pig food, where it does not matter whether the protein comes from meat, soya beans or potatoes, as long as the proportion of protein in the end product is right. They also exclude products with a negative marginal utility.

Conclusions derived by Lancaster

In the Lancaster model and its descendants all characteristics of a product must meet these assumptions and the consumption technology must be as assumed. There can be very few products, if any, that meet these assumptions. It is very disturbing that, far from recognizing these limitations, Lancaster should assume that the assumptions are universally true, so much so that he can work from them to produce generalizations about 'welfare, variety and the GNP', 'intra-industry trade between identical economies', 'variety in capital goods', 'the optimal division of labour', and 'variety and economic development'.[16]

OTHER PROBLEMS WITH HEDONIC THEORY

Point quality, grades and brands

Nearly all of the hedonic literature assumes point quality, with all items in a product line having identical characteristics. The discussion of product variation, brands, grades, sorting, search and uniformity earlier in this book suggests that this assumption is invariably wrong.

What indifference curves?

There are several rather different concepts of indifference curve floating round. For example, they may be thought of as lines joining combinations of characteristics that give *consumers* equal satisfaction, or as lines joining combinations of characteristics that give *buyers* equal satisfaction or, a very different concept, lines joining combinations of characteristics that buyers are equally likely to buy if the price is the same. Lancaster (1979) says 'It will be assumed here, as in traditional welfare economics, that the "true" preferences are those that would be revealed by actual choice'. This only has any meaning within his very restrictive assumptions: for example, he has assumed that the buyer is the consumer, so the question of which he is talking about is fudged.

Indeed this innocuous seeming sentence is extremely confusing once its implications are considered. It suggests that we are no longer considering what choice will maximize utility with a given consumption technology, but rather we are describing what the choice actually is. If we are talking of 'what will be revealed by actual choice' as preferences, then it does not matter that a consumer consistently makes a choice that does not maximize utility, whether because of poor perception of characteristics or inappropriate appraisal methods: what he buys is his preference, not what would have maximized his utility.

One may ask, though, whether revealed preference utility theory has any meaning in a situation where preference cannot be revealed. In two-good indifference theory, with convex indifference curves, it is formally possible to identify the curves. One can rank the effects of increasing one good, to get the level of a curve, and one only has to identify three points on the curve and apply a little imagination to produce a credible curve. This is not possible when dealing with two characteristics: there is no reason to suppose that the higher indifference curves lie further from the origin, so a ranking procedure is inadequate; the curves are not convex to the origin so many points have to be identified. The difficulty of calculating a two-dimensional curve for iced tea was described above: this was not a revealed preference indifference curve, but the much more easily measured iso-preference curve, using sixteen choice situations (which were controlled experimentally) and analysing five complex types of information. To

calculate the revealed preference indifference curve, one would
have to use only the information of whether they bought or not, so
far more observations would have had to be monitored. The effect
of changing prices would have to be taken into account. It will be
shown in the next chapter that the price assumptions in Lancaster
are wrong, and that very complex price surfaces are normal.

The time assumptions of hedonic theory have been questioned
in Chapter 13. The assumption that everything is consumed as
soon as it is bought in spite of different products being consumed
together is difficult to sustain, but the whole concept of the
indifference curve changes if a stew is made of meat bought
yesterday, vegetables bought last week, garlic bought last month
and spices bought last year. It then becomes extremely difficult to
relate an indifference surface for the ingredients of a stew to
Lancaster's 'It will be assumed here, as in traditional welfare
economics, that the "true" preferences are those that would be
revealed by actual choice', when the actual choice is spread over
many shopping expeditions and, indeed, when the actual choice
on what meat, vegetables and spices are to be bought is made
before the buyer, or the consumer, has any idea what meal is to be
cooked.

Another time-dependent assumption is the explicit assumption
that there is constant demand, with people buying the same
shopping list each day. Again, this has been questioned in Chapter
13. The hedonic approach also assumes away the fact that buyers
(and consumers) typically have different preferences when
buying, when actually consuming and when remembering what
they consumed.

For some purposes economists and marketing professionals
make use of concepts which are formally very different to the
indifference curves of revealed preference utility theory, but which
are intuitively similar. These include:

- The results of a controlled blind tasting test like Huber's iced
  tea.
- Asking consumers to draw their own indifference curves, or
  provide the data necessary for someone else to do this, by
  stating their perceptions of a series of product lines or brands.
- Laboratory experiments to see what consumers purchase when
  presented with selected product lines at controlled prices.
- Social indifference curves, indicating what combinations

society is indifferent between. While I have come across these, using exactly the same diagrams and analysis as the Lancaster model, the conceptual problems do not appear to have been tackled. Even if Lancaster's approach is taken to be correct, the analysis that applies for a single individual cannot be applied to society as a whole merely by changing the labels on the axes.

Subjective or objective?

In Chapter 14 and throughout this book, great emphasis has been laid on the difference between subjective and objective characteristics in quality theory. Consumers' decisions must be based on their subjective assessment of the quality of the product, which may or may not be closely related to the objectively measurable characteristic.

Hedonic theory formally assumes away this difference, assuming that subjective beliefs are identical to the objectively measurable characteristics. It does accept that consumers vary in their preference for characteristics mixes and therefore vary in their indifference curves. The theory also assumes, implicitly,

- that the consumer is perfectly informed at a conscious level about (a) his own wants, and (b) the efficacy of each possible characteristics mix in meeting these wants;
- that he is perfectly informed about (a) the characteristics mix of each product line in the market, and (b) the satisfactions he could get from each;
- that he is perfectly informed about (a) the price of each product on the market and (b) the price of each characteristic. There is a range of implicit assumptions here on the type of characteristic we are talking of and the market that can exist for a characteristic as opposed to a product: these are discussed in the next chapter;
- that he has constant and immutable indifference curves;
- that there are no differences between subjective and objective, no brand awareness, no perceptions of quality except ones with corresponding characteristics.

In previous chapters it has been shown that much of marketing in the real world depends on the belief that all these assumptions are wrong.

It may or may not be a valid simplification to assume away the difference between subjective and objective in two-good indifference theory. In two characteristic theory it certainly is not: there are always substantial disagreements about what the characteristics are, what level they are and what attributes they correspond to.

Can we use objective characteristics on the axes?

It has been argued throughout this book that consumers' purchase decisions and the satisfactions they gain from a product are subjective, and may not be closely related to objective characteristics. This means that no two people need agree on the attributes of a product or the satisfactions it gives. Under these circumstances, how can we plot their subjective beliefs against objective quality as is normally done in hedonic theory? If this is not possible, then one must give up any hope of

- comparing individuals' indifference curves;
- deriving demand curves related to objective characteristics;
- aggregating demand for quality;
- presenting normative or descriptive optimizing models based on characteristics;

If these are impossible, hedonic theory seems rather pointless. What comparison is possible when one consumer believes that tobacco is harmless, another that it is very dangerous; when one believes that garlic has a characteristic that cures a cold, another believes that it has a characteristic that keeps away werewolves and another believes that it has a characteristic that restricts one's love life; when one consumer believes that Miller Lite beer is low alcohol, like Swan Light and another that it is 4 per cent alcohol?

A consumer can *never* plot his own indifference curve against objective characteristics: he can only plot an indifference curve against his subjective perception of what these objective characteristics are. Two stages may be distinguished:

- plotting what he believes is his indifference curve against what he believes are objective characteristics. For instance, I may believe that I am indifferent between a sweet, low aroma, white wine and a dry, aromatic wine;
- plotting what he believes is his indifference curve against products. There may be a substantial difference between this indifference curve and the one in the last paragraph, because

the characteristics content of the product may not be consistently related to what he believes it is. He may like Brand X
more than Brand Y, when, from their physical characteristics
and his belief about his characteristics requirements (in the
last paragraph) he should prefer Brand Y. His perception of
what he likes in the product may be wrong: he may like it for a
characteristic that affects its taste, but which he does not know
exists. There is also a placebo effect: he may like Brand X
because he thinks it has the characteristics he thinks he likes.

Conceivably an omniscient outside observer could plot indifference curves of an individual against objective characteristics, or
recalibrate the axes so that preferences for brands were plotted
against objective characteristics. (By definition, the buyer's
indifference curve would change if he knew the objective
characteristics of the product.) The curves then become extremely
odd. The buyer in the detergent commercial who will nòt take two
packets of Brand X in exchange for her normal brand (with
identical objective characteristics) would have a curve which
breaks the normal criteria for utility theory. Similarly, a consumer
who is indifferent between brands which have very different
objective characteristics, but which he believes to be identical, will
have a very peculiar indifference surface when it is plotted against
objective characteristics. Again, it is difficult to see how the
assumptions of convexity, non-intersection, transitivity, and non-
satiation would hold in these extremely common situations.

When we are talking of branded products, we may assume that
the perception of the quality is significantly changed by the fact of
branding – which is a major reason for branding a product. If one
plots the buyer's indifference curve for characteristics to meet a
want against objective level of characteristic, one might get a
smooth and 'reasonable' curve. If, on the other hand, one plots
the buyer's indifference curves between branded product lines
against the objective level of characteristic, the curves cannot be
expected to be 'reasonable'.

Any businessman, any marketing professional, is extremely
interested in differences between buyers' perceptions of the products
on the market and their objective characteristics. It is strange that
one school of economics should want to assume them away.

Yet another possible indifference curve would exist where the
consumer is not consciously aware of what his wants are or how

they could be met, but is perfectly informed of the characteristics of the product. He could then plot what he perceived as his indifference curve, though it might bear little relation to the indifference curve revealed by purchasing.

The most common situation in the real world is probably one where the consumer does not know his own wants, how to satisfy them or the degree to which the products in the market have the required characteristics.

Is it possible to ignore these subjective elements, and plot actual purchases against characteristics mix to derive indifference curves? In practice, no. There are very few commodities for which an individual makes sufficient purchases covering a sufficient range of qualities to derive even a single curve of a two-dimensional indifference curve. Changes in supply over time alter the price of the product lines and their alternatives. Changes in demand and changes in purchase within a consistent demand pattern (for example, having a different main course for dinner every day) further complicate the issue.

MEGA-ATTRIBUTES

Is it possible to get round these problems by introducing a set of 'mega-attributes' like attractiveness, performance, safety, reliability or quality index, which combine a number of characteristics in such a way as to meet the assumptions of convexity, and so on? Lancaster specifically ruled them out in his theory, but some of his followers lack his rigour, and relax his very proper restrictions without justification. There are many reasons why it is not possible to use such 'mega-attributes' in a hedonic analysis.

These mega-attributes are purely subjective and have no objective parallel. The performance of a car cannot be described by a single, objective measure. The components of performance might be top speed, initial acceleration, acceleration at 60mph, cruising speed, performance in slow moving traffic, cornering, road holding, braking, turning circle, and so on.[17] Each individual consumer can be expected to have different weightings for these characteristics, and indeed to include different characteristics in the concept of performance.

It is by no means certain that the mega-attributes would conform to the requirements of convexity, transitivity, and so on any more than ordinary attributes. Certainly one can have too much safety, too much performance, too much comfort. Certainly, the relationship between performance, status and comfort is not the one that would be expected for two-good problems. If an economist defines the mega-attributes to conform to the assumptions, then the probability must be that he is using concepts such as 'integratedness' which exist only in his own mind and bear no relation to what individual consumers think.

The use of a mega-attribute as a summary of several characteristics implies that there has been some system of evaluating the characteristics and of combining the evaluations to rank possible choices within this aspect of quality. The combination will normally be quite complex, with linear or additive combinations being rare (consider the importance of brake power in relation to top speed, for example). This means that even if it were possible to define mega-attributes so that they met the criteria of hedonic theory, this would not avoid the problems discussed in this paper. Instead of one final decision being modelled, as in standard hedonic theory, the decision would have to be modelled for each mega-attribute. There would be a complex model for safety, another for performance, another for reliability and so on. It is unlikely that any one of these decisions would meet the assumptions of hedonic theory. This means that assuming mega-attributes compounds the problems of hedonic theory, rather than removing them.

It would be wrong for an economist to dream up indices or concepts which do not directly relate to the concepts used by the consumer. If he thinks in terms of acceleration, cruising speed, cornering, and so on, it would be wrong to dream up a measure of 'integratedness'. This would be simply a matter of replacing a consumer's perception of an objective characteristic with the subjective perception of the economist (and indeed it may be an artifact of his model rather than his perception). If it has no relation to any consumer's perceptions or actions, it can have no value.

Individual preference and market demand

Hedonic theory has had to assume away virtually all of marketing economics and marketing theory and much of micro-economic theory in order to define a situation in which it is theoretically possible to derive market demand from individual preferences. It has assumed away complications like the difficulties of aggregating and disaggregating (including brands, grades, advertising, quality cues, segmentation, market structure, monopoly, multi-use products, elasticity, search, information, income, the psychology of pricing, price as an indicator of quality, and so on). In marketing, in fact, it is usually believed that it is not possible to derive market demand from individual consumers' preferences: the causal chain is too long, too complex and too obscure.

CONCLUSION

The hedonic approach is only one possible approach to quality, and this book does not rely on it. This chapter has shown that the approach is not formally consistent: it is wrong in attempting to transfer the two-good approach to a two-characteristic approach, and some of its formal assumptions are shown to be incorrect. In general, its assumptions have the effect of limiting its application to the vanishing point. Rigour requires more than that the conclusions of an analysis follow logically from the formal assumptions – that is trivial. To be really rigorous, a theory's assumptions must not clash with reality.

The reliance on the indifference curves of revealed preference theory is of questionable value when it is not possible to plot curves according to the requirements of revealed preference utility theory. There are many other concepts which might be called indifference curves or iso-preference curves, which do not require that consumers are perfectly informed about their needs, the characteristics that meet these needs, and the products that have these characteristics.

This chapter has shown that hedonic theory, by assuming away the difference between subjective and objective, has therefore assumed away brands, advertising, information, search, and so on, and it can apply to very few products. If, however, the theory were to recognize the difference, all sorts of problems would arise, like aggregating the subjective beliefs of individuals and relating beliefs to manufacturing specifications.

Lancaster's theory suffers from the assumption of a consumption technology that is, at best, extremely rare in practice, and from confusion on satiation, as well as the other problems mentioned above. This, plus his confusions on indifference curves and his restrictive assumptions, makes his theory have no application.

This chapter has presented a whole series of indifference curves of new and interesting shapes. Undoubtedly, these provide important insights when one is looking at the quality of products. It must be asked, though, whether they can be incorporated into the traditional economic analysis. It has been suggested in this chapter that introducing this level of realism into the analysis very soon leads to an unmanageable level of complexity. This will be looked at further in the next chapter.

Chapter 16

The misuse of hedonic prices and costs[1]

INTRODUCTION

In the last chapter the use of indifference curves in hedonic theory (following Lancaster 1966, 1971, 1979, and Rosen 1974) was examined and was shown to be incorrect. In this chapter another key part of the theory is examined, hedonic prices and costs. It will be shown that with these, as with indifference curves, the basic assumptions are wrong, and that they are so restrictive as to mean that the theory can have little or no practical application. Most of the papers in the literature mention some of the weaknesses mentioned here, and accept that these are significant errors in the theory presented. There is, however, a limit to the number of errors you can accept in a theory before discarding it. In this chapter the weaknesses accepted by various economists will be brought together, and new ones will be shown. The question will be asked 'In view of the errors and weaknesses in the theory, would it be better to avoid it and work in some other tradition of quality economics?'

In this chapter 'quality prices' are the set of prices for different qualities of a product or for different product lines at different times; a price list in effect. Hedonic prices are the 'implicit prices of attributes [Characteristics in the terminology of this book] . . . revealed to economic agents from observed products and the specific amount of characteristics associated with them'.[2] They are calculated by regressing the price of a product line on the level of its characteristics.

In most markets we do have price data, though it is often so unreliable and inaccurate as to be unusable.[3] It is often harder to obtain data on quantity, and this is even less reliable. The data, if it exists, is only available intermittently, and not at each point in time. However, for the purpose of this chapter, it will be assumed that perfect information is available.

PRICE TAKERS

Prices give information which may be used for economic analysis such as this, but the information a price gives depends on the market and market circumstances that formed the price. In this chapter, two contrasting market types will be examined, price taking and price making. Hedonic theory assumes price taking under perfect competition, with sellers putting all they produce on the market, and taking the going market price. It is assumed that the market is cleared in any period, with nothing unsold or stored until the next market period. The following assumptions are often made in hedonic theory, often implicitly:

- There is no difference between subjective and objective quality, there are no brands and no advertising (see Chapter 14 for a critique of this assumption).
- Price reporting is based on characteristics which both buyers and sellers consider relevant.
- There is product differentiation, but not product variation (see Chapter 2).
- Time is assumed away. This explicit assumption introduces a lot of contradictory implicit assumptions. For example, price formation as a dynamic process is ignored. The distinction between the market period (when supply is fixed), the short run, and the long run is ignored.
- There is perfect information about quality, quantity and prices at all times.
- There are very many qualities or product lines. Rosen, in fact, assumes a continuous spectrum covering all possible characteristics mixes, with supplies of each mix being available at all times – an infinite number of qualities.
- There are so many buyers and sellers that no one buyer or seller can affect the price. The assumption is that there are a large number of buyers and sellers for each possible quality.

The assumption of very many qualities (or even an infinite number), with very many buyers and sellers for each, implies a vast number of buyers and sellers and this does not occur in any market. It is not possible to juggle definitions to avoid this problem, arguing that everyone in the market is a potential buyer or seller for each quality, so there are many buyers and sellers for each grade, even if there are only a few hundred buyers and sellers in the market: there is a world of difference between a market with a hundred buyers and sellers for a hundred qualities, and one where there are a hundred buyers and sellers for each line.

The assumptions are put there to preserve the illusion of perfect competition. One must question though, whether perfect competition is possible, as Chamberlin, having argued in *Monopolistic Competition* that perfect competition was not a very useful concept at the best of times, argued (1953) that when quality or product variation was taken into account it was completely meaningless (see Chapter 2 on the product as a variable for part of the argument). Economists who do not deal with markets with large numbers of buyers and sellers, often do not realize the complexities of these markets, and assume that there is perfect competition. Those of us who do work with such markets are well aware that markets cannot operate with the large numbers assumed. In practice even the large commodity markets have a limited number of brokers or wholesalers as intermediaries, and a limited number of grades are used instead of an infinite number of qualities. If this were not so, buyers of a particular quality would not know how to locate sellers of that quality, and the amount of information produced would be unmanageable. In these markets, there are a limited number of buyers and sellers for the rarer qualities. Some markets like the housing market and the labour market may appear at first sight to be competitive, but on examination it becomes clear that the product variation and the market imperfections are such that they cannot be taken to have even that limited degree of competition to be found on commodity markets.

Snapshot prices

The buyer entering a market faces a set of prices, the 'quality prices'. This is a snapshot of a moving target, as prices are constantly changing throughout the day.

Hedonic theory makes strange assumptions about prices. Rosen, for instance, assumes that the set of prices facing the buyer is *at the same time*

- a market clearing price *and*
- an average equilibrium price at the end of a day's trading *and*
- the price facing each buyer and each seller at all times throughout the market period.

The hedonic models assume prices that are constant over the period *and* that are market clearing. In practice, these conditions do not exist at the same time: those markets like fruit and vegetables which are competitive and which are at the same time market clearing (because of perishability), are characterized by prices that fluctuate wildly, often doubling or halving over a day's trading. If the opening price happens to be below a market clearing price, too much will be bought by early customers, so there will not be enough for latecomers, and prices will shoot up. Throughout the day prices rise and fall because of changes in expectations of what will happen to prices over the rest of the market period. The only way to avoid this contradiction between the two assumptions would be to assume that all buyers and sellers have perfect knowledge of present and future supply and all have the same perfect ability to forecast prices.

There are other reasons why prices change in the course of a market period. There may be a switch in the quality demanded as different buyers visit the market later in the day. There may be supply changes. The 'quality price' is ephemeral; the fact that irises are in short supply today while gladioli are plentiful, or that roses are wanted for St Valentine's Day, establishes the relative price for one period but does not determine any long-term relationship. Similar fluctuations in the supply of different colours or grades of roses will occur.

The 'quality price' is a marginal price in the sense that it is the price that the next buyer in the market will have to pay if he buys at that moment in time. It is not a marginal price in the sense that it is the price that would be obtained for any extra supply reaching the market: under Rosen's assumptions, the whole set of quality prices (including quality premiums) would instantly adjust, and the new supply would get a lower price – in a fruit and vegetable market, for instance, there would be oversupply at the end of the period, and a very low price for some product, not necessarily the marginal items. It is not an average price, and nor does it indicate an average quality premium: it applies to a single purchase at one moment in time. Neither the price nor the premium can be expected to hold in the face of changed supply or demand. Nor can they be expected to hold in the face of changed global supply of a characteristic common to many lines, as nitrogen is an ingredient of many fertilizers (an unusual example, to be sure, but this is the sort of product assumed by Lancaster).

Empirical work since Waugh (1929) and the sometimes amateur market research of producers often forecasts that perceived regularities in quality premiums and in prices in the past will be the same as in the future. While it is often a good prediction to say that the future will be the same as the past, it is a weak prediction when there is no explanation. It is not supported by hedonic or any other economic theory of quality.

The scatter of prices

Hedonic theory assumes that price is positively related to level of characteristic. Here it is shown that it need not be so, and that for most products there will be some characteristics for which it is not the case. For example, as was shown in detail in the last chapter, the individual's indifference curve for sweetness and acidity in a Moselle could well be a bull's eye, as in Figure 16.1, so a well-balanced wine, with medium sweetness and moderate acidity is preferred. Too much or too little sweetness will make the wine less acceptable, and the 'right' sweetness with too much or too little acidity, will be less acceptable than something with a 'worse' sweetness, but better balance. It is reasonable to assume that if most consumers have similar tastes, aggregate demand will also form a rough bull's eye, looking just like Figure 16.1, except that the curves are iso-price lines rather than indifference curves. This is so even when there are many different preferred points, but each has a bull's eye. There are many possible iso-price contours that could arise from such curves, three of which arise in the following situations:

1 The supply of wines of all qualities is much the same, because climate and soil prevent all growers from changing to the quality most in demand. Since demand is concentrated at the centre of the bull's eye, prices will be highest there, and iso-price curves will fall away from the centre, as the indifference curves do.

2 Most of the wine in a region is of one quality, because of soil and climate, so supply is greatest at the centre of the bull's eye

and falls away gradually. Consumers' preferences are scattered, with some preferring dry, some sweet, and so on, though market demand forms a bull's eye. Where there is a small supply there is also a small demand. Prices are the same for all qualities.

3 Economies of scale mean that producers concentrate on producing for the most popular taste, and can do so cheaply. Prices are then lowest in the centre of the bull's eye, and rise for the rarer qualities, as people with rarer tastes pay higher prices.

The bull's eye is only one set of indifference curves – others were presented in the last chapter. It is quite certain, though, that there are many products in our daily lives where price is not positively related to a quality characteristic. For example, a salad costs more

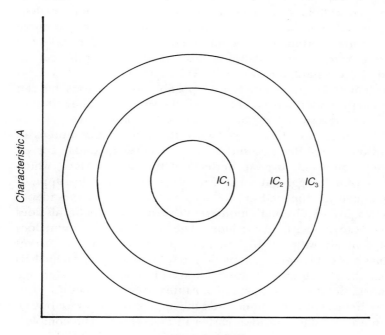

Characteristic B

Figure 16.1

than its ingredients, but pure chemicals cost more than impure. Black coffee costs the same as white. Some cafes charge for the first cup of coffee but not for refills. Price may vary positively with the level of one characteristic, but not with others – gold in ore, for instance – but this implies a negative value for waste. The fact that the marginal price of a characteristic is zero or negative does not mean that it is unimportant: ball-point pens are priced on status, appearance, and so on at the margin, but in the final analysis, if they do not write, they are useless.

Classical two-good indifference analysis involves superimposing lines showing what can be bought for a fixed sum of money on top of indifference curves (Figure 15.1). Where the constant outlay curve is tangential to an indifference curve there is an optimum, and from this result a considerable body of theory has been derived. Hedonic theory has used identical analysis with identical diagrams.

However, once one accepts that preferences are different when the characteristics are consumed together, this whole analysis changes. Let us take the simplest type of indifference curve demonstrated in the last chapter, the bull's eye (Figure 16.1). Let us than take it that, as shown in this section, the iso-price curves, and the constant outlay curves will also form a bull's eye. A constant outlay curve indicates the possible combinations that can be bought for a given sum of money, the various combinations of sweet and less sweet that you can buy for £7, for instance.

One then gets a figure like Figure 16.2 if one superimposes an individual's indifference surface on the constant outlay curves. (They would only overlap perfectly if the price surface, which arises from the aggregate of individuals' demand and the supply of each quality, happened to produce constant outlay curves identical to a given individual's indifference surface: no doubt this does happen to one buyer in a million.) The individual's optimum does not coincide with the highest price point, the one the market values most. It is a great temptation to start building up an analysis from these diagrams in the tradition of two-good indifference analysis, but it should be resisted. At this stage one does not even know if the central point indicates the highest or the lowest outlay: both are possible, as shown earlier in this section. The complexities increase if one introduces some of the realistic indifference curves set out in the last chapter, instead of the simple bull's eye. A fuller analysis would take into account quantity as well as mix of characteristics, allowing for the fact that wine is sold in discrete units, bottles. (It is difficult to see how, in the real world, we could accept Lancaster's assumption that two bottles of dry wine is the same as one bottle of sweet, and so put quantity on the simple two-dimensional model.) This would imply surfaces like those in Figures 15.3, 15.4 and 15.5. The complexities of this analysis are obviously far greater still. This enormous degree of complexity arises even in the simple two-characteristic model, and it increases manifold if even a third characteristic is introduced. Any attempt at a model would require empirical data on both indifference curves and constant outlay curves for each pair of characteristics – it is *not* acceptable to assume a convenient curve as in hedonic

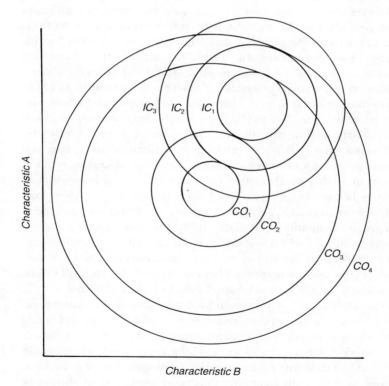

Figure 16.2 Possible indifference curves (*IC*) and constant outlay (*CO*) curves for a product with two characteristics

theory. The complexities soon become unmanageable, and the idea of n-dimensional indifference and outlay curves being manipulated to determine optima is beyond credibility.[4]

Hedonic prices

The 'implicit prices' for each characteristic are calculated by regression on the quality prices – the price list for the product lines on the market. If, however, the prices have the limited meaning discussed above, it is not clear why one should want to derive a statistic, itself subject to error, from them. The regressions are a description of the prices at one point of time and are necessarily a less accurate description than a price list, particularly if the assumption of many qualities and a single price for each is retained.

Regression can be used to aggregate records from different time periods, but the exercise is fraught with danger. One must ask, too, what is the purpose, and what is the justification for this aggregation. It requires the heroic assumption that there is a constant relationship between price and level of each characteristic in a dynamic, price-taking market. A regression as a description of prices is merely a less accurate but compact alternative to a price list. The fact that it is compact does not mean that it is particularly useful: anyone who has bought a new house will appreciate that it is a very quick job to identify the cheap and expensive areas and to get an idea of the price of certain types of house in each area from the advertisements (and inspection of sample houses in the preferred area is necessary, rather than reliance on an estate agent's description, or, if one can imagine it, a regression equation). Similarly, in the job market, one can get a pretty good idea of what someone with certain qualifications can get from reading the Situations Vacant columns for a week or two, while a regression equation will not be up to date, and will not be statistically significant for unusual mixes of qualifications.

The alternative, of presenting a regression as an explanation rather than as a description, requires an explanatory model taking into account supply and demand changes, dynamic price formation, market structure, and so on – all aspects which are normally covered by marketing economics but are assumed away in hedonic theory. It is formally necessary that regression analysis should be preceded by an *a priori* justification of the shape of the curve if it is to be anything more than a very crude description of the scatter of the observations. For example, if the price pattern follows the bull's eye and the prices are scattered all over the diagram, a linear regression will show no correlation. If most observations are in the bottom left quadrant, a positive slope will be found, and in the top right, a negative slope (or *vice versa* if the centre point is a minimum price).

This problem cannot be got round by redefining the variable as 'balance'. This would be dishonest when most people think in terms of acid and sweet rather than balance. It would also invalidate other dimensional analyses, that between acidity and fruitiness for instance. In any case, to start redefining the variable, one would first need to know how indifference curves actually lay – in which case regression curves might be better specified. It has been argued above that there are few indifference relationships for which a linear regression would be reasonable. Some important characteristics, like wheels on a motor car, will not even show up in a regression, because all cars have them, but they are still both costly and important.

In the last chapter it was shown that a consumer may consume more of a characteristic in several different ways:

- consuming more of the identical product;
- switching to a product line which is identical except that it has more of characteristic A;
- switching to a product line which has more of several, or all, characteristics, including characteristic A;
- changing the product mix to get more of characteristic A, eating more potatoes and less meat to increase fibre intake, for instance;
- consuming the same product more frequently.

It was argued that each of these increases in characteristic A can be expected to change satisfaction in a different way, and certainly one can expect that the cost of each change is different. It is most unlikely that the same regression curve would fit each expansion.

This section has shown that hedonic theory, because it assumes that price is a positive and non-decreasing function of level of characteristic, has assumed away virtually all real products. It is questionable whether there are many products for which this assumption would be valid for most of the important characteristics, and it is questionable whether there is any product for which this is true for all characteristics in a price-taking market.

PRICE MAKERS

So far this chapter has concentrated on a price-taking market with some of the features of perfect competition, though it has been suggested that where quality is important it is unlikely that anything like perfect competition will be seen. Now attention will be turned to another extreme form of market, price making, where firms set prices for their products, and leave it to the market to buy as much as it wishes. This can occur in the classic monopolistic competition situations, where the seller has a degree of monopoly over a quality with no close substitutes, or where he has a locational monopoly, for instance. It is particularly likely to be the case, though, where there is a discrepancy between attributes and characteristics, where there are strong brands, for instance, and where, as a result, products with identical characteristics can fetch very different prices.

Hedonic theory was based on price-taking markets, and it would be necessary to make substantial changes to the theory to adapt it to price-making markets, changes which do not appear to have been made in practice.

In the price-making market, prices must be interpreted differently. They are not just the prices faced by the next buyer to enter the market-place: they are short- to medium-term prices, which can be expected to change only slowly. Competitors as well as buyers can see these prices as fixed in the short to medium term. Competition is predominantly an attempt to increase market share at a given level of price, rather than price cutting. These prices may tend towards equilibrium in the long run, but they are not short-term or market-period equilibrium prices.

The quality price or list of prices on the market cannot be taken as an indication of what the next supplier to enter the market will get for his product, so it is not a marginal price in that sense. If the product is one where attributes and characteristics are identical (implying at least that they are unbranded) a new firm entering the market at the same price for the same characteristics mix would split the market with competitors. If the product was branded, the new brand would compete with established brands of the same characteristics mix, and if the price were the same, the brand would be lucky to survive. It should be noted that the assumption of a great many buyers and sellers is difficult to sustain where there is price making: it has to be explained why buyers would not buy from the cheapest seller.

The scatter of prices

In price-making markets, prices are not determined by supply and demand in the market at one particular time, but rather are set by the seller, and are based on considerations like:

- the perceived elasticity of demand facing the firm (not the elasticity of market demand). If there is a strong brand or there are no close substitutes, this can be expected to be less elastic.
- the firm's perception of its cost curves.
- the expected fluctuations in output. With cost-free storage, zero interest rates, unlimited finance and no risk, it might pay to produce at a constant level of output, holding a reserve stock, but normally output will fluctuate.

The long-term decision on what qualities to produce requires an assessment of alternative qualities. Quality changes in the short run are not desirable when they require investment or when they would put the brand image at risk.

In price-taking markets, short-run prices need not be related to production costs at all, but in price-making markets the relationship should be stronger. While prices are intended to be higher than the cost of production, this may not be achieved if at any time output is below the break-even level, perhaps because of seasonal shifts in demand, perhaps because the product is not competing effectively. If there is a strong brand or a monopoly, it may be possible to hold the price well above the cost of production. It seems then that the scatter of prices with price making will be far less, and that the prices will be closer to (expected) cost of production. However, in price-making markets there will necessarily be a big discrepancy between characteristics and attributes. At one level, where there is no branding, the product variation (see Chapter 2) is of key importance: differences in location, for example, will not show up in a normal hedonic price analysis. Where there is branding there can be a significant difference between actual characteristics and consumers' perceptions of them. If these differences between characteristics and attributes did not exist, it is difficult to see how a price-making market could operate: consumers would just switch to the cheapest supplier.

This makes it difficult to describe quality prices even in the form of a price list: should the product be described in terms of characteristics or attributes? should location be described? and so on.

Hedonic prices

The same questions about hedonic prices arise with a price-making market as with a price-taking market. There is no reason to prefer a regression to quality prices (i.e. a price list):

- as there are four distinct ways of increasing consumption of a characteristic (five if you include time);
- as ratios between characteristics rather than absolute level of characteristic determine satisfaction for most goods;
- as uniformity, precision, reliability, and so on are also elements of quality;
- as there is not a positive or constant relationship between price and level of characteristic.

In addition, though, in price-making markets there are major discrepancies between subjective attributes and objective characteristics, and monopoly pricing also disturbs other regularities that might otherwise exist. Putting in extra variables to allow for these factors removes degrees of freedom: with a house, a holiday, a job or a meal, there are so many characteristics and so few product lines that it is not possible to use regression to determine the cost of each. It has been shown above that it is not valid to confine the analysis to those characteristics that differ, as stated by Lancaster. Similarly, it is not acceptable to use regressions to measure the strength of brands, with the unexplained error giving the strength of the brand.

Perceptions of price

Hedonic theory assumes that all consumers have perfect knowledge of the price of all products on the market, that they have perfect knowledge of the prices of all characteristics of these products, and that they have perfect knowledge of their own budget constraints. It will be argued here that these assumptions are unrealistic in price-taking markets and impossible in price-making markets.

Earlier chapters have spelt out some of the difficulties and costs of obtaining information, and the fact that consumers cannot have perfect information (with poor memory, and differences in perception over time – before, during, and after consumption). The problems are particularly intractable in a price-taking market because prices are so volatile and because there are so many buyers and sellers.

Most price-making markets exist only because consumers' perceptions of products are not the same as their objective characteristics. Sellers use many strategies to change buyers' perceptions of the price of products, strategies like 'Special Offer', '25 per cent extra free', 'Interest-free loan' or '99p', as well as deceptive packaging and presentation. These strategies do not necessarily reduce utility, as consumers may well value the product higher as a result.

If buyers' or consumers' perception of the price of a product is incorrect, then the perception of the price of its constituent characteristics is incorrect. If the perception of the price of the product is correct, but the perception of its characteristics is incorrect, then the perception of the price of its characteristics will be incorrect. It is remotely possible that these two misperceptions may cancel each other out. It has been argued in this chapter that even a statistician could not usefully derive the price of a characteristic from price data, and it seems unreasonable to expect the average consumer to do any better.

Differences between buyers and consumers have been emphasized in earlier chapters.

Perceptions of budget constraints are also likely to be imperfect. Perceptions of constraints are seldom absolute, as the time over which the budget must be balanced is elastic. Buyers may also have ill-defined budgets for housing, food, clothing, and so on, even within a tight overall budget. Sellers may attempt to change the time horizon of the budget by offering credit, and try to persuade buyers to devote a greater proportion of the budget to one type of product.

THE RELATIONSHIP BETWEEN PRICE AND COST OF PRODUCTION

The hedonic theorists, following Lancaster and Rosen, assume that price is directly related to costs of production. They base their analysis on 'the costs of producing characteristics' and 'what consumers ought to want to choose', with the interface being 'hedonic prices'. This implies that the production function touches the indifference curve at the hedonic price.

In other traditions of economics such a simplistic approach would be unthinkable: Table 16.1 shows the relationship normally

Table 16.1 Some factors affecting quality price

SUPPLY   PRODUCTION ECONOMICS

Costs of producing different characteristics mixes at different levels of output.

Supply curves of individual firms.

Gross margin, joint products, multiproduct production.

Market period, short run, long run.

Variations in quantity produced.

Variations in quality produced.

Perceptions of present and future costs, future quantities.

Reliability, consistency, tolerances, adherence to specification.

Grading.

New products.

Intermediate products.

Alternative production technologies.

Validity of aggregation.

MARKETING ECONOMICS

Number of firms, market structure.

Substitution, alternative products.

Attributes or characteristics.

Grades, brands.

Location.

Imports, exports, alternative markets.

Information, cues.

Search.

Wholesaling, retailing, transport and distribution.

Elasticity.

Aggregation.

QUALITY PRICE

Quality price

Hedonic price.

Reporting methods.

Relationship of price to market environment.

Statistical validity.

DEMAND

MARKETING ECONOMICS, MARKETING

Subjective, objective.
Grades, brands.
Brand loyalty, repeat buying.
Number of product lines on the market.
Substitution, cross-elasticity.
Segments.
Elasticity.
Monopsony, number of firms, differentiation.
Price as indicator of quality.
Alternative sources of supply.
Alternative products, product lines.
Special prices.
Search, information, cues.
Market period, short run long run.
Learning.
Dynamic price formation.
What people buy.
Long-term and short-term decisions.
Purchasing strategies.

PSYCHOLOGY

Why people buy.
Deviation between purchases and preferences.

CONSUMPTION THEORY

What people ought to want to buy.
How consumers ought to appraise quality.

accepted between production and consumption, and hedonic theory assumes away most of these steps – virtually all of marketing and marketing economics, and much of production economics. Marketing economists, for example, think that the relationship between the production function and the quantity hitting the market is so distant and so complicated that they ignore production functions and production costs unless they have a very good reason to include them in an analysis. Production economists think that production decisions are influenced by the probable premium for quality and the cost of producing different quality mixes, and do not pay any attention to individual consumers' utility maximization processes.

Production costs

In the traditional, two-good, indifference curve analysis, it is normally assumed that the price of each good is fixed, so the combinations that can be bought with a given sum of money can be shown by a straight line between the axes. With hedonic analysis, one approach has been to use a similar straight line constant outlay curve, implicitly assuming that there is a perfectly elastic supply of each separate characteristic (which leaves one wondering what product it applies to). An alternative is to derive a curve from an assumed cost function. For example, in Lancaster (1979: 31) this is a 'product differentiation curve' a curve joining combinations of two characteristics which can be produced with a single unit of resource. He believes that, for some unstated reason, it is likely to slope downward to the right 'having the same property of concavity toward the origin as the traditional production possibility curve'. Rosen (1974) assumes convex total cost functions such that 'marginal costs of increasing each component of the design are also positive and non decreasing' and produces a somewhat similar ' family of production "indifference surfaces"' joining combinations of qualities and unit prices that give the firm the same profit. In neither case is any empirical support for the assumption given, nor any theoretical case for believing that one shape of the curve rather than another is correct. This is surprising, since the assumption is absolutely fundamental to their analysis. There is virtually nothing in the literature on the costs of producing quality (see Chapter 12).

Is there in fact any *prima facie* case for believing in any one shape for production functions for a characteristic rather than another? The level of characteristic may be increased (or its uniformity increased) in any of the following ways:

- Increasing the level of characteristic A only.
- Increasing the level of characteristic A and some or all other characteristics at the same time.
- Providing more of the product – for example, a bigger pack size.
- Switching to a process with closer tolerances and so reducing risk, waste, repairs under guarantee, and so on.
- Sorting a mixed product into grades or changing the specifications of grades. This can result in a product with a different probable level of characteristic A and changed variance and risk.
- Advertising, to change consumers' perception of the amount of characteristic A in the product, or to change their perceptions of the need for characteristic A.
- Developing new products.

Obviously each way of increasing the level of the characteristic or attribute will lead to a different production function, both in relation to the level of characteristic A and in relation to the level of output of the product. Obviously, too, neither the production function of the firm nor production function of the industry will follow just one of these routes: at one level of characteristic, increasing the level of characteristic A may be most profitable, at another, changed specifications, and at another a totally new product.

In calculating production functions it is also necessary to allow for the range of production methods through the industry, the range of raw material costs (which fluctuate over time), joint products, technically fixed ratios and multiproduct manufacture.

The production functions above do not imply that the unit cost is a simple function of the level and uniformity of a single characteristic. The normal production function still applies, where the unit cost is related to the volume produced, so there is an added dimension to each production function.

This is not all. Typically, for each level of characteristic A there will be a different set of production functions for increases in characteristic B. The cost of putting different sizes of engine in a very small car and in a large car will not be the same. The cost of increasing the dietary fibre content of a meal will be affected by the meat content required, as meat has no dietary fibre. This is even more marked when there are technical or chemical constants: one cannot produce crisp potato crisps without using fat; one cannot make bronze without copper, one cannot produce sulphuric acid without combining the elements in the ratio H_2SO_4.

In the next few pages the effect of different types of product on production functions will be looked at.

Ingredient products

Hedonic theory has concentrated almost entirely on ingredient products, products which are manufactured by combining characteristics or by combining raw materials which are themselves combinations of characteristics. Two types will be looked at here, those for which input characteristics are the same as output characteristics, and those for which they are not.

Input and output characteristics the same

It is usually assumed in hedonic analysis that the input characteristics are the same as the output characteristics. This would mean that the level of characteristics in the ingredients of a product is directly related to the level of characteristic in the final product. For some products, particularly intermediate products like fertilizer, this may be a fair approximation, but more generally it is likely to apply to only one or two characteristics of a product.

It cannot be assumed that when a product is an ingredient product, the cost of increasing the level of a characteristic is a straight linear function of quantity of ingredient. For example, the cost of producing a pure chemical is seldom a straight linear function of percentage of that chemical. Indeed, it sometimes would appear to be geometrical. Similarly, increasing the carrot content of a stew implies reducing the amount of other ingredients. If the carrots replace meat, the marginal cost of the characteristics is negative: if they replace potatoes, positive. If the balance of meat and potatoes is maintained, the marginal cost could be positive, negative, or zero.

Another example is a mixed product like a lawn fertilizer, which is compounded out of different 'straight' fertilizers, like urea, sulphate of ammonia, muriate of potash and superphosphate. Each of these straights contain one or more of the basic plant nutrients N, P and K, in different proportions. The compounder might see his problem as to produce a mix which gives the right proportion of N, P and K, say 7:7:7, at the lowest price. This would normally be done by running a linear programme. To work out the marginal cost of N, for instance, it would be necessary to run programmes for a range of mixes. It is unlikely that the marginal cost would be the same at 7:7:7 as at 15:15:0, or at 20:20:20, as different straights might be used to add the N and as more concentrated nitrogen straights would replace less of the other fertilizers. In practice, of course, the problem is more difficult than this, as some combinations of straights are chemically unstable, and some combinations are not suited for a given crop. Again, the cost of increasing the N content to move from 7:7:7 to 15:7:7 would be very different to the cost of increasing N together with the other nutrients to get 15:15:15. The fact that fertilizer is used on crops with a range of requirements means that there is no unequivocal value in relation to the output of a single crop. For these reasons, again, it is not possible to accept the basic postulates of hedonic theory.

Input and output characteristics different

Generally, though, the characteristics used for evaluating the raw material inputs are not the same as those used for evaluating the final product. This is true even when a product is named after an ingredient: garlic sausage is not considered better the more garlic it has and nor are pepperoni pizza, potato salad, or dandelion wine judged primarily on the one ingredient. Generally, in fact, the consumer does not know what the ingredients are, or what the proportions of each are, or the way in which they are mixed or combined. They evaluate the product rather on taste, texture, and so on.

With cooking and with some manufacturing it is the process that determines quality, rather than the characteristics of the raw material. A good cook can make a good meal out of cheap ingredients.

This makes it very difficult to accept the production functions postulated by hedonic theory, where the level of the output characteristic is a simple function of cost.

Component goods

A car or a computer cannot usefully be considered to be a mix of ingredients, an assembly of characteristics. Instead, they are assembled from components, and the product may perhaps be described largely in terms of its components (Chapter 14).

However, the product may have very different performance characteristics: a car is constructed of components like wheels, springs and shock absorbers, but its road-holding depends on how these components perform in conjunction with each other and other components. Improving springs, say, while leaving other components unchanged, could make road-holding worse. Similarly, it is possible to attach high capacity storage devices to a computer, only to find that the computer, or its software, cannot access that storage – the performance characteristic has not changed in line with the component. There are also components which are excellent in the right machine, but useless elsewhere. This means that hedonic theory's assumption of 'a positive and non-decreasing cost' for each characteristic cannot be accepted. Spending more on components does not necessarily imply better quality.

The performance of components themselves, as opposed to the product, cannot be assumed to be positively and non-decreasingly related to the cost. For example, in a recent computer journal, Western Digital hardcards were advertised by one firm at £175 for 21 Mb, £199 for 32 Mb and £199 for 42 Mb.

Quality control

If the product is manufactured to closer tolerances it is 'better' in some respects: risk, search costs and in-store losses might be reduced, for instance. This improved quality is ignored in hedonic theory. There is no reason to believe, though, that there is the production cost relationship generally assumed in hedonic theory. Indeed quality assurance engineers will argue that it is usually possible to improve quality without cost, any increased production cost being compensated for by reduced rejects, returns, and so on.[5] There is an important point here, that increasing the costs of the manufacturing division of a firm can reduce the costs of the marketing division, and of the retailers it sells to, without, perhaps, altering the quality perceived by consumers. This implies a production function for quality which is not at all straightforward.

Grades

The importance of grades, uniformity and tolerances has been stressed throughout this book. These aspects of quality can be changed by sorting and by different production methods. The costs of sorting, and the more complicated costs of grading, cannot be expected to be related to the level of these quality characteristics in any simple way.

Advertising

Consumer perceptions of a product line can be changed by advertising, so a production function exists here. Where hedonic theory assumes away the difference between attributes and characteristics, it assumes away brands and advertising too.

CONCLUSION

In this chapter the theoretical foundations of hedonic theory have been examined and its assumptions challenged. I have asked whether the assumptions are mutually compatible and whether the theory can have any application to the real world, in view of its simplifying assumptions. I have also brought together criticisms which are generally accepted by economists working in the paradigm.

Hedonic theory usually assumes a price-taking market. In such a market there is no reason to believe that there will be a 'positive and non-decreasing cost' for each characteristic. If a price-making market were assumed instead, there would be somewhat more chance of a positive cost, but it would not be a close relationship because of market structure, monopolistic competition, the difference between attributes and characteristics and the range of production functions.

A price list provides more information, and probably more useful information on the price/quality relationship than a regression curve. There are major problems in fitting regression curves to the data. A fundamental one is mis-specification, because of the arbitrary assumption of a positive and increasing relationship between price and level of characteristic.

A more accurate specification would require a proper market study including all those elements assumed away by the hedonic theory. Hedonic theory also assumes, on no discernible theoretical or empirical basis, that there are convex total cost functions, positive and non-decreasing marginal cost curves and convex, downward-sloping, product differentiation curves. This chapter has shown that very different curves are probable and do exist for some products at least.

The simplifying assumptions made by hedonic theory assume away most of marketing and marketing economics, and some of production economics. It is difficult to see the purpose of models that assume that producers sell directly to buyers who are themselves consumers (Rosen) or that assume consumers are themselves producers (Lancaster).

The indifference theory which underlies the hedonic price approach was shown to be fatally flawed in the last chapter.

Hedonic theory is not fundamental to quality theory, and indeed it is open to question whether it would be of more than peripheral importance even if it were correct. There are other traditions of quality which do not have these fatal flaws, which do correspond closely with the real world, and which are capable of development. How many errors, weaknesses, and limitations can one accept in a theory and still continue to use it? I believe that the time has come to abandon it and move to more productive traditions.

Chapter 17

Approaches to the economics of quality

This book has made use of most of the different approaches to the economics of quality. It has seldom been appropriate to work with one single approach: instead, several ways of looking at the same problem have been combined. Most people doing practical work on quality do the same, applying several approaches which may be formally quite distinct.

In this chapter some of the distinct approaches will be identified and they will be classified according to several criteria. It will come as no surprise to anyone who has read this far to be told that the classification used is one individual's subjective classification system, and that other classification systems are possible. Nor will it come as a surprise to find out that there are a great many possible categories defined by the handful of criteria used. As a result it is not possible to describe every category in this subjective category system. Instead, systems in a few categories will be described, and many of the approaches in the literature will, of necessity, be left out because they fall in other categories. What is important is not to describe all possible categories but to show why the criteria used are relevant.

The approaches are classified here by four criteria:

1 Do they deal with characteristics, attributes, brands or products?
2 Do they operate at market level, at the level of the individual, or both?
3 Are they normative, descriptive or explanatory?
4 Do they deal with a variable product or a differentiated product?

This gives seventy-two possible categories but, as will be shown below, some approaches fit into several categories. Some economists have intermixed two or more approaches, so the classification I give to, say, the hedonic approach, may not fit all models based on it. Similarly, a lot of the models based on the hedonic approach have dropped some of its assumptions (usually without realizing it, apparently) so they may be normative, perhaps, where the hedonic approach is only descriptive.

The question arises 'Which approach is best?'. Broadly speaking, the answer is 'It depends what you want to do with it'. However, it must be said that an economics of quality that does no more than build up logical models from carefully specified but unrealistic assumptions can be of no practical value. To be of value, a theory should

1 have realistic assumptions;
2 be capable of analysing real world problems;
3 be logically correct;
4 be capable of making falsifiable predictions;
5 make use of observable data.

The questions a theory may be required to answer are many and various, including

Sellers   What happens to sales of my product when I change specifications but keep the price the same?

What is the optimum quality to produce?

What is the optimum sorting strategy for a mixed product?

Should I tighten tolerances, raise specifications, or introduce guarantees?

Should I brand my product?

Regulators   Are minimum standards desirable, or would compulsory labelling be better for the consumer?

There is clearly no price competition in the industry: does this mean that there is no competition, or is there cut-throat quality competition?

Buyers   What is the optimum strategy for industrial raw material procurement?

Producers   What are the costs and benefits of producing different qualities?

Why is the marketing department always complaining about quality when everything leaving the production division meets specifications?

THE CRITERIA

Characteristics, attributes, products and brands

The importance of differentiating between objective characteristics and subjective attributes, and between quality of items, quality of product lines and quality of brands has been made clear throughout this book, and especially in Chapters 14 and 15. It was shown that there was ample scope for confusion and it was very difficult indeed to avoid double counting in any analysis.

The distinction is seldom made in the literature, and it is common for authors to slip from characteristics to attributes and back again without noticing it. Lancaster states that his approach can only work with objective characteristics, and with a very few types of objective characteristics at that, but his restrictions are ignored (without being shown to be unnecessary) in most later work in this paradigm. Some market research approaches are concerned entirely with what the buyer thinks about the product, or with the relationship between attributes and characteristics. Some approaches seem to be capable of working with either characteristics or attributes, but not with both at the same time.

It does not seem likely that a single model can deal with characteristics (or attributes) of items, product lines and brands at the same time. In practice, a researcher might wish to run separate models in parallel, one on consumer perceptions of an item, another on the performance of a brand for instance, rather than attempting to integrate the two into a single model.

Market level or consumer level

Models may be constructed to run at several levels:

1 Individual level, to describe behaviour or preferences of individuals.[1]
2 Individual level, to provide hypotheses for market level studies,

including econometric analyses, and to avoid specification error in these studies (see Chapter 16 for examples of mis-specification).

3 Individual level, to explain or predict behaviour of markets.
4 Market level, to describe, explain or predict market behaviour.
5 Market level, to identify problems to be tackled by individual level studies, and to provide hypotheses for testing.
6 Market level, to explain what individuals choose or how they choose.

There are, of course, intermediate stages which could be mentioned, such as moving from individuals to market segments, or from markets to sub-markets and to market segments.

Of these approaches, 1 and 2 are quite straightforward, and so too are 4 and 5. However, 3, which aggregates from the individual to the market, and 6, which disaggregates from the market to determine how individuals behave, do cause problems. Any economist who built a macroeconomic model from assumptions about the behaviour of individual producers and consumers would be a joke in the profession. Any economist who looked at the national accounts and produced conclusions on how individuals behaved and how they made decisions would be considered extremely eccentric. Economists recognize that the causal chain from balance of payments to the shopping habits of Mrs Jones is so long and is affected by so many other influences that one cannot derive one from the other. The question then arises of how short and how simple the causal chain must be before aggregation or disaggregation is meaningful:

– Can one aggregate from consumer beliefs or consumer behaviour to behaviour of a single market segment or to behaviour of the market as a whole?
– Can one aggregate for a product, a line or a brand?
– Can one disaggregate? From a single firm's sales, from sales of a brand or from market level data can one draw conclusions about what individual consumers want?

Aggregation

Is aggregation necessary? It is quite legitimate to use aggregate data to answer aggregate questions – economists have used elasticities for years without making any attempt to link them to individual behaviour. It is also perfectly legitimate to use the results of individual level studies to derive realistic hypotheses and specifications for market level studies. This means that, whether or not aggregation is valid, it certainly is not necessary for an economics of quality.

The problems of aggregation from individual level to market level when dealing with homogeneous goods, not qualities, are well known. Marketing economists exercise extreme caution before doing this, because of the extremely long, complex chain between producer and consumer (see Table 16.1). Almost never does one deal with the very simple market structures, distribution systems and production systems which make such aggregation possible. For most markets it is necessary to use market level data to tackle market level problems.

Throughout this book it has been shown that there are further intractable difficulties that arise when one tries to aggregate behaviour if one takes quality into account as well. In Chapters 14 and 15, for example, it was shown that there must be major difficulties in aggregating individual consumers' subjective perceptions of quality. In Chapter 16 it was shown how difficult it is to aggregate individual producers' cost curves. In Chapter 4 it was shown that search for quality is a function of an individual's subjective belief. In Chapters 5, 8, 9 and 14 it was shown that the quality of a brand and of the item actually bought are very different. In Chapter 13 some of the complications introduced by the time dimension were set out. Chapters 6 and 7 showed complications introduced once it is accepted that in real life a producer's output is not homogeneous, so quality control, sorting, grading and uniformity have to be taken into account. Some of the perverse relationships that arise from market effects were set out in Chapter 11. The increase in the complexity of the analysis is enormous when several characteristics are introduced and when several methods of valuing characteristics are taken into account, as shown in Chapters 15 and 16.

Few of the approaches I have seen recognize most of these difficulties, let alone attempt to overcome them. Few even overcome the difficulties that arise when aggregating behaviour towards a single, homogeneous product. It would be unwise to make any attempt to work on such aggregation models when alternative methods, using market level data for market level problems, are available.

Disaggregation

Disaggregation is certainly not necessary either, when there is such a wealth of market research techniques for examining individual preferences and behaviour. Examination of market data on prices, qualities and volume of sales to determine the optimum characteristics of a motor car, for instance, can only be justified if it gives results that are as accurate and as meaningful as the direct methods.

Disaggregation methods suffer all the weaknesses of aggregation methods. There is the difficulty of relating market data to individual behaviour, which is usually insuperable even with homogeneous goods. There are the enormous complexities and conceptual difficulties that arise when quality elements such as attributes and characteristics are introduced.

There is a further problem with disaggregation. With a given set of consumer preferences, a given market, and a given set of supply functions, aggregation will give a single unique result in terms of market price, sales and so on (though it is not suggested that anyone will have the data or the capacity to calculate this unique result). However, a given set of market prices, sales and so on will be compatible with many different sets of individual behaviours and preferences. No disaggregation procedure can be relied on to produce the one, correct, set of behaviours and preferences. Even if one takes the very simple problem of deriving individual retailers' behaviour on margins from market wholesale and retail prices for a homogeneous good, it proves impossible because so many policies on margins are compatible with one end result.[2]

Again, I am not aware of any study that successfully addresses these problems. Most could be shown to be incorrect in a matter of minutes by a marketing economist.

Normative, descriptive or explanatory

Normative models showing what people ought to want to buy can be very helpful to institutional or industrial purchasers. So can normative models of search. The linear programming models used by farmers and industrialists in the 1940s and 1950s were the precursors of today's hedonic theory. Formal quality control at purchase has been in use for over a hundred years.[3]

There has been a certain amount written on how consumers

ought to choose – subject to arbitrary assumptions on preferences. These models are to be seen in one tradition of hedonic theory, for instance. While it may be amusing to model the processes, the models are of limited value: we know that people do not act as they 'should'; we know that they have different ways of assessing products; we know that their subjective perceptions of quality do not normally square with objective quality; we know that our assumptions on preferences, weightings, consumption technology, and so on are wrong. Normative models of search can be equally useless in describing what consumers actually do, but the best of them show that observed behaviour which appears erratic, and the acceptance of purchases which are clearly not of the best possible quality, may well be rational.

Some normative work has been done on how producers ought to grade a mixed product or what they ought to produce, with a given set of costs and demand.

Descriptive information, such as what people do buy, how they react to price changes, what they think of alternative products, and so on is the basis of marketing. Other descriptive information like elasticities, volume of sales, repurchasing habits and so on are widely used in marketing and marketing economics.

One is never entirely happy working from description alone, without an underlying explanation. For instance, one might react to the descriptive statement that a new line of salad dressing sold very much better in the South-East than in Scotland by berating the sales force and distributor for inefficiency and lack of effort. If one has even a partial explanation, that people in the South-East eat three times as many salads as the Scots, one reaches a very different conclusion. Similarly, if normative and descriptive models agree on what quality will be bought, one has a lot more confidence in future sales than if one only has a description of last month's purchases. Combining or comparing different models gives more explanation. So too does building a quality model into a marketing model.

Variable or differentiated

Chapter 2 spelt out the difference between a differentiated product, 'in which the products of different sellers, though different, are all *given* so the only variables studied are price and quality'[4] and the product as a variable, where all quality elements are taken into

account including aspects 'arising from the materials or ingredients, mechanical construction, design, durability, taste, peculi-
arities of package or container, service location or seller, or any
other factor having significance to the buyer'.[5] Throughout the
book it has become increasingly evident that the variable product
is the norm.

It is, of course, much easier to model product differentiation:
often a simple characteristics approach will suffice, so
mathematical models have tended to work in this way. However,
marketing generally tries to take in as many elements of variation
as possible, brand image, shop image, perception of the product
and so on. Marketing economics and location economics, again,
try to take in the product as a variable.

THE HEDONIC APPROACH

The hedonic approach is the most visible in the literature. It has
been criticized in some depth in Chapters 15 and 16, and much of
the rest of the book challenges the concepts it is based on, from
the concepts of quality in Chapter 1 to search in Chapter 4, and
subjective and objective quality in Chapter 14.

The approach is based on objective characteristics as the sole
source of utility. It is not applicable to taste, touch, smell, beauty,
and so on and it is not applicable to brands or to the quality of
product lines. It is applied to differentiated products, but not to
the product as a variable.

While Lancaster appears at times to be using a purely descriptive approach, with indifference curves indicating what people
buy rather than their preferences, both he and many of his
followers, appear to use it as a normative approach at times.

The model operates at the level of the individual rather than
the market. It is sometimes used for specification of market level
models, with unfortunate results (Chapter 15).

EVALUATION AND CHOICE STRATEGIES

In Chapter 6 some evaluation and choice strategies were discussed,
AVE, CONJ, LEX and so on. They were discussed in the context of
sorting though they are more usually thought of in relation to
purchase. These strategies apply equally to characteristics and
attributes, and could be applied to variable as well as differentiated

products. They are not applicable to product or brand level quality.

The strategies are ways of evaluating and selecting purchases. Some are capable of selecting the best item, others make sub-optimum selections, but economize in search. Often the solution is satisfactory, but it is not suggested that the trade-off between the cost of search and increased utility from further search is optimal (as is the case with normative search models). It would be inter-esting, but not useful, to relate these search, evaluation and choice strategies to different utility functions and to different sorting systems. The strategies can be used as normative methods of evalu-ation for an industrial purchaser or as normative methods of sorting (Chapter 6). More commonly, though, these models are descriptive of how choices are in fact made rather than how they ought to be made. Attempts are sometimes made in the marketing literature to see whether such non-optimizing strategies provide a better explanation for observed choice than optimizing strategies.[6]

The models apply at individual level only, and it is not suggested that all individuals share the same models or weighting, so aggre-gation to market level is impractical.

These models model a choice process rather than being a description of individuals' preferences or how they evaluate when consuming. If one were to relax a few assumptions of hedonic theory, it would be just another possible evaluation and selection model, like LEX, CONJ and so on, and, indeed, it is sometimes used in this way.

HEURISTICS

Heuristics may be thought of as the decision rules and methods which reduce the complex task of assessing quality and selecting purchases to a relatively simple process. The simple decision rules may not be very good for identifying the optimum purchase, but this may be compensated for by a saving in time or effort. The evaluation and selection rules discussed in the last section are heuristics, and so are the habitual purchase strategies of Chapter 4.

However, in many cases a heuristic is chosen which leads to virtually random choice or to severe and systematic errors, and marketing research shows that what appear to be irrational choices are common. There is a large and very interesting psychological literature on heuristics and biases.[7] These heuristics are almost

totally ignored in the economics of quality because if one recognizes them, there are limitations to the analysis that is possible. If
these heuristics are common or widespread, theories based on
optimizing, on the utility functions of the individual, or on formal
evaluation and choice strategies are meaningless. If people do not
act in a certain way, any theory based on the assumption that they
do is meaningless. It is even more difficult to imagine a method of
aggregating the various heuristics described in the literature to
give market demand.

SEARCH THEORY

Search theory presents formal search models showing how a buyer
could make an optimal or satisfactory choice, balancing the probable cost of further search against the probable benefit from that
search. The assumption of most search theory is that the buyer
starts the search with a knowledge of his own quality preferences
and the range of qualities available. There is also a range of
unrealistic assumptions about the amount and type of information
available.

The variant of search theory presented here, particularly in
Chapters 4, 5, 8, 9 and 13, is more flexible in these respects. First,
it does not start with the assumption that consumers know their
own preferences. It accepts that there is a trial and error process
for most products and that both preferences and choice patterns
will evolve. It accepts that where this is not possible, buyers will use
a variety of heuristics like buying in a shop that usually sells the
type of product they like or buying a brand that they like. It accepts
that buyers are often not aware of all the lines on the market, and
that they very seldom can try all the lines available and determine
preferences between them. This means that the search approach
to quality can model consumer choice without requiring a theory
of how people relate characteristics or attributes to their own
preferences, or why they like one product rather than another.
The approach also means that full information is not assumed, and
that consumer choice is explained more by memory (imperfect
memory at that) than by computer-like processing of vast amounts
of data and probability functions in relation to multi-dimensional
preference functions.

Search theory throws a lot of light on to the difference between
attributes and characteristics: why one brand is perceived to be

better than an objectively identical brand, why an item in one shop is perceived as being better than an objectively identical item in another shop. It also throws a lot of light on the difference between product differentiation and product variation.

The approach is based on the individual's search process. Aggregation of the results of this search to market level does not seem to be a promising approach, but aggregation of people with similar processes may prove enlightening. An example of a market level application of one aspect of search theory is location economics.

The approach is descriptive and explanatory rather than normative, though there are a lot of models in the literature that are purely normative.

INDIVIDUAL CONSUMER BEHAVIOUR

Marketing makes use of techniques of observing individuals' preferences and their behaviour. The results can be extremely valuable in product design, in planning marketing strategies and in providing hypotheses and specifications for market-level studies. Economic theory is not very obvious in these models, and the economic base is usually not made explicit. Careful examination shows that many of these models implicitly make use of economic models such as hedonic theory in drawing up specifications, particularly for multicharacteristic models. The use of unrealistic heuristics in analysing data can cause serious biases.

REGULARITIES IN CONSUMER BEHAVIOUR

There are approaches to quality based on regularities in aggregate consumer behaviour which are commonly used in marketing. Information gathered on repeat purchases, response to new products, and so on can be used to predict response to new product launches. The assumption is that people will continue to display the same regularities in the future as in the past. The approach is product or brand based, rather than item based, and tends to be descriptive rather than explanatory. It is never normative. The approach may well produce very accurate forecasts.

The approach is characterized by sophisticated data analysis and rather simple descriptive models.

Notes

Introduction

1 Garvin (1988).
2 Shingo (1987).

1 What is quality?

1 I have borrowed from Garvin (1988) the idea of concepts of quality,
and some of the concepts he uses. I prefer not to use his categories of
transcendent (self-evident), product-based, user-based, manufac-
turing-based and value-based, as some of them do not easily fit the
idea of a concept of quality. The idea of conflicting ideas of quality,
with officials, traders and marketing boards having different concepts
was expressed very interestingly by Bauer and Yamey (1954a, 1954b).
2 Bowbrick, (1983).
3 See Bowbrick, (1977, 1978, 1979, 1981) for detailed critiques of such
schemes.
4 BS 6143, BS 4778 and BS 4891. The 'economics of quality' referred to
in BS 6143 bears no relation at all to any of the economics of quality
to be found in economics journals. It aims to measure, but not
analyse, some of the costs of not conforming to specifications. The
weakness of this approach will be discussed in Chapter 12 below.
5 This section draws on Bowbrick (1983).
6 Ogilvy (1978: 49).

2 The product as a variable

1 Chamberlin (1953: 3).
2 Chamberlin (1953: 3).
3 Chamberlin (1953: 3).
4 Fieldhouse (1986), following work by Bass, Wakefield and Kolosa,
cited in Ray, (1991).

5 A very well-documented example: see, for example, Plumer's *An Irregular Corps in Matabeleland* (1897).
6 For example, see Lancaster (1979).

3 What are brands and grades?

1 Oxford English Dictionary. However, quality control engineers use the word in a different sense, or rather in several rather confusing senses (BS 4778). They may use grade, where marketing would use quality, and vice versa. In one of the senses used 'an hotel with few public rooms, no bars, no lift, and so on, could be low on a grade scale, but its quality could be high if the limited services which it did provide were exemplary' (BS4778, 1979: 9), a useful concept.
2 See Conniffe (1976).
3 Here price can be discontinuous, with the same price for all chickens in a weight range, while weight is a continuous characteristic.

4 What is search?

1 This chapter draws heavily on Bowbrick and Price (1991d). I am indebted to David Price for his contribution.
2 Cigno (1979).
3 Readers wishing to follow up the literature on these will find many recent reviews such as Murray (1991), Mohr and Nevin (1990), Tellis and Gaeth (1990), Dickson and Sawyer (1990), Mahajan, Muller and Bass (1990), Hoch and Deighton (1989) or McInnis and Jaworski (1989). In view of its limited relevance to the economic implications and its limited contributions to economic thinking, it is felt that a detailed review of the marketing literature on search, and particularly on the behavioural models of search would be unwieldy and not constructive here.
4 'Although consumer search has been investigated for years, nearly all of the many studies have been focussed on pre-purchase events – that is, information relevant to a specific consumption problem' (Bloch, Sherrell and Ridgway 1986: 119). 'Papers addressing the problem of consumer search for information about price (or quality) of goods have considered typically the choice of the best search strategy for a particular consumer when the price of a single good is a random variable' (Barron and Peterson 1978).
5 There are obvious possibilities for constructing amusing, but rather pointless, models of paradoxical responses here.
6 It is sterile to argue that certain types of people are more likely to search for certain types of good, as it is impossible to generalize from non-random studies of specific markets. See Bloch, Sherrell and Ridgway (1986) for a useful survey of the literature, followed by a rather pointless empirical study attempting to find out what determines ongoing search for computers and clothes.
7 See Mahajan, Muller and Bass (1990), for a review of new product

diffusion models – most of which derive from pioneering agricultural extension and epidemiology models.

8   It will be noted that the examples of credence goods are ones where buyers may give no credence to claims unless there is some legal sanction against false claims or there is some special reason to believe the seller. Service goods are particularly likely to be experience goods because of difficulties in search.

9   Nelson (1970).

10 For example, Hey and McKenna (1981) and Chan and Leland (1982). Some problems arise from the way they treat price as though it were just another characteristic. In reality, price is valued negatively, as a cost; it is valued positively as an indication of quality; it may actually *be* quality, as with designer jeans where it is the indication of the price paid that gives the satisfaction; it is additive over the market basket; it can be changed by the seller. These are discussed more fully below.

11 Nelson (1970).

12 For example, Lenahan *et al.* 1972, McCulloch and Padberg 1971.

13 See Dickson and Sawyer (1990) for a review and experiment.

14 The knowledge that Grade A is always the best of what is available, but is of a different level of quality depending on what quality is available on the market may be of some value for some habitual purchases, even though grade specifications vary. However, it gives very misleading indications of value for money, compared with fixed specifications.

15 Ellis and Uncles (1989) quoting AGB (1988).

16 Though Carlson and McAfee (1984) and Devine and Marion (1979) are of some interest.

17 *Supermarketing*, May/June 1976.

18 Job search models tend to assume that if someone once turns down a job, he cannot come back for it if he is unsuccessful in finding another (as in Telser 1973), while least cost purchase models usually assume that the product will be available if they come back. One or two models have an uncertain probability of finding the product if they come back (for example, Karni and Schwartz 1977).

19 The same point arises with TV shopping, catalogue shopping and electronic markets. This point is missed in much of the literature, which concerns price search alone. Chan and Leland (1986) explore the different equilibria possible when price information is cheap and quality information dear, and vice versa. Models can also take into account the fact that quality uncertainty is greater than price uncertainty.

20 Carlton (1977) suggests that there is a belief with some goods that prices must be there a significant time before customers notice them and come to believe that they are normal.

21 Bowbrick (1972); Parish (1967); Preston (1962).

22 See, Chan and Leland (1982), Salop and Stiglitz (1977).

23 Goldman and Johansson (1978).

24 See Devine and Marion (1979), for example.

25 See Devine and Marion, (1979).
26 For example, Chan and Leland (1982); Salop and Stiglitz, (1977).
27 See, for instance, Oliver (1977); Olshavsky and Miller (1972); Anderson (1973); Cohen and Goldberg (1970); Deighton (1984); Hoch and Ha (1986); Dellarosa and Bourne (1984).
28 J.D. Power and Associates (1984).
29 See, for example, Jacoby, Speller and Kohn (1974) for an early example, and Jacoby (1984) for a more recent review.
30 See Wilkie (1974) and Summers (1974) for innocuously phrased, but totally damning, comments on Jacoby, Speller and Kohn (1974). See also Malhotra (1982), Malhotra, Jain and Lagakos (1982) and Jacoby (1984).
31 Jacoby (1984: 435).
32 See Kahneman, Slovic and Tversky (1982), for instance.

5 Brands as search

1 Interestingly, the attempts by IBM to establish sub-brands seem to have failed, because PC, XT and AT 'compatibles' have been taken up by the rest of the industry as technical specifications, and are not seen to be IBM brand names.
2 It is emphasized that the retailer buying from a wholesaler or manufacturer is seldom in the position of a retail customer making a single, one-off purchase, with no pre-purchase search.
3 It might be interesting to calculate the pay-off to a manufacturer of having some of his product lines of top quality, others cheap and nasty. It is possible to conceive of a situation where this would pay him. It would also be interesting to calculate the trade-off between having a multi-product brand where 80 per cent of customers actively avoid the brand, and having a completely different single-line brand for each product line, on the grounds that customers would then try each line as part of their random search strategy. Segmentation might mean that the latter was preferable.
4 Bowbrick and Twohig (1979).

6 Sorting

1 As a rule, the more tightly one characteristic is controlled in a sorting process, the more variable other characteristics will be.
2 See Bowbrick (1977, 1979, 1981) for an exhaustive analysis of the EEC standards for fruit and vegetables. It is concluded that the system is misconceived: there is no theoretical basis for it nor can the system possibly achieve any of its stated objectives (which conflict with each other). The standards themselves were dreamed up in an office, and any empirical research that has been done shows them to be wrong. There are minimum standards in the regulations which have the effect of raising prices to consumers, without noticeably benefiting producers. The system prevents the development of aggressive

marketing, using grades as a method of developing new market segments. If the system were enforced, the market would collapse.
3 See Wright (1975) for a taxonomy of consumer choice strategies. I have adapted this for sorting rules.
4 See Dalrymple (1958) and Kohls (1961) for examples of cases where the US grade specifications did not reflect consumer demand and where, in fact, the higher grades were given a lower rating by consumers. See Bowbrick (1981) for a review of the evidence of variable ratings for horticultural produce in the EEC countries and the USA.
5 Conniffe (1976) analysed this problem.
6 This distinction between grading and sorting costs is difficult to make where the sorting is integrated into a manufacturing process, but is quite clear where the sorting is a discrete process.
7 Smith (1956).
8 There are many implicit assumptions here: the statement is true, for instance, when customers buy the product on description, using the grade label as the only description, but it is not of general application when, for instance, the customer can look at the oranges in a supermarket shelf and select out the quality he desires. Formal proofs of similar propositions are presented in Abbott (1956), Freebairn (1967), Zusman (1967) and Lancaster (1975), though Lancaster now accepts his argument was wrong.
9 See Abbott (1956) and Kuehn and Day (1962), and their followers.
10 Young, Ott and Feigin (1978).
11 Michman, Gable and Gross (1977); Wind (1978).
12 Young, Ott and Feigin (1978).

7   Uniformity

1 It is assumed here that efficiency is constant, as is normal in economic analysis. The assertion sometimes found in quality control literature that 'Quality is Free', is trivial: certainly you can produce greater uniformity at a lower cost by improving quality, but equally you can produce the same quality at a lower cost by improving efficiency.
2 This may be completely justified by the use to which the product is to be put, as with the nuts and bolts example, but in some grade specifications it appears to have been slipped in inadvertently by a committee.
3 Weatherburn (1961: 195).
4 Wilson (1975).
5 But this is diversity within a rigid framework of what fashions are acceptable: a few years ago it was 'anything goes as long as it is loose, crumpled and black'.
6 Formally this means that all the cauliflowers are at the bottom of the grade specifications. If sorting was according to one characteristic only, this would mean that they were very uniform indeed, and their appearance and value might even be better than that of the run of the grade. However, the fact that several characteristics are taken into

account means that there is not as much increase in uniformity as there would be if there were only one characteristic. In addition, they may be of low quality because they are inferior in characteristics not mentioned in the grade specification (for example, they are just scruffy): this type of deviation is discussed later in this chapter. In practice, the items that are left on display for long periods are damaged by heat, dryness, and repeated examination during the search period.

7 Brunk, M., personal communication.
8 See Weatherburn (1961: 195) for the sampling distribution of the range of a large sample taken from a normal population.
9 See Garvin (1988: 53), citing Sullivan (1984), Hall (1983) and Taguchi and Wu (1979).
10 The example is from BS 4778 (1979: 9). However, I cannot accept either their terminology or their analysis.
11 The most attractive approaches here are locational approaches in the tradition of Hotelling and Smithies. However, the simpler models using an equal preference for each level of quality, and assuming a constant trade-off between level of characteristic and price, do not appear to have any practical application.

8   Grades and search

1 The objectives of the grading scheme never seem to have been spelt out. The statements made by officials involved are confused and contradictory, and the aims cannot be achieved by the system that was introduced (Bowbrick 1981). This seems to be typical of such schemes.
2 In practice, such a scheme would normally be combined with branding and some more general grading scheme, which opens the possibility of a more complex, but less generalizable, analysis.
3 Grossman and Stiglitz (1976).

9   Compulsory minimum standards: good or bad?

1 This paper draws heavily on 'The case against compulsory minimum standards' (Bowbrick 1977) and 'Justifications for compulsory minimum standards' (Bowbrick 1990). The first was an attack on the approach then in vogue of having minimum standards for virtually everything sold in the EEC. This battle is now won, with the theory being accepted, and the empirical predictions proved correct, and most Directorates of the EEC have now switched to another approach. However, there is a danger that the baby might be thrown out with the bathwater, as the British Government of the 1980s cut the enforcement of all standards, evidently in the belief that 'market forces' make them unnecessary, or that, because consumers' interests were mentioned when they were introduced, they are not in the interest of the producer. Accordingly, the second paper was written.

2 OECD (1978).
3 Martin (1977).
4 The impact on the market of removing one quality will, however, be different from that of removing a randomly-chosen selection (Price 1967a, b, 1968; Waugh 1971).
5 Besanko, Donnenfeld and White (1987).
6 See Bond (1982), Heinkel (1981) and Kambhu (1982).
7 See Bowbrick (1981), for a review of research on horticultural products.
8 See Gold and van Ravenswaay (1984).
9 Garvin (1988) points out that a totally different production line with higher unit costs often proves cheaper when costs of taking goods back under guarantee and repairing them is taken into account. However, we should not be comparing efficient and inefficient here, rather efficient with and without minimum standards.
10 See Fallows (1985).
11 The term 'quality assurance' is used here not in its quality control sense, but in a sense sometimes used in marketing.
12 See, for example, Tellis and Fornall (1988), and Parsons (1975).
13 Carter, Loyns and Ahmadi-Esfahani (1986).
14 Bockstael (1984) used much more restrictive and unrealistic assumptions to examine the same hypothesis for much the same market as my 1977 paper and came up with more extreme conclusions. She concluded that minimum quality standards *cannot* increase total social welfare where the characteristics are discernible to the customers before purchase. I cannot accept the assumptions or the analysis. Besanko, Donnenfeld and White (1987) show one situation where minimum standards can cause social welfare unambiguously to decrease.

10   Price as an indicator of quality

1 This follows Bowbrick (1980) very closely. Before this paper was written there were frequent publications on the subject, but the subject has since become unfashionable.
2 A high proportion of the articles contain lengthy reviews of the literature so, rather than produce another, I refer the reader to the full reviews in Monroe (1976) and Monroe (1973). The most widely quoted papers on the subject are Tull, Boring and Gonsior (1964), Gardner (1970, 1971), and Shapiro (1968).
3 For example, Leavitt (1954).
4 Bowbrick (1988a: 75).
5 For example, Monroe and Gardner (1976) and Gabor and Granger (1966). There have been rather more studies examining the relationship between price and quality to see how effective the marketing system is in communicating consumers' preferences to producers or to identify those quality characteristics for which people are willing to pay, but these are part of a different research programme and are not

considered in this discussion. Related subjects like consumers' perception of quality in the absence of price cues, the relationship between price and actual quality, and the economics of information are also ignored here.

6 See, for example, Stiglitz (1987).
7 Popper (1972).

11 Market effects

1 This section draws on Bowbrick and Feeney (1981), and Sam Feeney's contribution is gratefully acknowledged.
2 See, for example, Bowbrick (1973-4a, 1973-4b, 1978).
3 This is drawn from Bowbrick (1976a).
4 O'Neill and Mitchell (1973/4).

12 The costs of producing quality

1 This chapter closely follows Bowbrick and Price (1991c) 'Weaknesses in the "cost of quality" approach', Working Paper, Henley, The Management College. I am indebted to David Price for his contribution.
2 See BS 4891 for definitions, Plunkett and Dale (1988) for a review and Fox (1989) for some criticisms. I am indebted to Plunkett and Dale for assembling the many types of diagram used and presenting them in a way which makes comparison easy, and I use their paper as a source for many of the references cited. They are not, however, responsible for the analysis and criticism that follows.
3 No attempt will be made here to quantify data from real firms or to find 'industry averages' or 'typical curves': this would be counter—productive, given the lack of any theoretical basis. Garvin's search of the literature concluded 'The data on quality costs . . . is largely anecdotal, often accounts by companies wishing to publicize successful quality programs' (1988: 82). Interestingly, he also found that 'The concept of quality costs is not widespread in Japan' (1988: 277).
4 Here, as elsewhere in the literature, it is not altogether clear how far there is a time element in the X axis.
5 BS 6143, for example, has the X axis labelled 'Quality awareness and improvement', but from the text it is a time axis.

13 The time dimension

1 Abbott (1956) gave prominence to novelty, but this line of research appears to have died out.
2 See Hendler (1975).
3 Pace McAlister and Pesseimer (1982)..
4 See, for example, Stigler and Becker (1977: 78).
5 Shepherd (1966).

14   Subjective attributes and objective characteristics

1 Notably Lancaster (1971, 1979).
2 See Ladd and Zober (1977).
3 Again, I do not want to stick to a single, formal definition, when the product is used in so many senses both by the layman and by the professional.
4 See, for example, West and McKie (1983) on the Austrian subjectivists.
5 Emsley (1989).
6 In his interesting classification Garvin (1988) talks of 'dimensions' as having a meaning rather like my 'characteristic groupings', though his are intended to be more objective. I avoid the term because it obscures the fact that there are, in fact, a great many dimensions within a single attribute groupings – the organic sulphides in onions for instance – and his terminology may encourage a simplistic approach. I have produced a rather different system, partly because he was concerned mainly with durable goods, partly because of a disagreement on the place of perceived quality, conformance to specifications, and value for money, and partly because I have brought in some new attribute groupings. His dimensions are performance, features, reliability, conformance to specification, durability, serviceability, aesthetics and perceived quality.
7 The French literature uses the word 'organoleptic' when describing these sense-related pleasures, but even though the word is in the Oxford English Dictionary, I cannot bring myself to use it.
8 Note that indifference curves used for the quality of a product and the associated price curves have very little in common with the indifference curves presented in the earlier chapters of economics textbooks. The ordinary curves trace the consumers' preference between different purchases of, say, bottles of brandy and gallons of petrol. The quality indifference curves imply that the brandy and petrol will be consumed in the same glass, and so the normal convexity and tangency conditions do not apply (see Chapter 15).
9 An unusual choice for someone to have, perhaps, but important in the literature.
10 This makes it possible to create models for consumer durables where all quality characteristics except durability are identical, so more durability is identical to more of the product. It does, however, assume away so much that it is questionable whether it leaves a quality problem at all.

15   Errors in characteristics theory

1 This chapter follows the line of argument of Bowbrick and Price (1991b) 'The misuse of indifference curves in quality theory'. I acknowledge my debt to David Price. I must also thank Arthur Money and Paul Anand for their helpful comments on an earlier draft.

2 Most economists appear to be quite happy to treat Lancaster and Rosen as being part of the same paradigm, calling it either hedonic theory or characteristics theory, and few emphasize the rather small differences in their approach.

3 This book is not attacking the concepts of utility theory as a whole, but only those concepts that have been incorporated into quality theory. Anand's (forthcoming) critique of utility theory (for goods rather than characteristics) is powerful and confirms many of the prejudices of those practical economists who find it both unconvincing and irrelevant to their work. He criticizes the assumptions of transitivity, completeness, continuity and so on in two-good utility theory as being inadequate on normative grounds, inaccurate in descriptive terms and unnecessary even for axiomatic models of consumer behaviour.

4 Since consumers think in terms of sweetness and sourness, it would be dishonest to replace these concepts with an invented characteristic like 'balance', which would, in any case depend on the perceptions of each individual consumer.

5 See Hendler (1975) for some major criticisms of the Lancaster/Rosen approach. Most of his criticisms have been taken on board by later workers in this tradition, so they will not be repeated here.

6 See Lancaster (1971), for instance.

7 For example, Lancaster (1979); van Tryp (1989).

8 Huber (1975).

9 Huber compared the results of this with a naïve model, an additive model, an ideal point in psychological space model and a weighted additive model.

10 Lancaster (1979: 18).

11 What the product does appears to be treated as a characteristic of the product when it is a mere feature of the product, but not when it is basic to what the product is.

12 Lancaster (1979: 18).

13 Lancaster (1979: 17).

14 Lancaster (1979: 25).

15 Lancaster (1979: 22).

16 Lancaster (1979, 314, 316, 322, 328).

17 Many different types of characteristic could be used, performance characteristics like those cited, ingredient characteristics, component characteristics (like engine size, air conditioning), or output characteristics among others.

16   The misuse of hedonic prices and costs

1 This chapter closely follows the argument in Bowbrick and Price (1991). I am grateful to David Price for his contribution. I must also thank Arthur Money and Paul Anand for helpful comments on an earlier draft.

2 Rosen (1974: 3).

3 Bowbrick (1988b).
4 It will be noted that those economists who have attempted *n*-dimensional models have not shown any understanding of two-dimensional indifference surfaces, so they lack credibility.
5 See Crosby (1979) for *Quality is Free* or Juran (1980) for *There is Gold in That Mine*. The message of an unusual production function for quality is obscured in the literature by the insistence that improved efficiency can usually reduce costs, which is not very exciting.

17 Approaches to the economics of quality

1 Another classification system might emphasize the difference between approaches based on preferences and approaches based on behaviour. This criterion is not included here, in order to keep the number of categories down.
2 Bowbrick (1973–4a, 1973–4b).
3 William Sealy Gossett (1876–1937), for example, built on the work of his predecessors at Guinness improving existing quality control measures and introducing new statistical techniques. He introduced among other techniques the '*t*' test, publishing under the *nom de guerre* of 'Student'.
4 Chamberlin (1953).
5 Ibid.
6 For example, Huber (1975).
7 For example, Kahneman, Slovic and Tversky (1982).

Bibliography

Abbot, L. (1956) *Quality and Competition*, New York, Columbia University Press (reprinted Westport, Conn, Greenwood Press, 1973).

AGB (1988) *TCA Databank*, London, Audits of Great Britain Ltd.

Akerlof, G.A. (1970) 'The market for lemons: quality uncertainty and the market mechanisms', *Quarterly Journal of Economics* 39, 489–500.

Akerlof, G.A. and Dickens, W.T. (1982) 'The economic consequences of cognitive dissonance', *American Economic Review* 72(3), 307–19.

Alba, J.W. and Hutchinson, J.W. (1987) 'Dimensions of consumer expertise', *Journal of Consumer Research* 13, 411–54.

Anand, P. (forthcoming) *The Normative Interpretation of Utility Theory: Towards a Philosophy of Mathematical Economics*, Oxford, Oxford University Press.

Anderson, R.E. (1973) 'Consumer dissatisfaction: the effect of disconfirmed expectancy on perceived product performance', *Journal of Marketing Research* 10, 38–44.

Barron, J.M. and Peterson, A.L. (1978) 'Consumer choice and search theory', *Journal of Economics and Business* 30(2), 162–4.

Bauer, P.T. and Yamey, B.C. (1954a) *West African Trade*, Cambridge.

Bauer, P.T. and Yamey, B.C. (1954b) 'The economics of marketing reform', *Journal of Political Economy* 62, 210–35.

Besanko, D., Donnenfeld, S. and White, S.J. (1987) 'Monopoly and quality distortion: effects and remedies', *Quarterly Journal of Economics* 102(4), 743–67.

Besterfield, D.H. (1979) *Quality Control*, Englewood Cliffs N.J., Prenctice Hall.

Bloch, P.H., Sherrel, D.L. and Ridgway, N.M. (1986) 'Consumer search: an extended framework', *Journal of Consumer Research* 13(1), 119–26.

Bockstael, N.E. (1984) 'The welfare implications of minimum quality standards', *American Journal of Agricultural Economics*, 66(4), 466–71.

Bond, E.W. (1982) 'A direct test of the "Lemon" model: the market for used pickup trucks', *American Economic Review* 72(4), 836–40.

Bowbrick, P. (1972) 'Price stabilization in a two-sector industry', *Acta Horticulturae* 40, 327–48.

Bowbrick, P. (1973–4b) 'Some limitations of market-margin analysis', *Irish Journal of Agricultural Economics and Rural Sociology* 4(2), 23–8.

Bowbrick, P. (1973–4a) 'Retail mark-ups and distributive margins – a critical analysis of Professor Allen's theory', *Irish Journal of Agricultural Economics and Rural Sociology* 4(2), 1–23.

Bowbrick, P. (1974) 'A new approach to the economics of grading', Paper to Irish Agricultural Economics Society.

Bowbrick, P. (1976a) 'Compulsory grading and the consumer', *Acta Horticulturae* 55, 335–9.

Bowbrick, P. (1976b) 'A perverse price-quality relationship', *Irish Journal of Agricultural Economics and Rural Sociology* 6, 93–4.

Bowbrick, P. (1977) 'The case against compulsory minimum standards', *Journal of Agricultural Economics* 28, 113–17.

Bowbrick, P. (1978) *A Bibliography on the Economics of Grading*, Dublin, An Foras Taluntais (updated in 1990).

Bowbrick, P. (1979) 'Evaluating a grading system', *Irish Journal of Agricultural Economics and Rural Sociology* 7, 117–26.

Bowbrick, P. (1980) 'Pseudo-research in marketing – the case of the price: perceived quality relationship', *European Journal of Marketing* 14(8), 466–70.

Bowbrick, P. (1981) *An Economic Appraisal of the EEC Fruit and Vegetable Grading System*, Dublin.

Bowbrick, P. (1982) 'The economics of grades', *Oxford Agrarian Studies* 11, 65–92.

Bowbrick, P. (1983) 'Stars and superstars', *American Economic Review*, 73, 459.

Bowbrick, P. (1988a) *Effective Communication for Professionals and Executives*, London/Dordrecht/Boston, Graham and Trotman.

Bowbrick, P. (1988b) 'Are price reporting systems of any use?', *British Food Journal* 90(2), 65–9.

Bowbrick, P. (1988c) *Practical Economics for the Real Economist*, London, Dordecht and Boston, Graham and Trotman.

Bowbrick, P. (1990) 'Justifications for compulsory minimum standards', *British Food Journal* 92(2), 23–30.

Bowbrick, P., and Feeney, P.J. (1981) 'The impact of cost-saving innovations with traditional margins', *Journal of Agricultural Economics* 32(2), 197–201.

Bowbrick, P. and Price, D. (1991a) 'The misuse of hedonic prices and costs', Working Paper, Henley, The Management College.

Bowbrick, P. and Price, D. (1991b) 'The misuse of indifference curves in quality theory', Working Paper, Henley, The Management College.

Bowbrick, P. and Price, D. (1991c) 'Weaknesses in the "cost of quality" approach', Working Paper, Henley, The Management College.

Bowbrick, P. and Price, D. (1991d) 'Towards a general theory of search', Working Paper, Henley, The Management College, February 1991.

Bowbrick, P. and Twohig, D. (1979) *The Fruit and Vegetable Wholesale Market* Dublin, Stationery Office.

British Standards Institution (1972) *BS 4891 A Guide to Quality Assurance*, London.

British Standards Institution (1979) *BS 4778 Quality Vocabulary*, London.

British Standards Institution (1981) *BS 6143 Guide to the Determination and Use of Quality Related Costs*, London.
British Standards Institution (1987) *BS 5750 ISO 9000: Quality Systems*, London.
Campanella, J. and Cocoran, F.J. (1983) 'Principles of quality costs', *Quality Progress* 16(4), 16–21.
Caplan, R.H. (1972) *A Practical Approach to Quality Control*, London, Business Books.
Carley, D.H. (1983) *Impact on the Georgia Dairy Industry of Increasing the Minimum Standards for Solids in Fluid Milk Products*, University of Georgia, College of Agriculture Exp. Sta. Research Report 440.
Carlson, J.A. and McAfee, R.P. (1984) 'Joint search for several goods', *Journal of Economic Theory* 32(2), 337–45.
Carlton, D.W. (1977) 'Uncertainty, production lags and pricing', *American Economic Review* 67(1), 244–9.
Carter, C.A., Loyns, R.M.A. and Ahmadi-Esfahani, Z.F. (1986) 'Varietal licensing standards and Canadian wheat exports', *Canadian Journal of Agricultural Economics* 34, 362–77.
Chamberlin, E. (1953) 'The product as an economic variable', *Quarterly Journal of Economics* 67(1), 1–29.
Chamberlain, E.H. (1949) *Monopolistic Competition*, 6th edn, London: Oxford University Press (Harvard Economic: Studies, vol 38).
Chan, Y-S. and Leland, H.E. (1982) 'Prices and qualities in markets with costly information', *Review of Economic Studies* 49(4), 499–516.
Chan, Y-S. and Leland, H.E. (1986) 'Prices and qualities: a search model', *Southern Economic Journal* 52(4), 1115–20.
Cigno, A. (1979) 'Search and consumer surplus: a generalization', *Bull. Econ. Res.* 31(2), 98–9.
Cohen, J.B. and Goldberg, M.E. (1970) 'The dissonance model in post-decision product evaluation', *Journal of Marketing Research* 7, 315–21.
Conniffe, D. (1976) 'Classification schemes for agricultural produce when the class specifications involve tolerances', *Irish Journal of Agricultural Economics and Rural Sociology* 6, 199–213.
Crosby, P.B. (1979) *Quality is Free*, New York, McGraw Hill.
Dalrymple. D.G. (1958) 'On the economics of product grading', *Journal of Farm Economics* 50, 157–9.
Dalrymple, D.G. (1968) 'Search and consumer surplus: a generalization', *Bull. Econ. Res.* 31(2), 98–9.
De Chernatory, L. (1989) 'Facilitating consumer choice decisions: the importance of branding cues', Paper to Conference on Food Marketing, Silsoe, Cranfield School of Management.
Deighton, J. (1984) 'The interaction of advertising and evidence', *Journal of Consumer Research* 11, 763–70.
Dellarosa, D. and Bourne, L.E. (1984) 'Decisions and memory: differential retrievability of consistent and contradictory evidence', *Journal of Verbal Learning and Verbal Behaviour* 23, 669–82.
Devine, D.G. and Marion, B.W. (1979) 'The influence of consumer price

326   Bibliography

information on retail pricing and consumer behaviour', *American Journal of Agricultural Economics* 61, 228–37.

Dickson, P.R. and Sawyer, A.G. (1990) 'The price of knowledge and search of supermarket shoppers', *Journal of Marketing* 54, 42–53.

Ellis, K. and Uncles, M.D. (1989) 'How private labels affect consumer choice', Paper to Conference on Food Marketing, Silsoe, Cranfield Institute of Technology.

Emsley, J. (1989) 'Onion rings around chemists', *New Scientist* 30 September, 32.

Emsley, J. (1990) 'How to "fine tune" a superconductor', *New Scientist* 20 October.

Fallows, S.J. (1985) 'Food standards in Britain: derivation and potential', *Food Policy* 145–54, May.

Fieldhouse, P. (1986) *Food and Nutrition: Customs and Culture*, London, Croom Helm.

Fox, M.J. (1989) 'The great "economic quality" hoax', *Quality Assurance* 15(2), 72–4.

Fairbairn, J.W. (1967) 'Grading as market innovation', *Review of Marketing and Agricultural Economics* 35, 147–62.

Gabor, A. and Granger, C.W.J. (1966) 'Price as an indicator of quality', *Economica*, 43–70.

Gardner, D.M. (1970) 'An experimental investigation of the price/quality relationship', *Journal of Retailing* 46(3), 25–41.

Gardner, D.M. (1971) 'Is there a generalized price/quality relationship?' *Journal of Marketing Research* 8, 241–3.

Garvin, D.A. (1988) *Managing Quality: The Strategic and Competitive Edge*, New York and London, The Free Press.

Gold, Marion S. and van Ravensway, E.O. (1984) *Methods for Assessing the Economic Benefits of Food Safety Regulations: A Case Study of PCBs in Fish.* Department of Agricultural Economics, Michigan State University, Report 460, November.

Goldman, A. and Johansson, J.K. (1978) 'Determinants of search for lower prices: an empirical assessment of the economics of information theory', *Journal of Consumer Research* 5(3), 176–86.

Grossman, S.J. and Stiglitz, J.E. (1976) 'Information and competitive price systems', *American Economic Review* 66(2) 246–53.

Hagan, J.T. (1986) *Quality Management Handbook* (in Walsh, Wurster and Kimber), New York, Marcel Dekker. Cited in Plunkett and Dale (1988).

Hall, R.W. (1983) *Zero Inventories*, Homewood, Ill., Dow Jones-Irwin.

Harrington, J.H. (1976) 'Quality costs – the whole and its parts' Part I, *Quality* (Illinois) 15(5), 34–5.

Heinkel, R. (1981) 'Uncertain product quality: the market for lemons with an imperfect testing technology', *Bell Journal of Economics* 12(2), 625–36.

Hendler, R. (1975) 'Lancaster's new approach to consumer demand and its limitations', *American Economic Review* 65, 194–200.

Hey, J. and McKenna, C. (1981) 'Consumer search with uncertain product quality', *Journal of Political Economy* 89(1), 54–66.

Hoch, S.J. and Deighton, J. (1989) 'Managing what consumers learn from experience', *Journal of Marketing* 53, 1–20.

Hoch, S.J. and Ha, Y-W. (1986) 'Consumer learning: advertising and the ambiguity of product experience', *Journal of Consumer Research* 13, 221–33.

Hotelling, H. (1929) 'Stability in competition', *Economic Journal* 39, 41–57.

Huber, J. (1975) 'Predicting preferences on experimental bundles of attributes: a comparison of models', *Journal of Marketing* 12, 290–7.

Huckett, J.D. (1985) 'An outline of the quality improvement process', *International Journal of Quality and Reliability* 2(2), 5–14.

Jacobson, R. and Aaker, D.A. (1987) 'The strategic role of product quality', *Journal of Marketing* 51, 31–44.

Jacoby, J., Speller, D.E. and Kohn, C.A. (1974) 'Brand choice behaviour as a function of information load', *Journal of Marketing Research* 11, 63–9.

Jacoby, J. (1984) 'Perspectives on information overload', *Journal of Consumer Research* 10(4), 432–5.

Juran, J.M. (1979) *Quality Control Handbook*, 3rd edn, New York, McGraw Hill.

Juran, J.M. and Gryna, F.M. (1980) *Quality Planning and Analysis*, New York, McGraw Hill.

Kahneman, D., Slovic, P. and Tversky, A. (1982) *Judgment Under Uncertainty: Heuristics and Biases*, Cambridge, Cambridge University Press.

Kambhu, J. (1982) 'Optimal product quality under asymmetric information and moral hazard', *Bell Journal of Economics* 13(2), 483–92.

Karni, E. and Schwartz, A. (1977) 'Search theory: the case of search with uncertain recall', *Journal of Economic Theory* 16(1), 38–52.

Kendall, K. and Fenwick, I. (1979) 'What do you learn standing in a supermarket aisle?', in W.L. Wilkie (ed.) *Advances in Consumer Research*. Ann Arbor, Association for Consumer Research, 153–60.

Kirkpatrick, E.G. (1970) *Quality Control for Managers and Engineers*, Chichester, Wiley.

Kohl, W.F. (1976) 'Hitting quality costs where they live', *Quality Assurance* 2(2), 59–64.

Kohls, R.L. (1961) *Marketing of Agricultural Products*, 2nd edn, New York, Macmillan.

Kuehn, A.A. and Day, R.L. (1962) 'Strategy of product quality', *Harvard Business Review* 40, 100–16.

La Scutio, L. (1966) 'Direct observation of purchasing behaviour', *Journal of Marketing Research* 3, 227–33.

Ladd, G.W. and Zober, M. (1977) 'Model of consumer reaction to product characteristics', *Journal of Consumer Research* 4, 89–101.

Lancaster, K.J. (1966) 'A new approach to consumer theory', *Journal of Political Economy* 74, 132–57.

Lancaster, K.J. (1971) *Consumer Demand: A New Approach*, New York, Columbia University Press.

Lancaster, K.J. (1975) 'Socially optimal product differentiation', *American Economic Review* 65, 567–85.

Lancaster, K.J. (1979) *Variety, Equity and Efficiency*, Columbia Studies in Economics, no. 10, New York and Guildford, Columbia University Press.

Leavitt, H.J. (1954) 'A note on some experimental findings about the meaning of price', *Journal of Business* 27, 205–10.

Lenahan, R.J., Thomas, J.A., Taylor, D.A., Call, D.L. and Padberg, D.I. (1972) 'Consumer reaction to nutritional information on food product labels', *Search* 2(15), 1–27.

Lockyer, K.G. (1983) *Production Management*, London, Pitman.

McAlister, L. and Pesseimer, E.A. (1982) 'Variety seeking behaviour: an interdisciplinary review', *Journal of Consumer Research* 9, 311–22.

McCullough, T.D. and Padberg, D.I. (1971) *Unit Pricing in Supermarkets: Alternatives, Costs and Consumer Reaction*, Ithaca, New York, Cornell University.

McGuire, W.J. (1973) 'The Yin and Yang of progress in social psychology: seven Koan', *Journal of Personality and Social Psychology* 26(3), 446–56.

McInnis, D. and Jaworski, B.J. (1988) 'Information processing from advertisements: toward an integrative framework', *Journal of Marketing* 53, 1–23.

Mahajan, V., Muller, E. and Bass, F.M. (1990) 'New product diffusion models in marketing: a review of directions for research', *Journal of Marketing* 54, 1–26.

Malhotra, N.K. (1982) 'Information load and consumer decision-making', *Journal of Consumer Research* 8, 419–30.

Malhotra, N.K., Jain, A.K. and Lagakos, S.W. (1982) 'The information load controversy: an alternative viewpoint', *Journal of Marketing* 46(2), 27–37.

Martin, E. (1977) 'Packaging and prepackaging of fresh fruit and vegetables for self-service and supermarkets', mimeo, London, Produce Packaging Association.

Mitchman, R.D., Gable, M. and Gross, W. (1977) *Market Segmentation: A Selected and Annotated Bibliography*, Chicago, American Marketing Association.

Mitchell, J.P. and O'Neill, F.K. (1973/4) 'Consumer perception of and objective assessment of the quality of fresh fruit and vegetables in supermarket chains', *Irish Journal of Agricultural Economics and Rural Sociology* 4, 51–60.

Mohr, J. and Nevin, J.R. (1990) 'Communication strategies in marketing channels: a theoretical perspective', *Journal of Marketing* 36–51.

Monroe, K.B. (1973) 'Buyers' subjective perceptions of price', *Journal of Marketing Research*, 10, 70–80.

Monroe, K.B. (1976) 'Objective and subjective contextual influences in price perception', Paper presented at a Symposium on Consumer and Industrial Buying Behaviour, College of Business Administration, University of South Carolina, Columbia SC.

Monroe, K.B. and Gardner, D.M. (1976) *An Experimental Inquiry into the Effect of Price on Brand Preferences*, mimeo, Amhurst, University of Massachusetts.

Morris, D. (1975) 'Household production theory, the Lancaster hypothesis and the price-quality relationship', Discussion Paper 19, Department of Industrial Economics, University of Nottingham.

Murray, K.B. (1991) 'A test of services marketing theory: consumer information acquisition activities', *Journal of Marketing* 55, 10–25.

Nelson, P. (1970) 'Information and consumer behaviour', *Journal of Political Economy* 78(2), 311–29.

Nguyen, D. and Vo, T.T. (1985) 'On discarding low quality produce', *American Journal of Agricultural Economics* 67, 615–18.

Oakland, J.S. (1989) *Total Quality Management*, Oxford, Heinemann Professional Publishing.

OECD (1978) *OECD Scheme for the Application of International Standards for Fruit and Vegetables: First Draft of the General Standard for Products for Which there are no Standards*, Paris, Organization for Economic Co-operation and Development.

Ogilvy, D.M. (1978) *Blood, Brains and Beer*, London, Hamish Hamilton.

Oliver, R.L. (1977) 'The effect of expectation and disconfirmation on postexposure product evaluations: an alternative explanation', *Journal of Applied Psychology* 62(4), 480–6.

Olshavsky, R.W. and Miller, J.A. (1972) 'Consumer expectations, product performance and perceived product quality', *Journal of Marketing Research* 9, 19–21.

Ouchi, W.G. (1981) *Theory Z*, New York, Avon Books.

Parish, R.M. (1967) 'Price levelling and averaging', *Farm Economist* 11(5), 187–98.

Parsons, L.J. (1975) 'The product life cycle and time-varying advertising elasticities', *Journal of Marketing Research* 12, 476–80.

Plumer, H.C.O. (1897) *An Irregular Corps in Matabeleland*, London, Kegan Paul & Co.

Plunkett, J.J. and Dale, B.G. (1986) 'Quality costs: the economics of some engineering practices', *CME*, 33.

Plunkett, J.J. and Dale, B.G. (1988) 'Quality costs: a critique of some "economic costs of quality" models', *Int. J.Prod. Res.* 26(11), 1713–26.

Popper, K. (1972) *The Logic of Scientific Discovery*, London, Hutchinson.

Power, J.D. and Associates (1984).

Preston, L.E. 'Markups, leaders and discrimination in retail pricing', *Journal of Farm Economics* 54, 291–306.

Price, D.W. (1967a) *The Marketing Order for Washington Apricots*, Technical Bulletin 56, Washington Agricultural Experimental Station.

Price, D.W. (1967b) 'Discarding low quality produce with an elastic demand', *Journal of Farm Economics* 622–33.

Price, D.W. (1968) *The Washington Sweet Cherry Industry and its Marketing Order*, Bulletin 701, Washington Agricultural Experimental Station.

Ray, D. (1991) 'Food, drink and the American dream', Paper to Agricultural Economics Society Conference, April.

Robertson, A.G. (1971) *Quality Control and Reliability*, London, Pitman.

Rosen, S. (1974) 'Hedonic prices and implicit markets: product differentiation in pure competition', *Journal of Political Economy* 82, 34–5.

Salop, S. (1977) 'Information and market structure', *American Economic Review* 66 (2), 240–5.

Salop, S.C. and Stiglitz, J.E. (1977) 'Bargains and ripoffs: a model of monopolistically competitive price dispersion', *Review of Economic Studies* 44, 493–510.

Scitovsky, T. (1944/5) 'Some consequences of the habit of judging quality by price', *The Review of Economic Studies* 12(2), 100–5.

Shapiro, B. (1968) 'The psychology of pricing', *Harvard Business Review* 41, 14–16.

Shepherd, G.S. (1966) *Agricultural Price Analysis*, 5th edn, Ames, Iowa State University Press, 64.

Shingo Shigeo (1986) *Zero Quality Control: Source Inspection and the Pokayoke System* Stamford, Conn. Productivity Press.

Shingo, Shigeo (1987) *The Sayings of Shigeo Shingo* (trans. A.P. Dillon), Productivity Press.

Smith, W.R. (1956) 'Product differentiation and market segmentation as alternative marketing strategies', *Journal of Marketing* 21, 3–8.

Smithies, A. (1941) 'Optimal location in spatial competition' *Journal of Political Economy*, 423–39.

Stigler, C.J. and Becker, G.S. (1977) 'De gustibus non est disputandum', *American Economic Review* 67, 76–90.

Stiglitz, J.E. (1987) 'The causes and consequences of the dependence of quality on price', *Journal of Economic Literature* 25(1), 1–48.

Sullivan, L.P. (1984) 'Reducing variability: a new approach to quality', *Quality Progress* July, p. 17.

Summers, J.O. (1974) 'Less information is better?', *Journal of Marketing Research* 11, 467–8.

Taguchi, Genichi and Yu-in Wu (1979) *Introduction to Off-Line Quality Control*, Nagaya, Japan, Central Japan Quality Association.

Tellis, G.J. and Fornell, C. (1988) 'The relationship between advertising and product quality over the product life cycle: a contingency theory', *Journal of Marketing Research* 25, 64–71.

Tellis, G.J. and Gaeth, G.J. (1990) 'Best value, price seeking, and price aversion: the impact of information and learning on consumer choices', *Journal of Marketing* 54, 34–5.

Telser, L.G. (1973) 'Searching for the lowest price', *American Economic Review* 63, 40–9.

Thoday, W.R. (1976) 'The equation of quality and profit', *Quality Assurance* 2(2), 48–52.

Tull, D.S., Boring, R.A. and Gonsior, M.H. (1964) 'A note on the relationship of price and imputed quality', *Journal of Business* 37, 186–91.

Urwick Group (1981) *Quality Costs: A Key to Survival*, Urwick Group Pamphlet.

Van Trijpp, H.C.M. (1989) *Variety Seeking in Consumption Behaviour: A Review*, Wageningen, Wageningen Agricultural University.

Van Trijpp, H.C.M. and Steenkamp, J-B.E.M. (1990) 'An investigation into the validity of measures for variation in consumption used in economics and marketing', *European Review of Agricultural Economics* 17, 19–41.

Veen, B. (1974) 'Quality costs', *Quality* (EOQC publication) 2, 55–9.

Waugh, F.V. (1929) *Quality as a Determinant of Vegetable Prices*, New York, Columbia University Press.

Waugh, F.V. (1971) 'Withholding by grade', *American Journal of Agricultural Economics* 53, 500–1.

Weatherburn, C.E. (1961) *Mathematical Statistics*, Cambridge, Cambridge University Press.

West, E.G. and McKie, M. (1983) 'De gustibus *est* disputandum: the phenomenon of "Merit Wants" revisited', *American Economic Review* 73(5), 1110–21.

Wilkie, W.L. (1974) 'Analysis of effects of information load', *Journal of Marketing Research* 11, 462–6.

Wilson, R.J. (1975) *The Market for Cashew Nut Kernels and Cashew Nut Shell Liquid*, London, Tropical Products Institute.

Wind, Y. (1978) 'Issues and advances in segmentation research', *Journal of Marketing Research* 15, 317–37.

Wong, V., Saunders, J. and Doyle, P. (1988) 'The quality of British marketing: a comparison with US and Japanese multinationals in the UK market', *Journal of Marketing Management* 4(2), 107–30.

Wright, P. (1975) 'Consumer choice strategies: simplifying versus optimizing', *Journal of Marketing Research* 12, 60–7.

Young, S., Ott, H. and Feigan, B. (1978) 'Some practical considerations in market segmentation, *Journal of Marketing Research* 15, 405–13.

Zusman, P. (1967) 'A theoretical basis for determination of grading and sorting schemes', *Journal of Farm Economics* 49, 89–106.

Name index

Subject index

34, 37; variation 13–27, 42, 48, 93, 108
production economics xvi, 124, 129, 174, 294, 300
production: cost 7, 90, 92, 105, 107, 108, 127–8, 160, 165, 182, 185–203, 287, 289, 291–9; cost and price 291–9; economics xvi, 124, 129, 174, 294, 300; process xiv, 8, 9, 28, 33, 66, 91, 92, 97, 98, 103, 106, 108, 109, 110, 112, 185–9, 218
programming 8, 25, 45, 222, 297, 306
proxy characteristics 26, 232–3, 234
public procurement 5
public policy xv, 72, 97, 147–68
purchasing costs 14, 20, 22, 26, 43, 225

quality assurance xvi, 8, 158, 158n, 185–203, 228, 298
quality: buyer-based 2, 5–6, 7, 8, 11, 15, 22, 27, 40, 42, 66, 68, 90, 214, 215, 217, 229, 242, 247, 269, 270, 291, 300; distributor-based 2, 6–7, 8, 10, 12, 22, 115, 177, 182–5, 225, 239; characteristics-based 9; concepts of 1–15, 42, 74, 212, 213, 219, 228, 238, 242; costs 185–203; definitions 1–12, 13–27, 212–95; producer-based 2, 7–8, 11, 42, 219, 229; product based 8; price 279, 280, 281, 286, 288, 289, 290; pure 28; 'Q. Is Free' 112n; inspector-based 2–3, 4, 7, 8; inputs-based 2, 8, 91; self-evident 2, 7, 106; time dependent 17–8, 49, 66; trader 17; transcendent 2n; user-based 2, 3–4, 5, 6–7, 8, 22, 115, 177, 182–5, 229; value-based 2n; why important xi
quality control xiii, xvi, 2, 3, 8, 34, 43, 55, 58, 68, 84, 85, 86, 92, 102, 103, 112, 113, 114, 119, 124, 153, 154, 158, 158n, 159,

185–203, 212, 216, 218, 230, 242, 298, 305, 306
random selection 111, 119, 144, 245, 309
random 21, 35, 54, 111, 119, 123, 134, 135, 142, 144, 145, 182, 245, 309
range (product) 47, 58, 60, 64, 65, 72, 75, 79, 80, 81, 83, 87, 126, 128, 135, 142, 143, 160, 168, 205, 207, 213, 220, 274, 297, 310
range (statistical) 34, 58, 60, 95, 113, 114, 119, 121, 230
rational choice 26, 45, 49, 52, 57, 66, 71, 76, 80, 103, 141, 152, 307
reduced value from sorting 104–6
regularities xv, 26, 46, 225, 227, 233, 282, 290, 311
regulation xvi, 12, 49, 72, 73, 96, 117, 163, 164, 167, 302
reliability xvi, 29, 30, 53, 76, 78, 79, 80, 81, 86, 138, 145, 152, 187, 206, 215, 227, 236, 237, 242, 258, 278, 286, 290
repeat purchases 53, 67, 78, 81, 85, 143, 144, 145, 146, 152, 159
reputation xii, 6, 16, 17, 42, 64, 67, 77, 86, 87, 125, 132, 137, 138, 163, 166, 171, 218, 237, 242
rework costs 7, 187, 188, 189
Right First Time 218
rigour xiii, 32, 276
risk xv, 9, 14, 16, 20, 21, 22, 29, 54, 55, 59, 71, 80, 90, 107, 117, 123, 124, 134, 135, 140, 143, 145, 149, 150, 152, 153, 154, 156, 157, 160, 172, 188, 206, 215, 216, 221, 224, 225, 233, 237, 242, 289, 295, 298

safety 29, 42, 43, 99, 141, 147, 152, 154, 155, 157, 167, 215, 236, 237–8, 239, 264
sample 21, 35, 70, 94, 99, 103, 114, 117, 119, 121, 124, 134, 137, 138, 142, 170, 182, 228, 286
sanctions 141, 143
satiation 18, 211, 251–3, 273, 274

tie-breaker 50, 80, 240
time xiv, xv, xvii, 1, 4, 5, 15, 17,
18, 20, 21, 22, 28, 30, 35, 42, 43,
45, 47, 49, 50, 51, 52, 53, 54, 57,
58, 59, 61, 62, 65, 66, 67, 68, 69,
70, 76, 78, 79, 80, 95, 103, 107,
111, 115, 116, 118, 121, 122,
123, 124, 125, 126, 127, 128,
129, 134, 135, 136, 137, 138,
141, 142, 150–1, 156, 159, 162,
164, 166, 167, 170, 174, 177,
178, 184, 186, 187, 188, 192,
202, 204–12, 216, 217, 228, 232,
233, 247, 252, 253, 270, 274,
278, 279, 280–1, 286, 289, 290,
291, 295, 305, 309
time dimension 204–11; delays
between buying and consuming
204–6; durables 5, 204, 206–7,
236, 239, 241–2; variation
in purchase 207–8;
characteristics or products
208–9; elasticities 209
tolerances 34, 35, 36, 92, 94, 95,
103, 105, 113, 114, 116, 117,
121, 133, 136, 138, 153, 154,
159, 167, 202, 203, 218, 295,
298, 299, 302
Total Quality Management xvi, 8
transparency 40, 236
turnover 6, 40, 56, 124, 128, 157,
163, 176, 181, 189, 227, 239

uniformity 7, 14, 33, 40, 65, 76,
80, 81, 92, 94, 97, 101, 103, 104,
105, 107, 111–29, 134, 135, 144,
145, 159, 162, 188, 218, 225,
291, 295, 299, 305; between

packs 117–21, 123, 188; costs of
122; define 113–5; over time
121–2, 123, 159, 188; search for
123–5; subjective 114–5; types
of 115–6; within grades 121–2;
within packs 115, 117, 118, 122,
123, 129, 188; within purchase
115–7
utility theory 4, 6, 244–77,
278–300, 309, 310

value for money 5, 29, 38, 51, 55,
57, 58, 59, 65, 66, 76, 80, 85, 86,
116, 135, 145, 151, 156, 205,
234, 237, 241, 242
variable, product as a 13–27, 28,
42, 74, 91, 92, 105, 112, 123,
131, 268, 279, 280, 289, 301,
307–8, 311
variance 43, 91, 295
variety 18, 19, 109, 125, 130, 155,
206–7, 209, 210, 226, 268, 310
vertical 35–6, 101, 102, 108, 139,
143, 145, 270–1

warranty 22, 188, 218, 225
waste 6, 7, 17, 23, 36, 40, 104, 107,
110, 116, 148, 176, 177, 178,
179, 182, 187, 188, 189, 190,
203, 212, 227, 228, 239, 284, 295
welfare economics 161, 269, 270
what it does 24–5
what needs it satisfies 25–6, 214,
216, 276
when to search 49

Zero defects 91–2, 187